BATMAN
THE BRAVE AND THE BOLD

THE FEARSOME FANGS STRIKE AGAIN!

J. TORRES LANDRY WALKER   WRITERS

J. BONE CARLO BARBERI ERIC JONES   PENCILLERS

J. BONE TERRY BEATTY ERIC JONES   INKERS

HEROIC AGE   COLORIST

TRAVIS LANHAM PAT BROSSEAU ROB CLARK JR.   LETTERERS

SCOTT JERALDS WITH HI-FI   COLLECTION COVER

BATMAN CREATED BY BOB KANE

Michael Siglain Rachel Gluckstern Editors-original series
Harvey Richards Assistant Editor-original series
Bob Harras Group Editor-Collected Editions
Anton Kawasaki Editor
Robbin Brosterman Design Director-Books

DC COMICS
Diane Nelson President
Dan DiDio and Jim Lee Co-Publishers
Geoff Johns Chief Creative Officer
Patrick Caldon EVP-Finance and Administration
John Rood EVP-Sales, Marketing and Business Development
Amy Genkins SVP-Business and Legal Affairs
Steve Rotterdam SVP-Sales and Marketing
John Cunningham VP-Marketing
Terri Cunningham VP-Managing Editor
Alison Gill VP-Manufacturing
David Hyde VP-Publicity
Sue Pohja VP-Book Trade Sales
Alysse Soll VP-Advertising and Custom Publishing
Bob Wayne VP-Sales
Mark Chiarello Art Director

BATMAN: THE BRAVE AND THE BOLD: THE FEARSOME FANGS STRIKE AGAIN!

DC Comics, 1700 Broadway, New York, NY 10019
A Warner Bros. Entertainment Company
Printed by Quad/Graphics, Dubuque, IA, USA (10/20/10)
ISBN: 978-1-4012-2896-5

BATMAN: THE BRAVE AND THE BOLD #7
Cover by Scott Jeralds with Hi-Fi

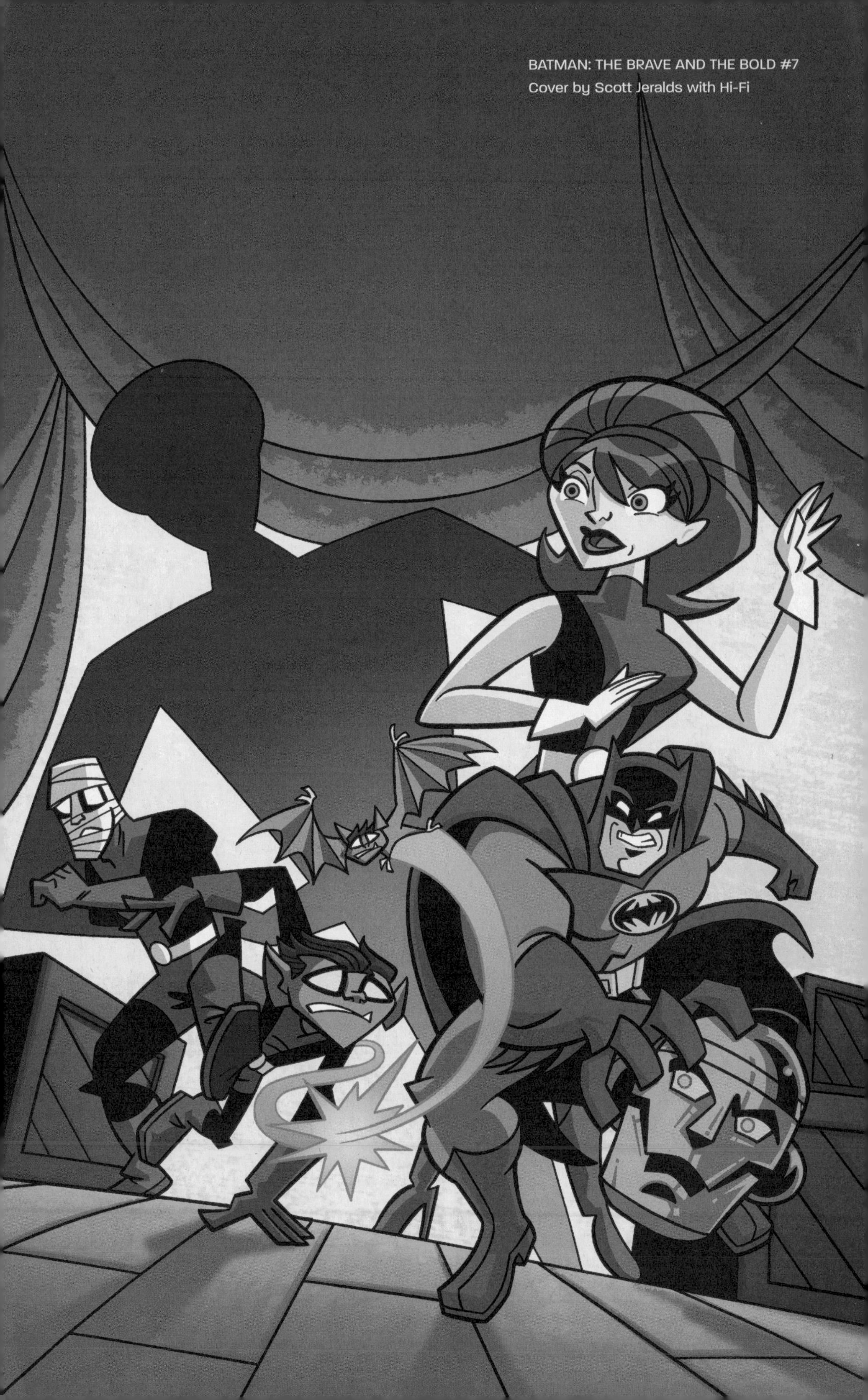

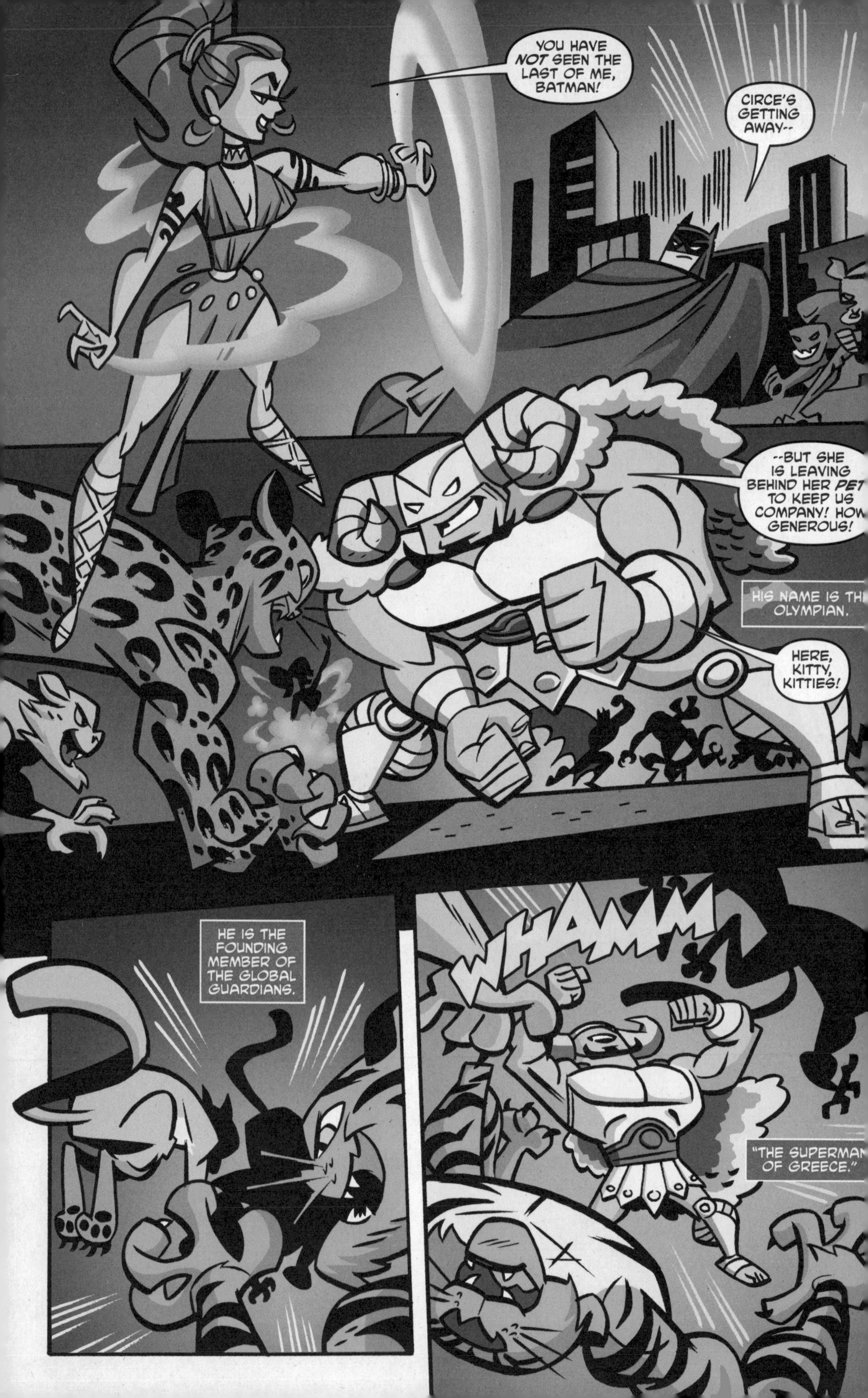
YOU HAVE NOT SEEN THE LAST OF ME, BATMAN!
CIRCE'S GETTING AWAY--
--BUT SHE IS LEAVING BEHIND HER PET TO KEEP US COMPANY! HOW GENEROUS!
HIS NAME IS THE OLYMPIAN.
HERE, KITTY, KITTIES!
HE IS THE FOUNDING MEMBER OF THE GLOBAL GUARDIANS.
WHAMM
"THE SUPERMAN OF GREECE."

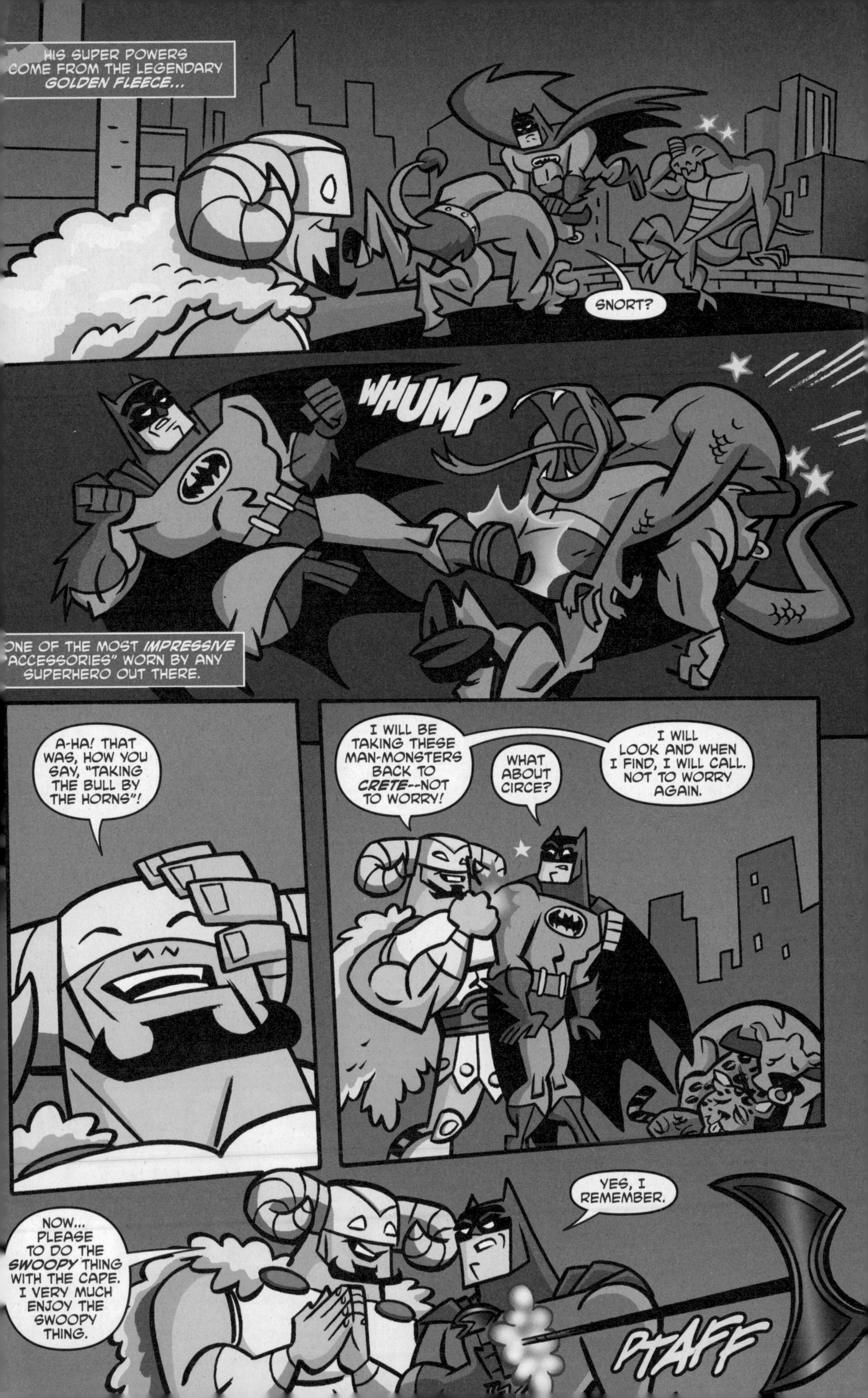
HIS SUPER POWERS COME FROM THE LEGENDARY *GOLDEN FLEECE*...
SNORT?
WHUMP
ONE OF THE MOST *IMPRESSIVE* "ACCESSORIES" WORN BY ANY SUPERHERO OUT THERE.
A-HA! THAT WAS, HOW YOU SAY, "TAKING THE BULL BY THE HORNS"!
I WILL BE TAKING THESE MAN-MONSTERS BACK TO *CRETE*--NOT TO WORRY!
WHAT ABOUT CIRCE?
I WILL LOOK AND WHEN I FIND, I WILL CALL. NOT TO WORRY AGAIN.
NOW... PLEASE TO DO THE *SWOOPY* THING WITH THE CAPE. I VERY MUCH ENJOY THE SWOOPY THING.
YES, I REMEMBER.
PTAFF

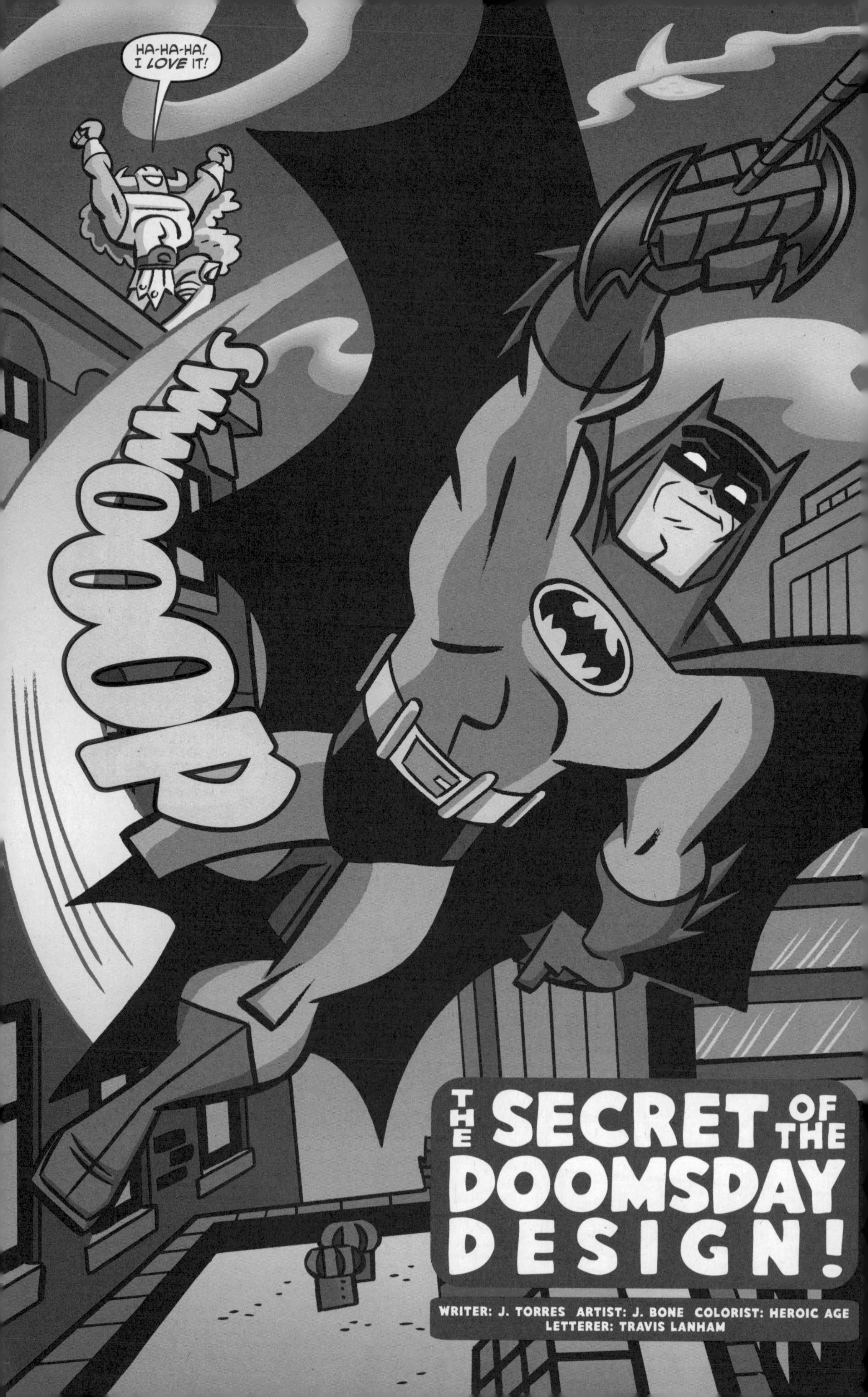
HA-HA-HA! I LOVE IT!
VOOOOOM
THE SECRET OF THE DOOMSDAY DESIGN!
WRITER: J. TORRES ARTIST: J. BONE COLORIST: HEROIC AGE
LETTERER: TRAVIS LANHAM

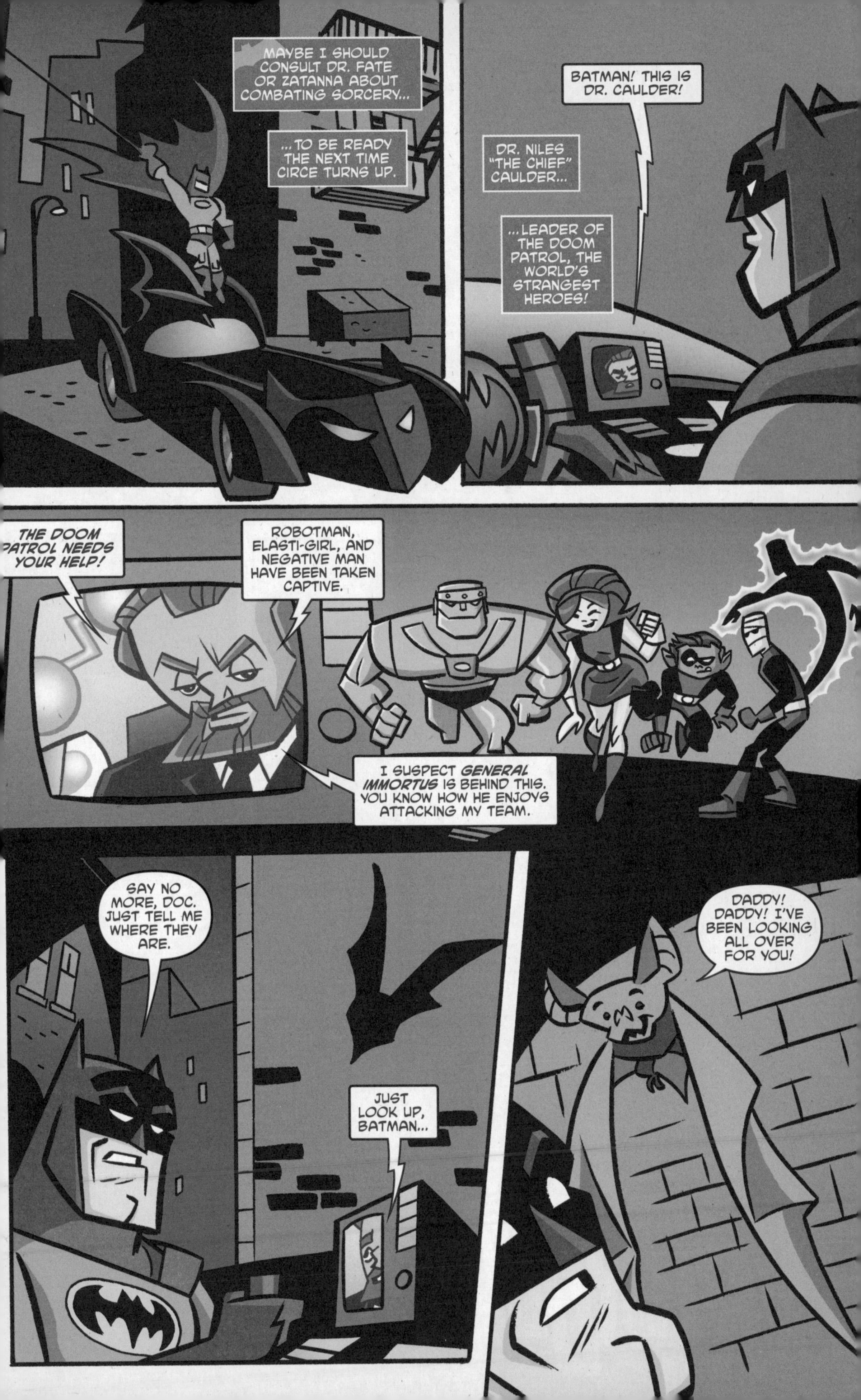
MAYBE I SHOULD CONSULT DR. FATE OR ZATANNA ABOUT COMBATING SORCERY...
...TO BE READY THE NEXT TIME CIRCE TURNS UP.
BATMAN! THIS IS DR. CAULDER!
DR. NILES "THE CHIEF" CAULDER...
...LEADER OF THE DOOM PATROL, THE WORLD'S STRANGEST HEROES!
THE DOOM PATROL NEEDS YOUR HELP!
ROBOTMAN, ELASTI-GIRL, AND NEGATIVE MAN HAVE BEEN TAKEN CAPTIVE.
I SUSPECT GENERAL IMMORTUS IS BEHIND THIS. YOU KNOW HOW HE ENJOYS ATTACKING MY TEAM.
SAY NO MORE, DOC. JUST TELL ME WHERE THEY ARE.
JUST LOOK UP, BATMAN...
DADDY! DADDY! I'VE BEEN LOOKING ALL OVER FOR YOU!

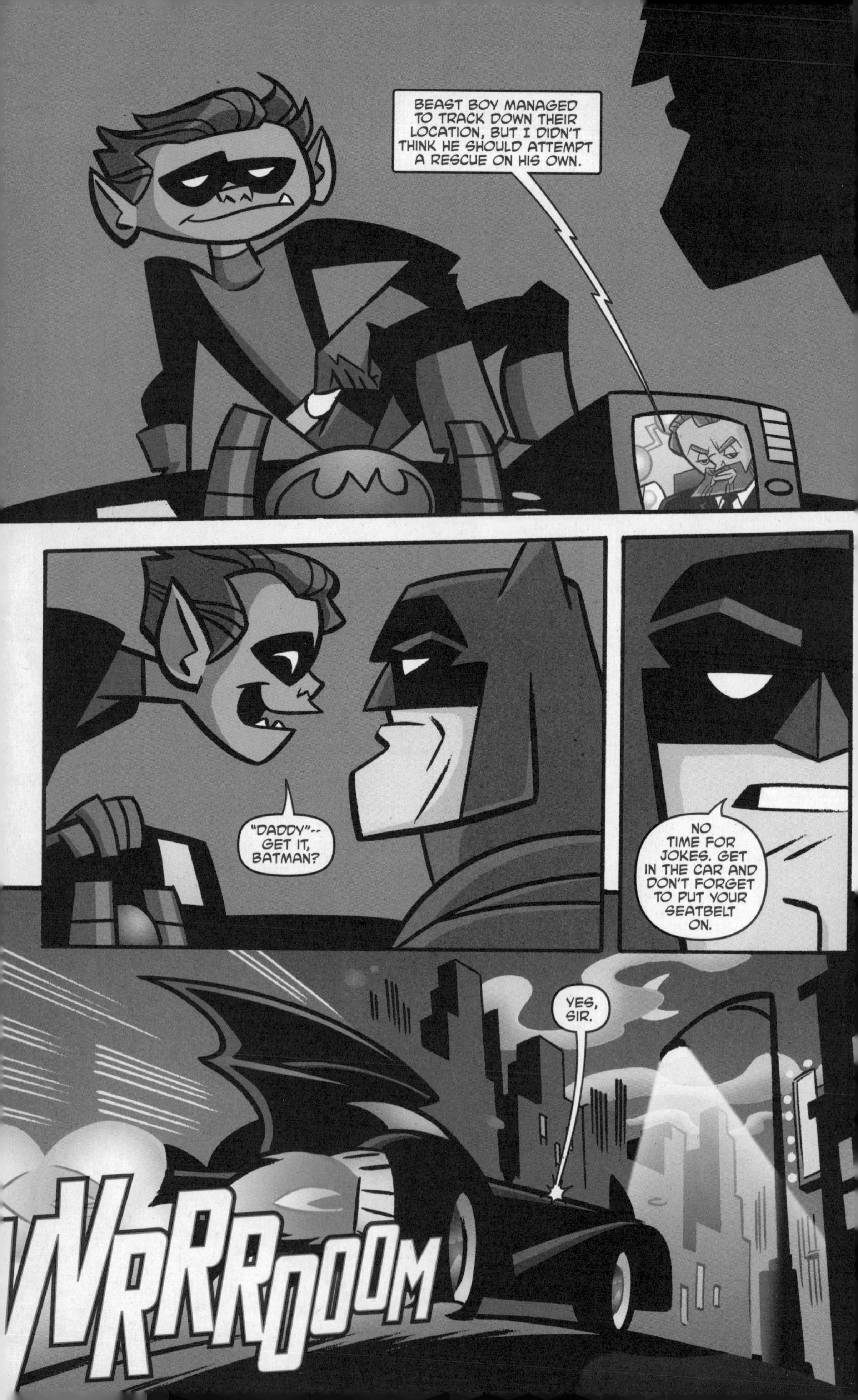
BEAST BOY MANAGED TO TRACK DOWN THEIR LOCATION, BUT I DIDN'T THINK HE SHOULD ATTEMPT A RESCUE ON HIS OWN.
"DADDY"-- GET IT, BATMAN?
NO TIME FOR JOKES. GET IN THE CAR AND DON'T FORGET TO PUT YOUR SEATBELT ON.
YES, SIR.
VRRROOOM

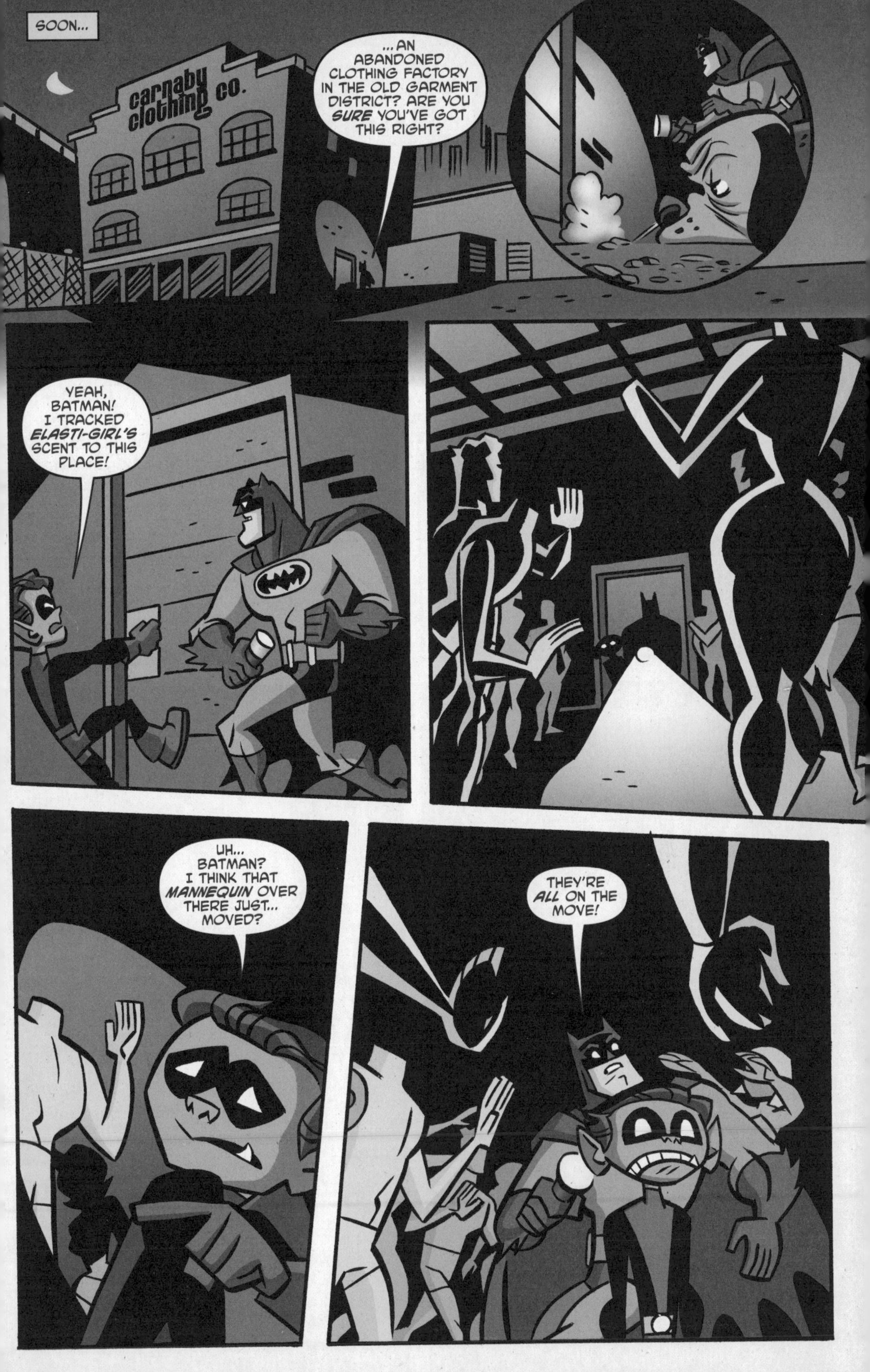
SOON...
carnaby clothing co.
...AN ABANDONED CLOTHING FACTORY IN THE OLD GARMENT DISTRICT? ARE YOU SURE YOU'VE GOT THIS RIGHT?
YEAH, BATMAN! I TRACKED ELASTI-GIRL'S SCENT TO THIS PLACE!
UH... BATMAN? I THINK THAT MANNEQUIN OVER THERE JUST... MOVED?
THEY'RE ALL ON THE MOVE!

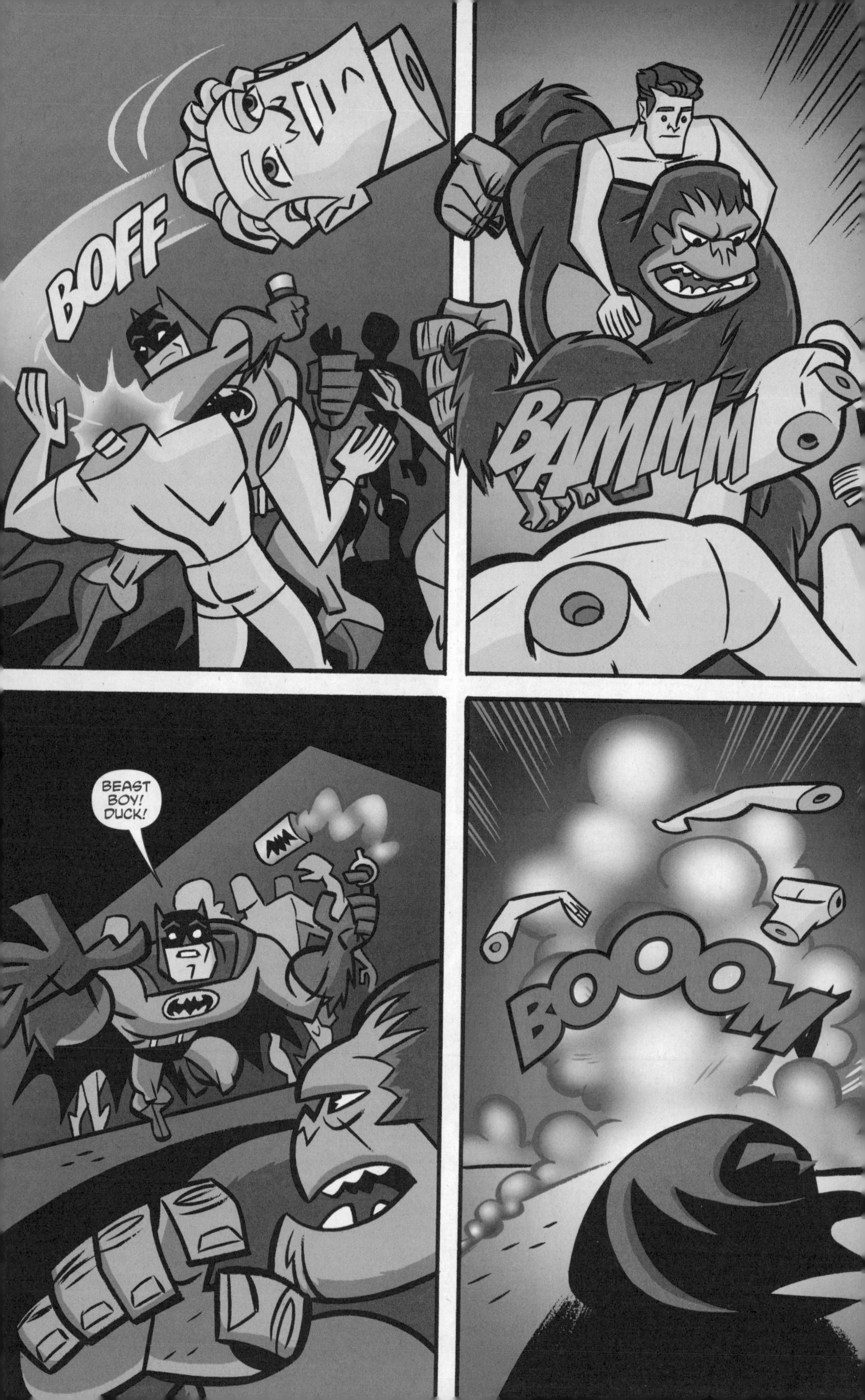
BOFF
BAMMM
BEAST BOY! DUCK!
BOOOOM

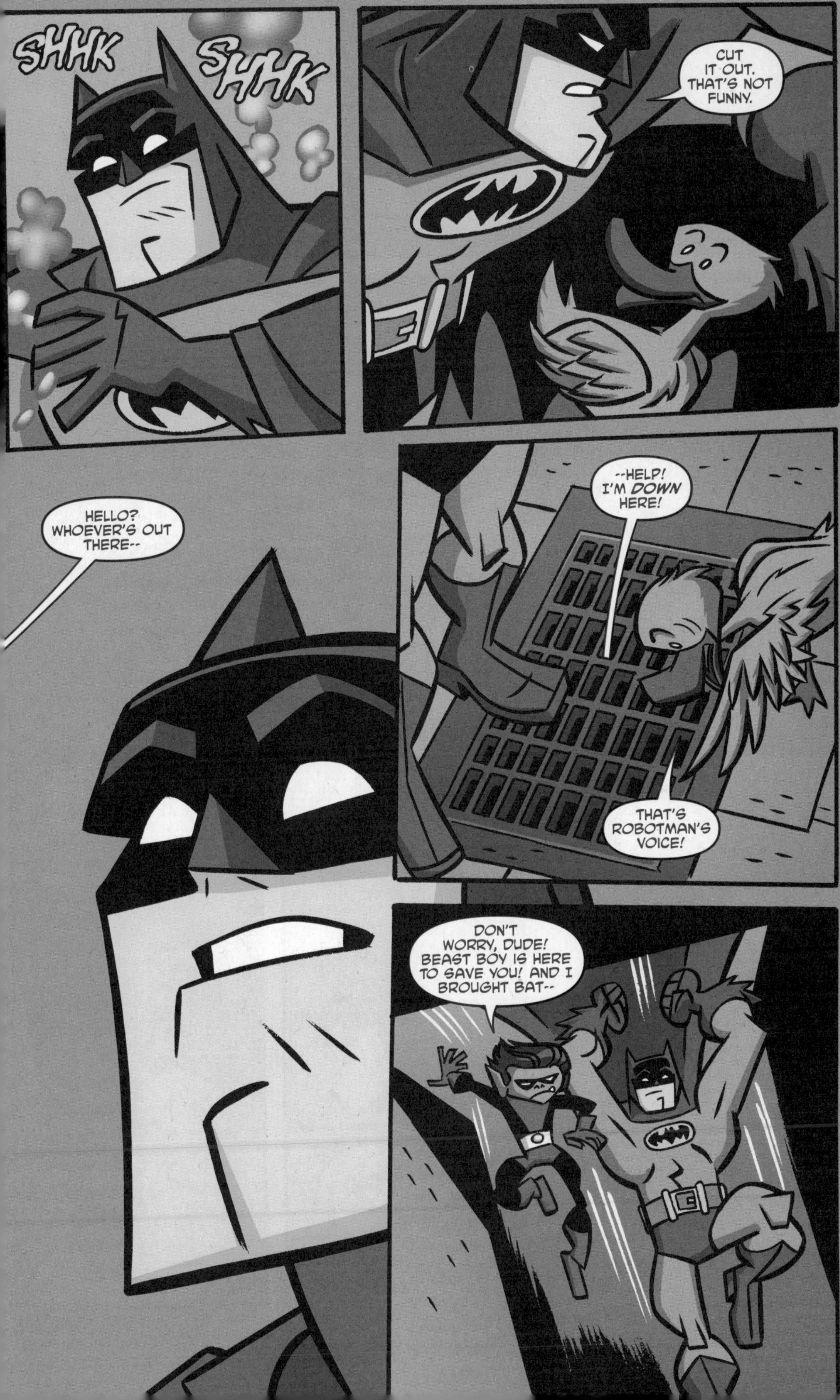
SHHK
SHHK
CUT IT OUT. THAT'S NOT FUNNY.
HELLO? WHOEVER'S OUT THERE--
--HELP! I'M DOWN HERE!
THAT'S ROBOTMAN'S VOICE!
DON'T WORRY, DUDE! BEAST BOY IS HERE TO SAVE YOU! AND I BROUGHT BAT--

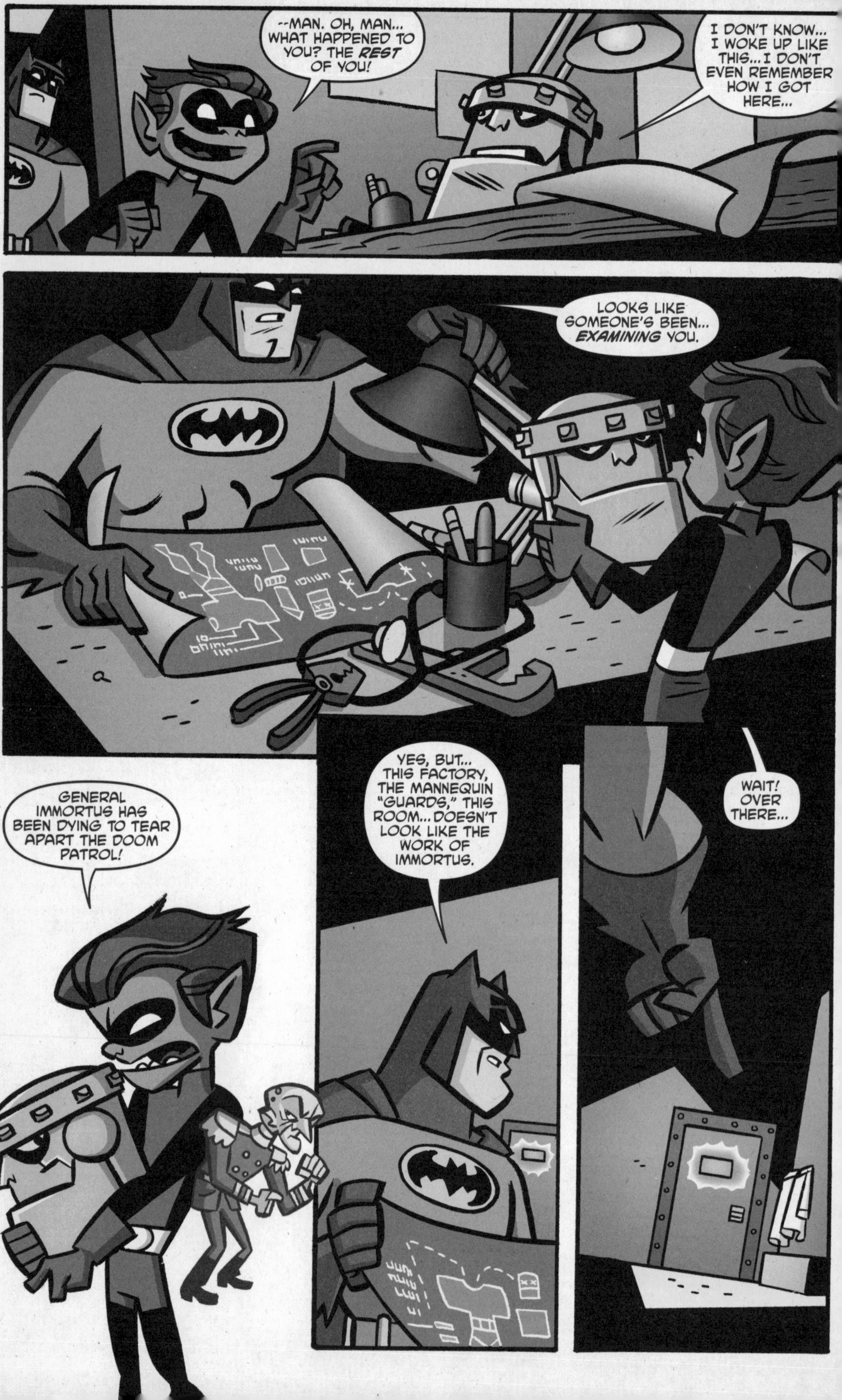
--MAN. OH, MAN... WHAT HAPPENED TO YOU? THE *REST* OF YOU!
I DON'T KNOW... I WOKE UP LIKE THIS... I DON'T EVEN REMEMBER HOW I GOT HERE...
LOOKS LIKE SOMEONE'S BEEN... *EXAMINING* YOU.
GENERAL IMMORTUS HAS BEEN DYING TO TEAR APART THE DOOM PATROL!
YES, BUT... THIS FACTORY, THE MANNEQUIN "GUARDS," THIS ROOM... DOESN'T LOOK LIKE THE WORK OF IMMORTUS.
WAIT! OVER THERE...

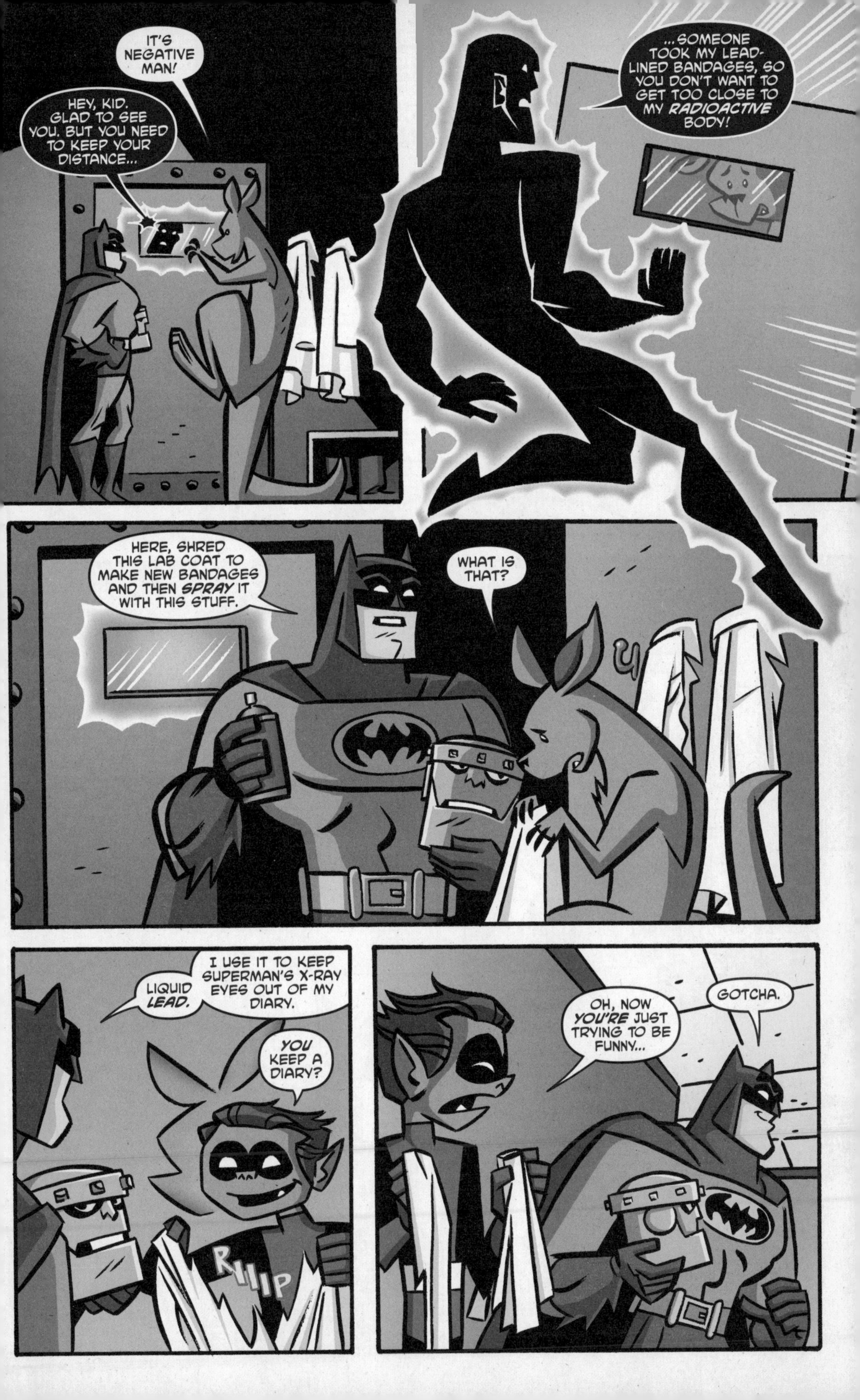
IT'S NEGATIVE MAN!
HEY, KID. GLAD TO SEE YOU. BUT YOU NEED TO KEEP YOUR DISTANCE...
...SOMEONE TOOK MY LEAD-LINED BANDAGES, SO YOU DON'T WANT TO GET TOO CLOSE TO MY *RADIOACTIVE* BODY!
HERE, SHRED THIS LAB COAT TO MAKE NEW BANDAGES AND THEN *SPRAY* IT WITH THIS STUFF.
WHAT IS THAT?
LIQUID *LEAD*.
I USE IT TO KEEP SUPERMAN'S X-RAY EYES OUT OF MY DIARY.
YOU KEEP A DIARY?
RIIIIP
OH, NOW *YOU'RE* JUST TRYING TO BE FUNNY...
GOTCHA.

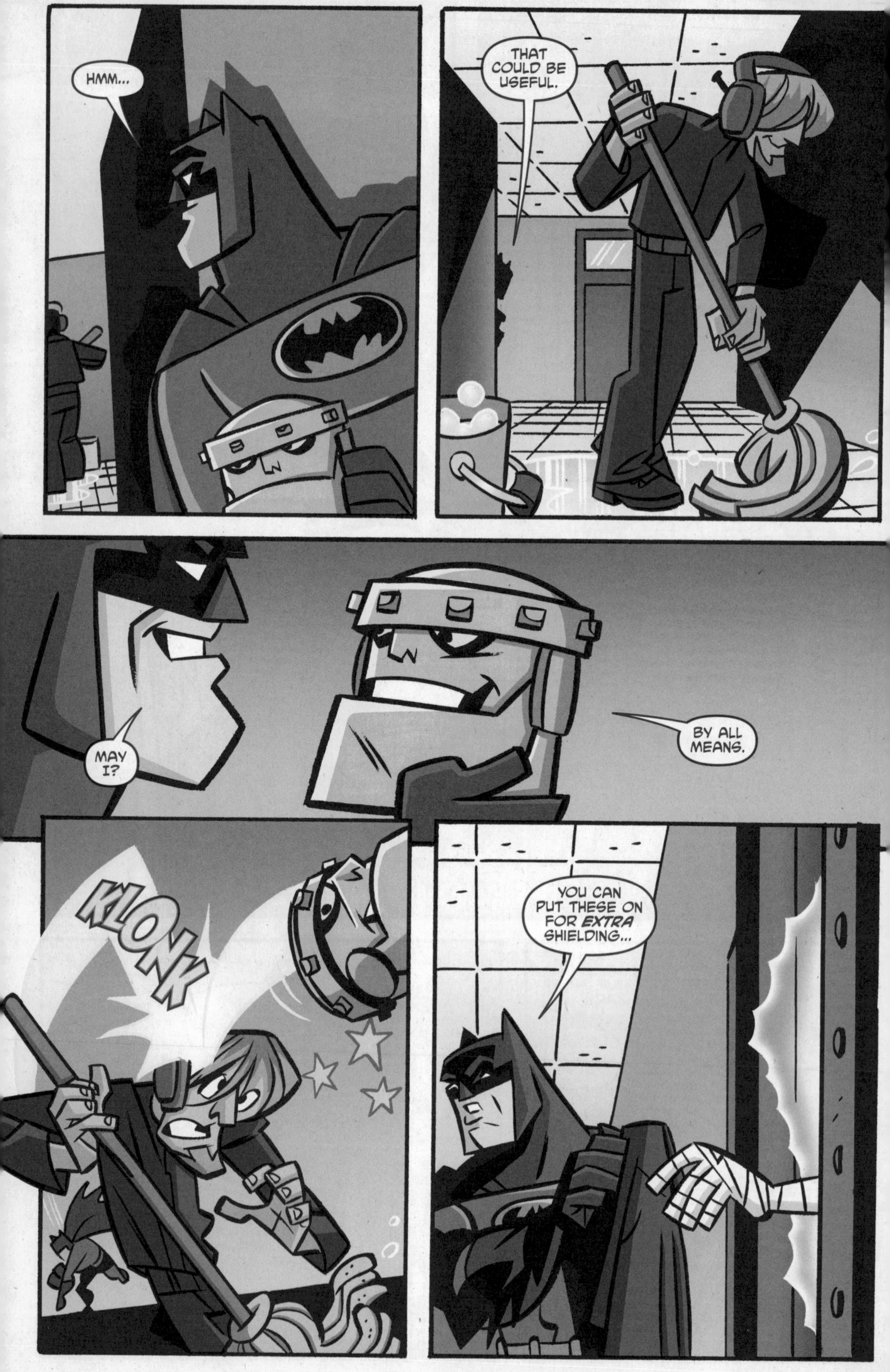
HMM...
THAT COULD BE USEFUL.
MAY I?
BY ALL MEANS.
KLONK
YOU CAN PUT THESE ON FOR *EXTRA* SHIELDING...

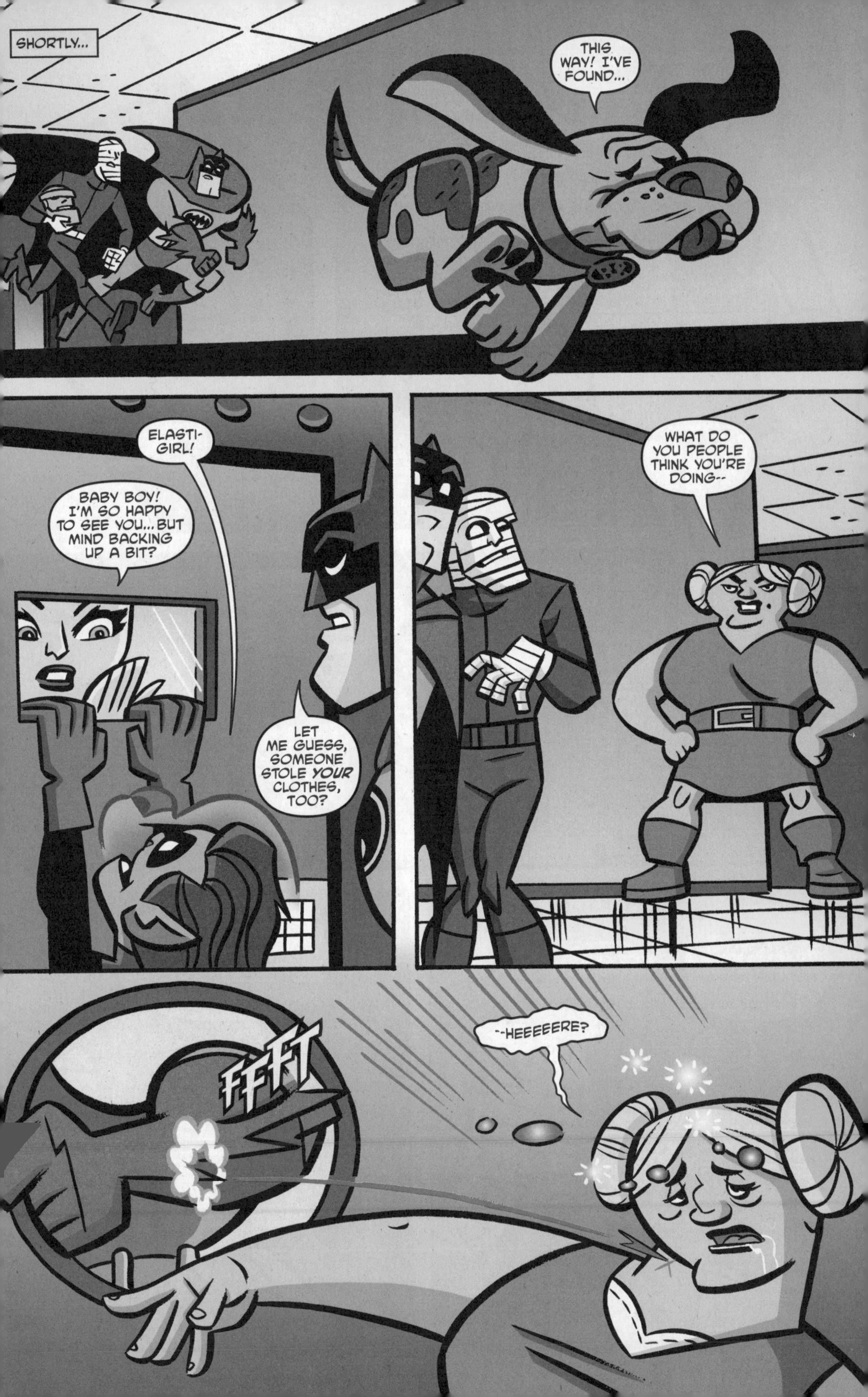
SHORTLY...
THIS WAY! I'VE FOUND...
ELASTI-GIRL!
BABY BOY! I'M SO HAPPY TO SEE YOU... BUT MIND BACKING UP A BIT?
LET ME GUESS, SOMEONE STOLE *YOUR* CLOTHES, TOO?
WHAT DO YOU PEOPLE THINK YOU'RE DOING--
FFFT
--HEEEEERE?

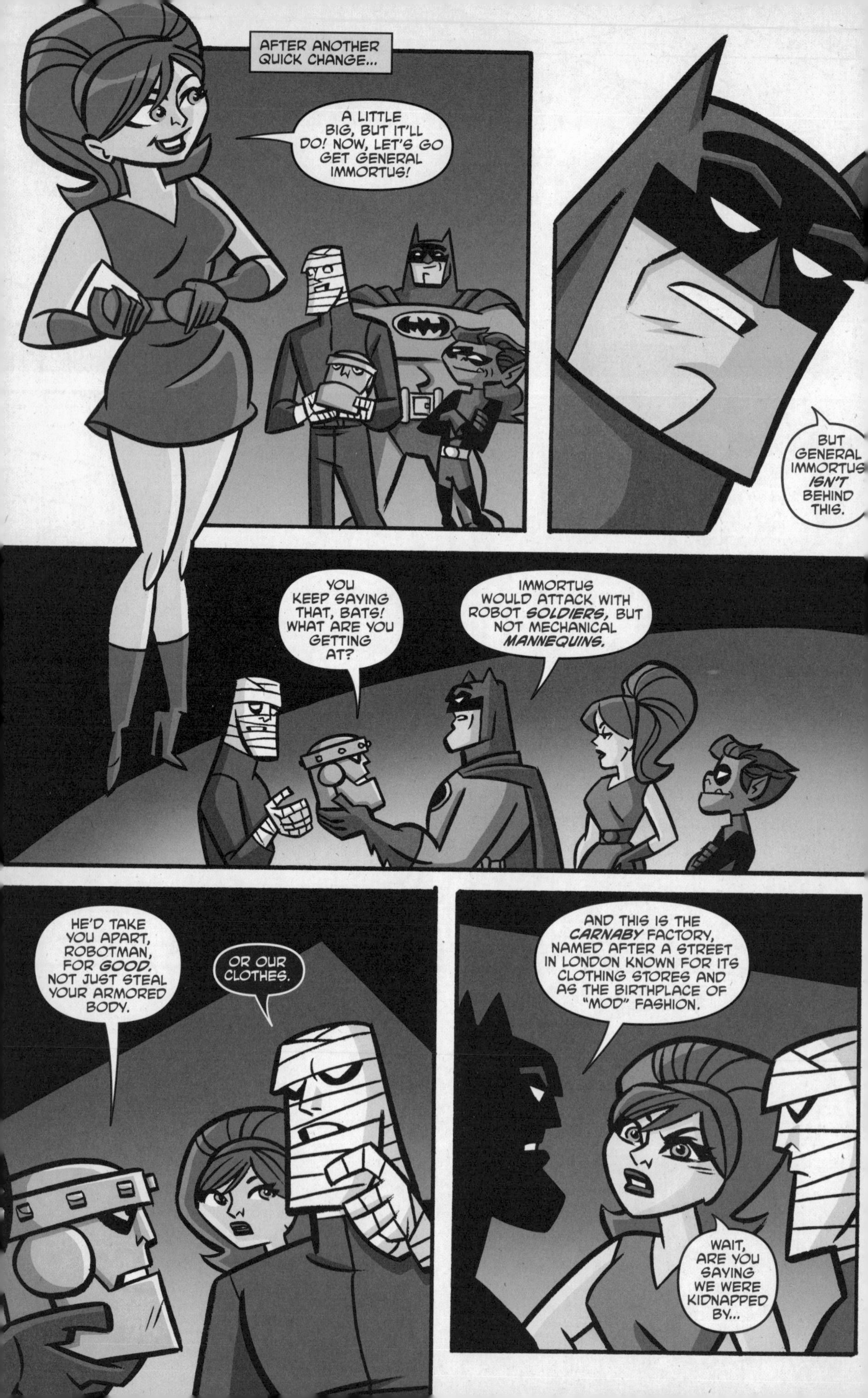
AFTER ANOTHER QUICK CHANGE...
A LITTLE BIG, BUT IT'LL DO! NOW, LET'S GO GET GENERAL IMMORTUS!
BUT GENERAL IMMORTUS *ISN'T* BEHIND THIS.
YOU KEEP SAYING THAT, BATS! WHAT ARE YOU GETTING AT?
IMMORTUS WOULD ATTACK WITH ROBOT *SOLDIERS*, BUT NOT MECHANICAL *MANNEQUINS*.
HE'D TAKE YOU APART, ROBOTMAN, FOR *GOOD*. NOT JUST STEAL YOUR ARMORED BODY.
OR OUR CLOTHES.
AND THIS IS THE *CARNABY* FACTORY, NAMED AFTER A STREET IN LONDON KNOWN FOR ITS CLOTHING STORES AND AS THE BIRTHPLACE OF "MOD" FASHION.
WAIT, ARE YOU SAYING WE WERE KIDNAPPED BY...

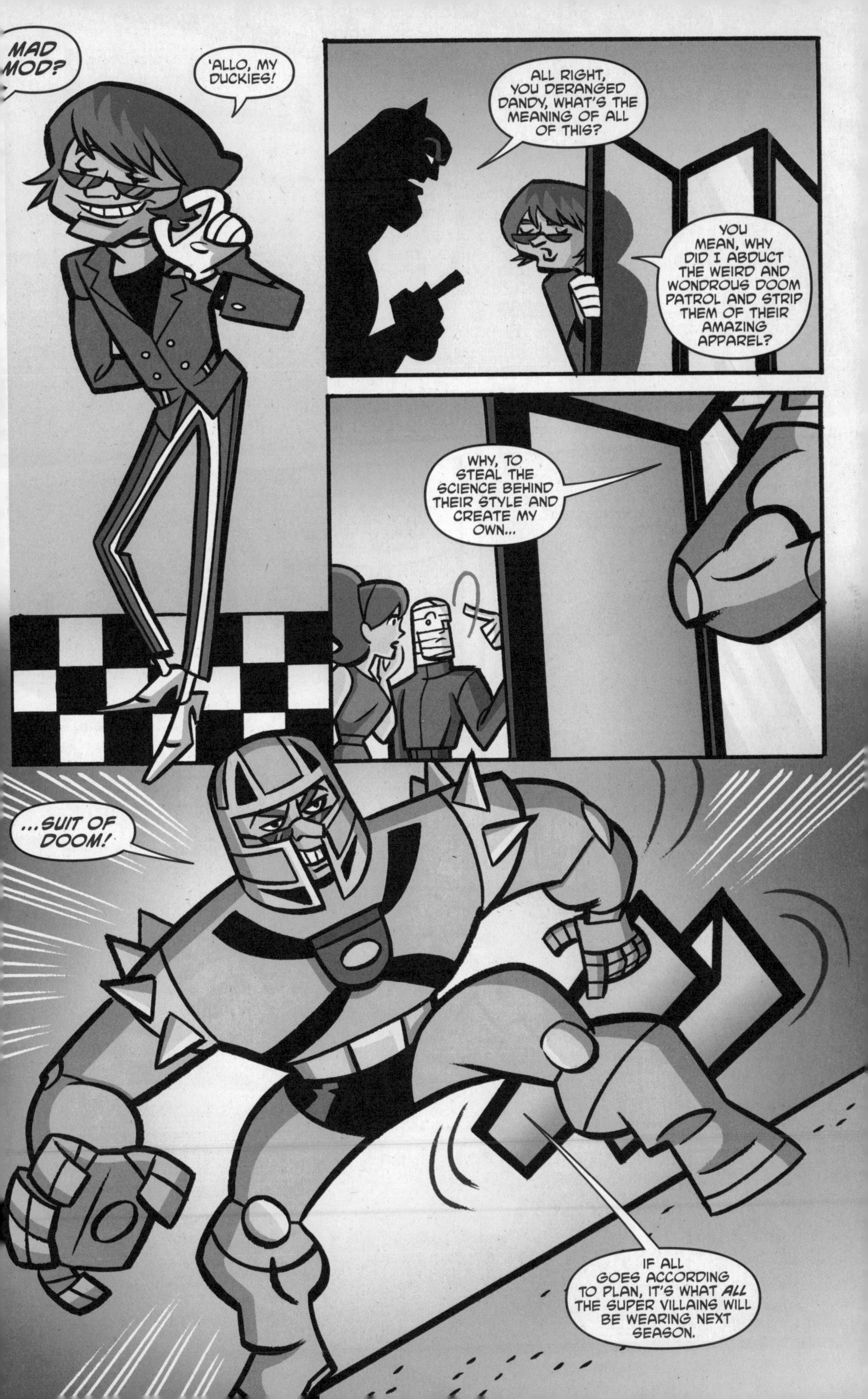
MAD MOD?
'ALLO, MY DUCKIES!
ALL RIGHT, YOU DERANGED DANDY, WHAT'S THE MEANING OF ALL OF THIS?
YOU MEAN, WHY DID I ABDUCT THE WEIRD AND WONDROUS DOOM PATROL AND STRIP THEM OF THEIR AMAZING APPAREL?
WHY, TO STEAL THE SCIENCE BEHIND THEIR STYLE AND CREATE MY OWN...
...SUIT OF DOOM!
IF ALL GOES ACCORDING TO PLAN, IT'S WHAT *ALL* THE SUPER VILLAINS WILL BE WEARING NEXT SEASON.

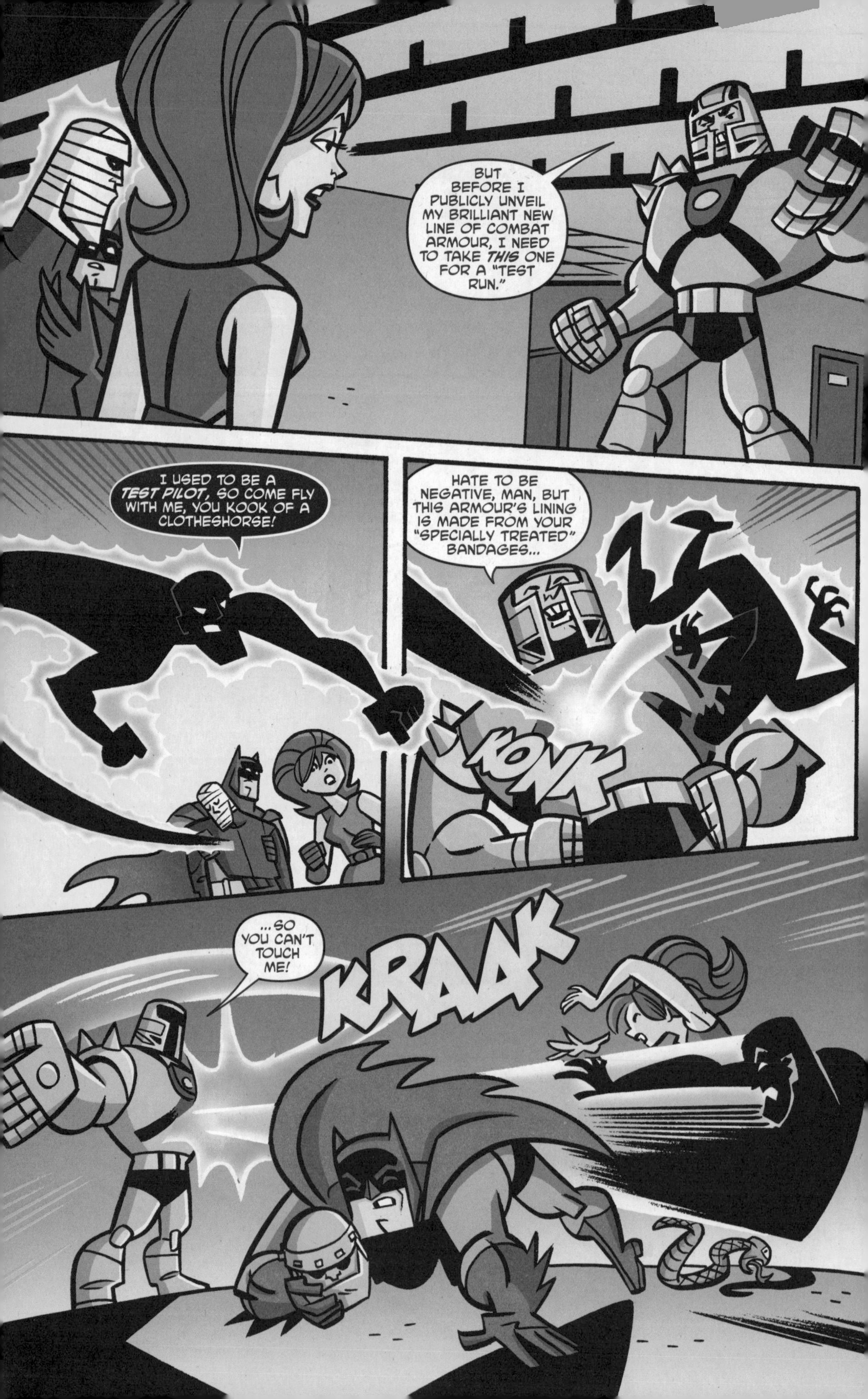

BUT BEFORE I PUBLICLY UNVEIL MY BRILLIANT NEW LINE OF COMBAT ARMOUR, I NEED TO TAKE *THIS* ONE FOR A "TEST RUN."
I USED TO BE A *TEST PILOT*, SO COME FLY WITH ME, YOU KOOK OF A CLOTHESHORSE!
HATE TO BE NEGATIVE, MAN, BUT THIS ARMOUR'S LINING IS MADE FROM YOUR "SPECIALLY TREATED" BANDAGES...
KONK
...SO YOU CAN'T TOUCH ME!
KRAAK

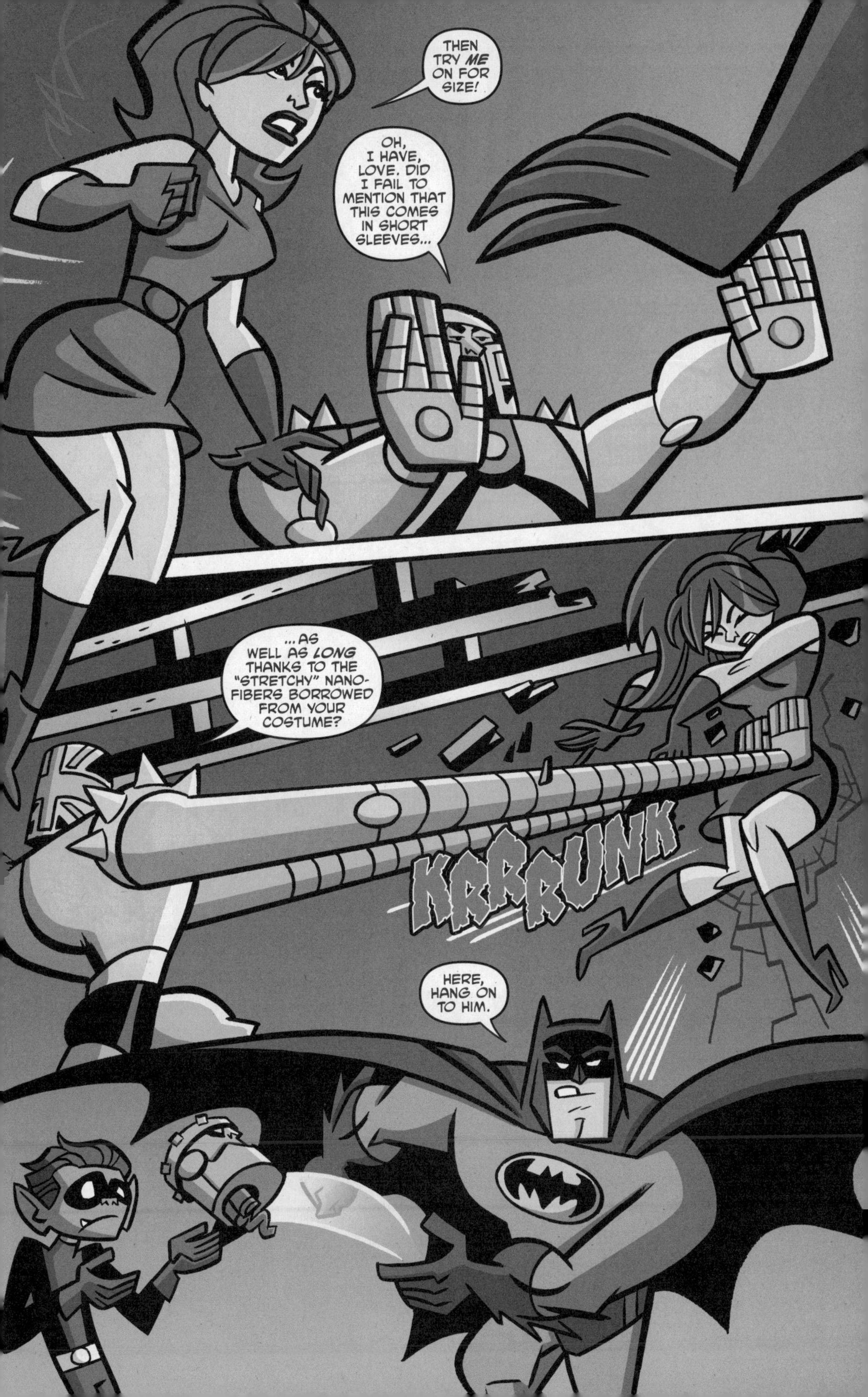
THEN TRY *ME* ON FOR SIZE!
OH, I HAVE, LOVE. DID I FAIL TO MENTION THAT THIS COMES IN SHORT SLEEVES...
...AS WELL AS *LONG* THANKS TO THE "STRETCHY" NANO-FIBERS BORROWED FROM YOUR COSTUME?
KRRRUNK
HERE, HANG ON TO HIM.

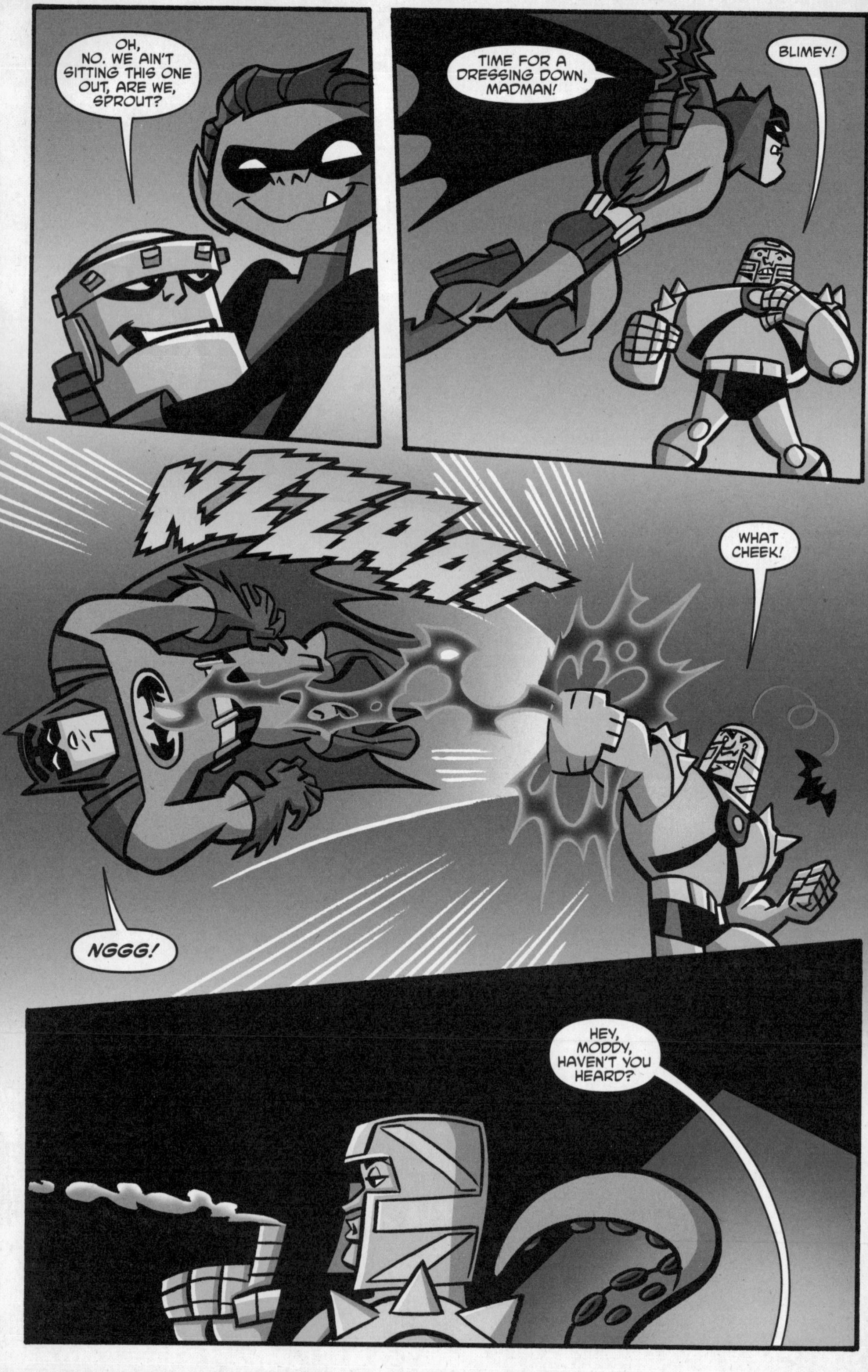
OH, NO. WE AIN'T SITTING THIS ONE OUT, ARE WE, SPROUT?
TIME FOR A DRESSING DOWN, MADMAN!
BLIMEY!
KZZAAT
WHAT CHEEK!
NGGG!
HEY, MODDY, HAVEN'T YOU HEARD?

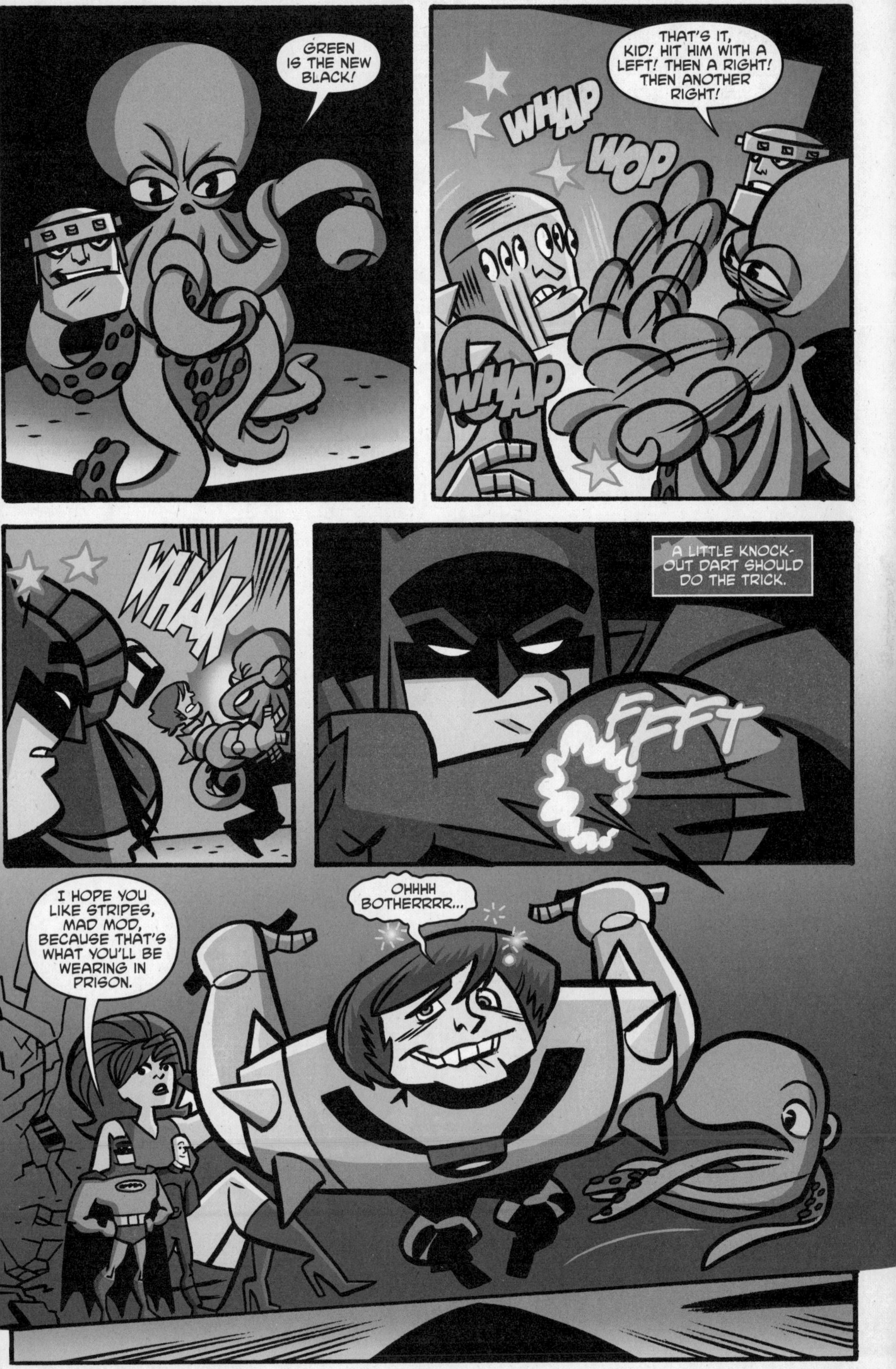
GREEN IS THE NEW BLACK!
THAT'S IT, KID! HIT HIM WITH A LEFT! THEN A RIGHT! THEN ANOTHER RIGHT!
WHAP
WOP
WHAP
WHAK
A LITTLE KNOCK-OUT DART SHOULD DO THE TRICK.
FFFT
I HOPE YOU LIKE STRIPES, MAD MOD, BECAUSE THAT'S WHAT YOU'LL BE WEARING IN PRISON.
OHHHH BOTHERRRR...

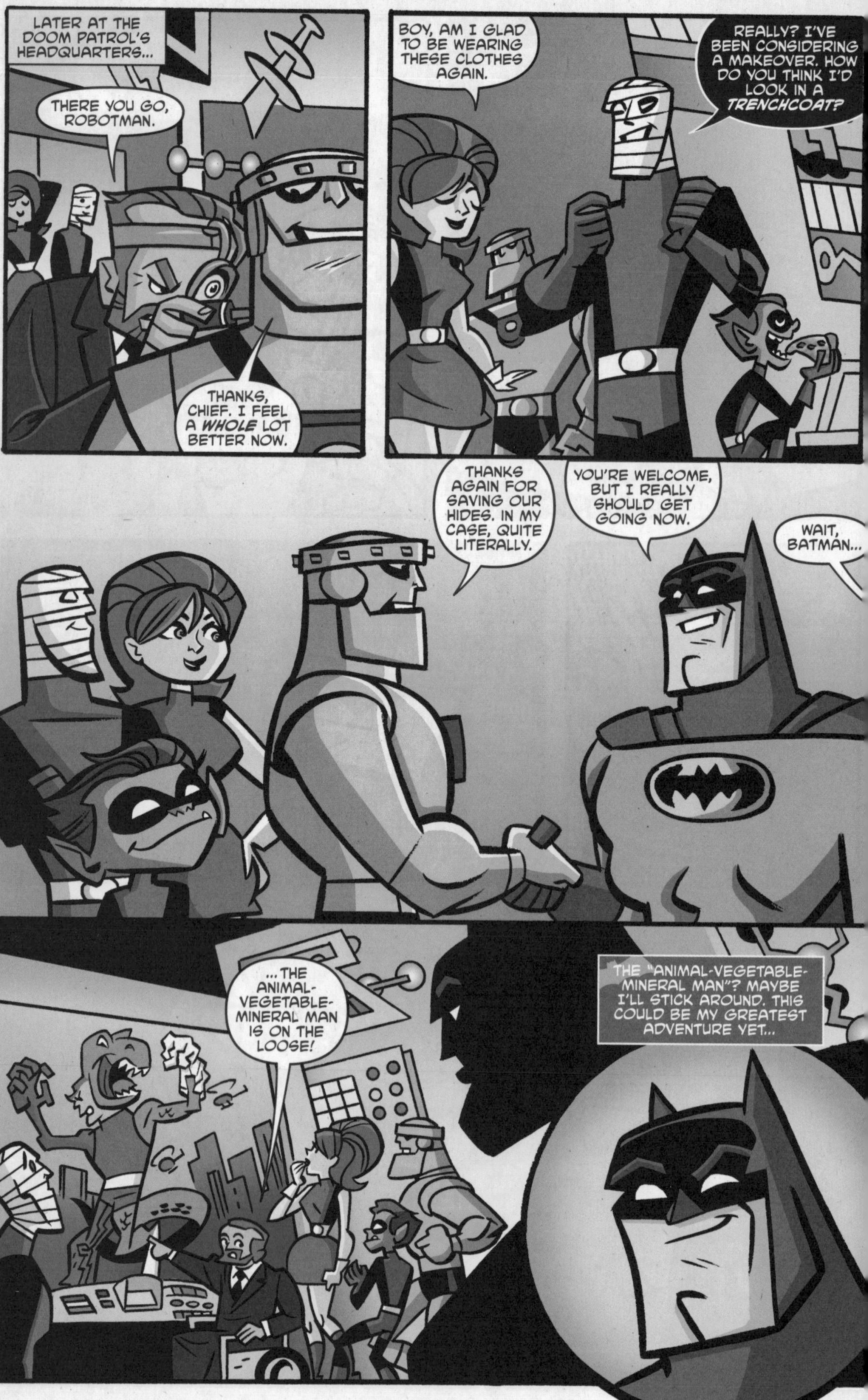
LATER AT THE DOOM PATROL'S HEADQUARTERS...
THERE YOU GO, ROBOTMAN.
THANKS, CHIEF. I FEEL A *WHOLE* LOT BETTER NOW.
BOY, AM I GLAD TO BE WEARING THESE CLOTHES AGAIN.
REALLY? I'VE BEEN CONSIDERING A MAKEOVER. HOW DO YOU THINK I'D LOOK IN A *TRENCHCOAT?*
THANKS AGAIN FOR SAVING OUR HIDES. IN MY CASE, QUITE LITERALLY.
YOU'RE WELCOME, BUT I REALLY SHOULD GET GOING NOW.
WAIT, BATMAN...
...THE ANIMAL-VEGETABLE-MINERAL MAN IS ON THE LOOSE!
THE "ANIMAL-VEGETABLE-MINERAL MAN"? MAYBE I'LL STICK AROUND. THIS COULD BE MY GREATEST ADVENTURE YET...

BAT-FILE

MAD MOD

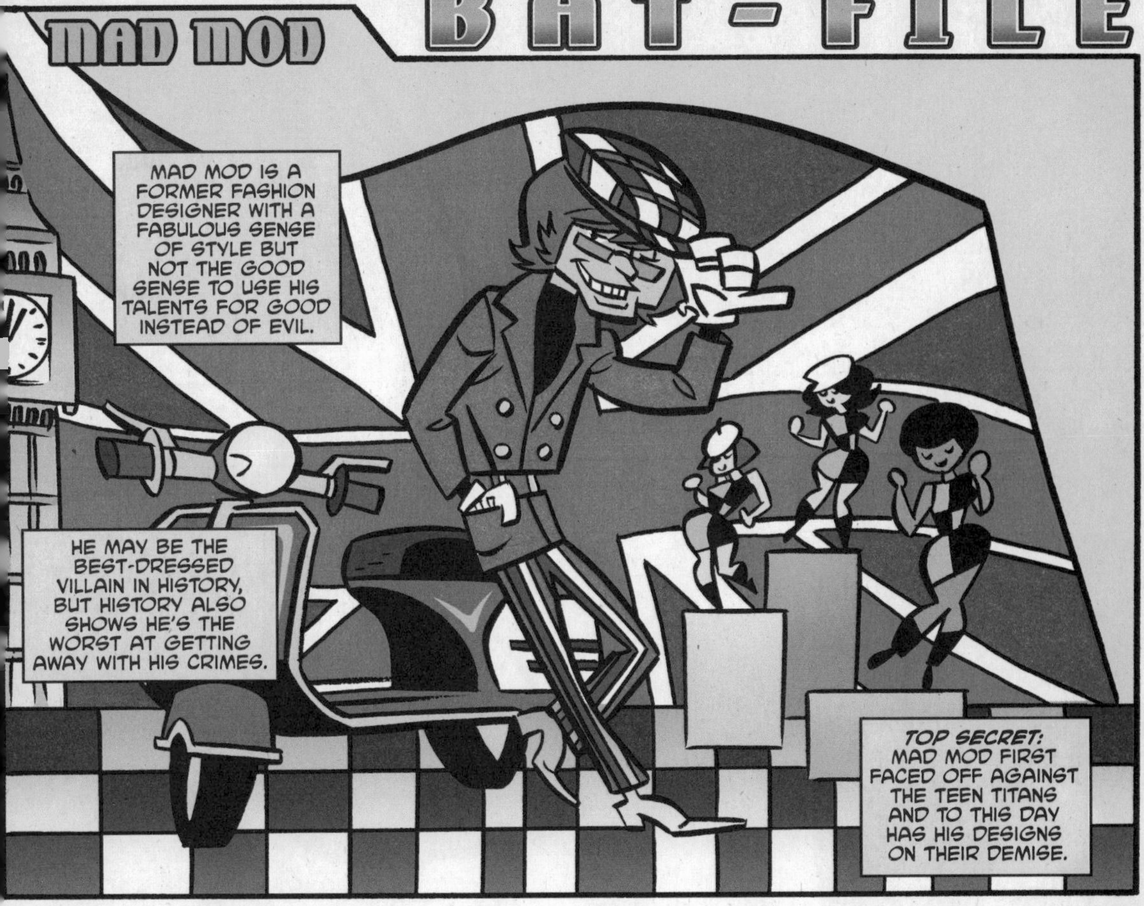
MAD MOD IS A FORMER FASHION DESIGNER WITH A FABULOUS SENSE OF STYLE BUT NOT THE GOOD SENSE TO USE HIS TALENTS FOR GOOD INSTEAD OF EVIL.
HE MAY BE THE BEST-DRESSED VILLAIN IN HISTORY, BUT HISTORY ALSO SHOWS HE'S THE WORST AT GETTING AWAY WITH HIS CRIMES.
TOP SECRET: MAD MOD FIRST FACED OFF AGAINST THE TEEN TITANS AND TO THIS DAY HAS HIS DESIGNS ON THEIR DEMISE.

DOOM PATROL

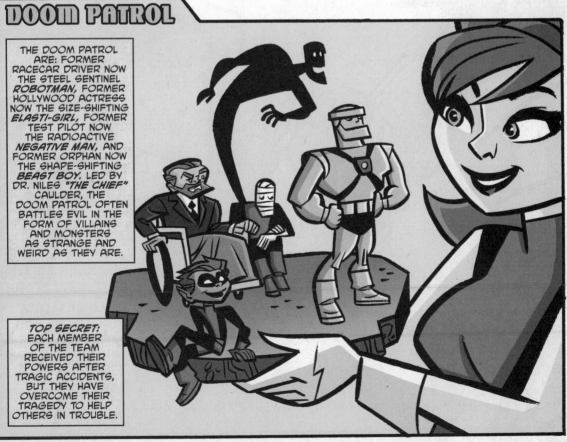

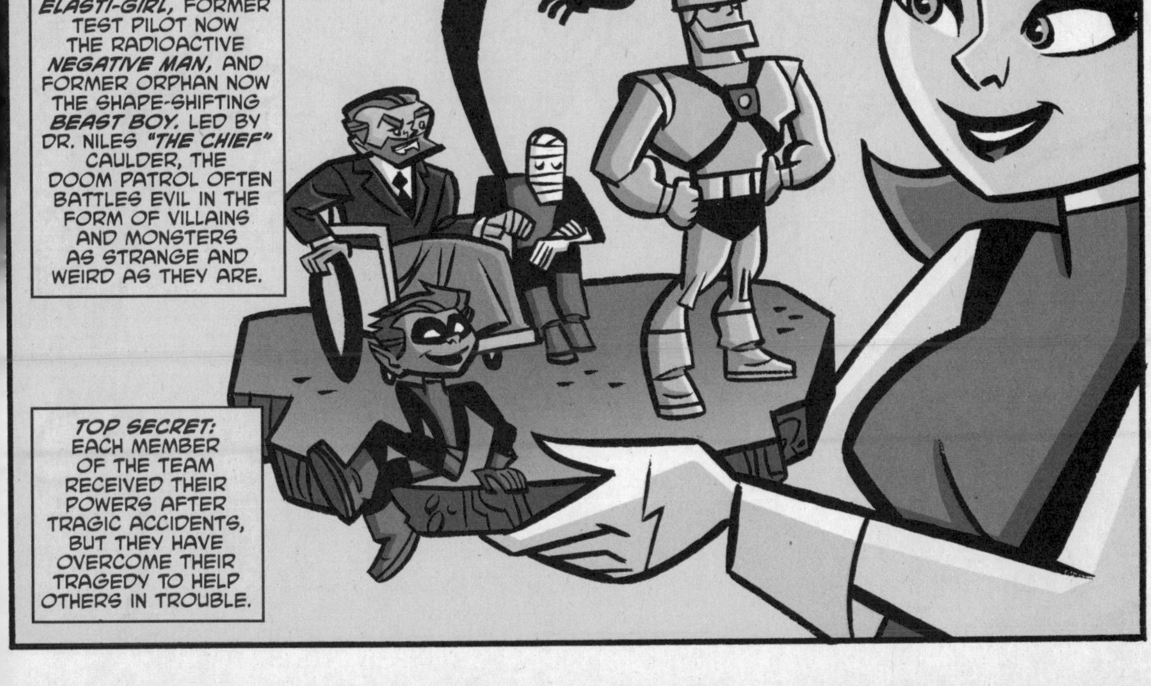
THE DOOM PATROL ARE: FORMER RACECAR DRIVER NOW THE STEEL SENTINEL ***ROBOTMAN,*** FORMER HOLLYWOOD ACTRESS NOW THE SIZE-SHIFTING ***ELASTI-GIRL,*** FORMER TEST PILOT NOW THE RADIOACTIVE ***NEGATIVE MAN,*** AND FORMER ORPHAN NOW THE SHAPE-SHIFTING ***BEAST BOY.*** LED BY DR. NILES ***"THE CHIEF"*** CAULDER, THE DOOM PATROL OFTEN BATTLES EVIL IN THE FORM OF VILLAINS AND MONSTERS AS STRANGE AND WEIRD AS THEY ARE.
TOP SECRET: EACH MEMBER OF THE TEAM RECEIVED THEIR POWERS AFTER TRAGIC ACCIDENTS, BUT THEY HAVE OVERCOME THEIR TRAGEDY TO HELP OTHERS IN TROUBLE.

BATMAN: THE BRAVE AND THE BOLD #8
Cover by Scott Jeralds with Hi-Fi

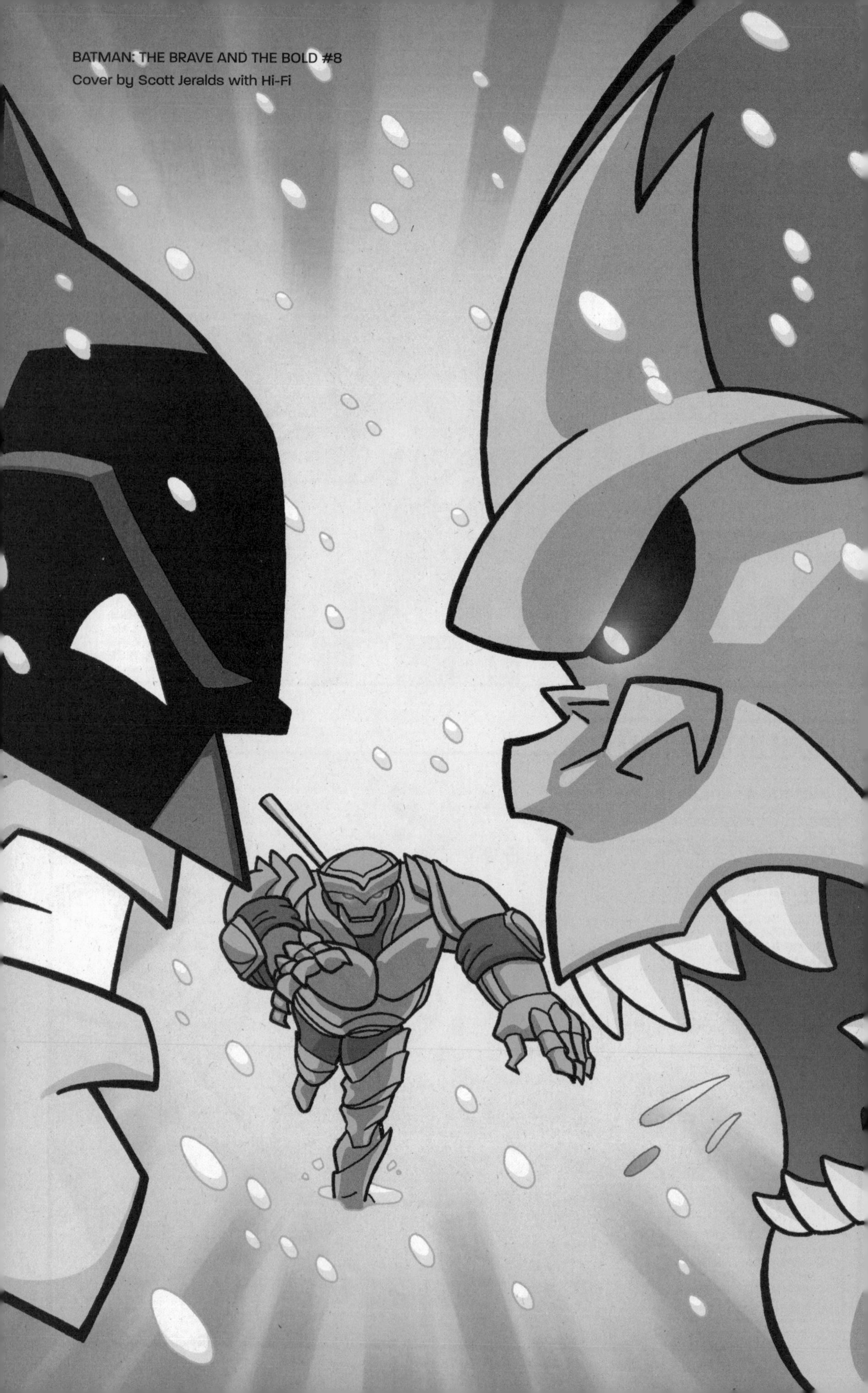

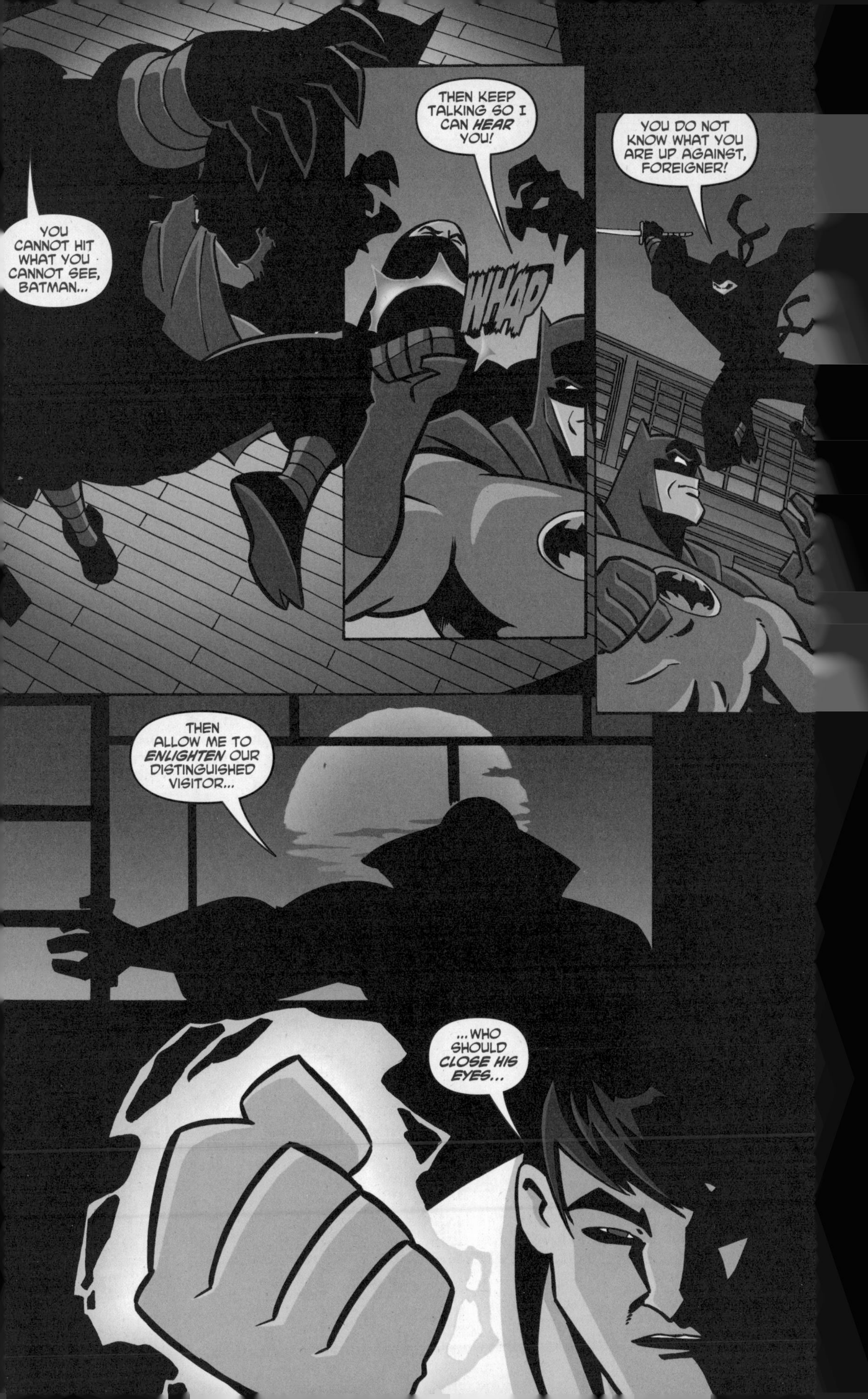
YOU CANNOT HIT WHAT YOU CANNOT SEE, BATMAN...
THEN KEEP TALKING SO I CAN HEAR YOU!
WHAP
YOU DO NOT KNOW WHAT YOU ARE UP AGAINST, FOREIGNER!
THEN ALLOW ME TO ENLIGHTEN OUR DISTINGUISHED VISITOR...
...WHO SHOULD CLOSE HIS EYES...

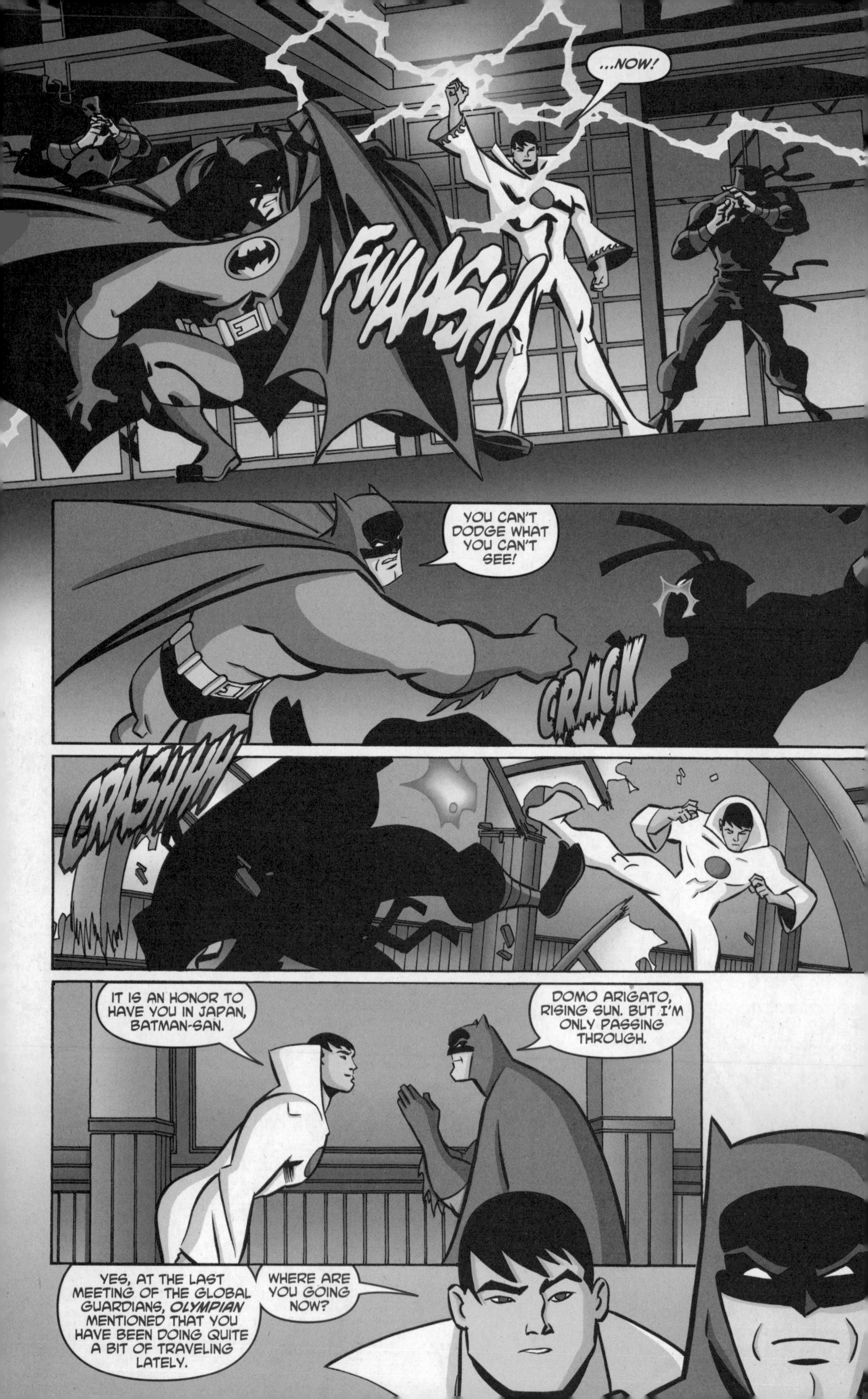
...NOW!
FWASH
YOU CAN'T DODGE WHAT YOU CAN'T SEE!
CRACK
CRASHH
IT IS AN HONOR TO HAVE YOU IN JAPAN, BATMAN-SAN.
DOMO ARIGATO, RISING SUN. BUT I'M ONLY PASSING THROUGH.
YES, AT THE LAST MEETING OF THE GLOBAL GUARDIANS, *OLYMPIAN* MENTIONED THAT YOU HAVE BEEN DOING QUITE A BIT OF TRAVELING LATELY.
WHERE ARE YOU GOING NOW?

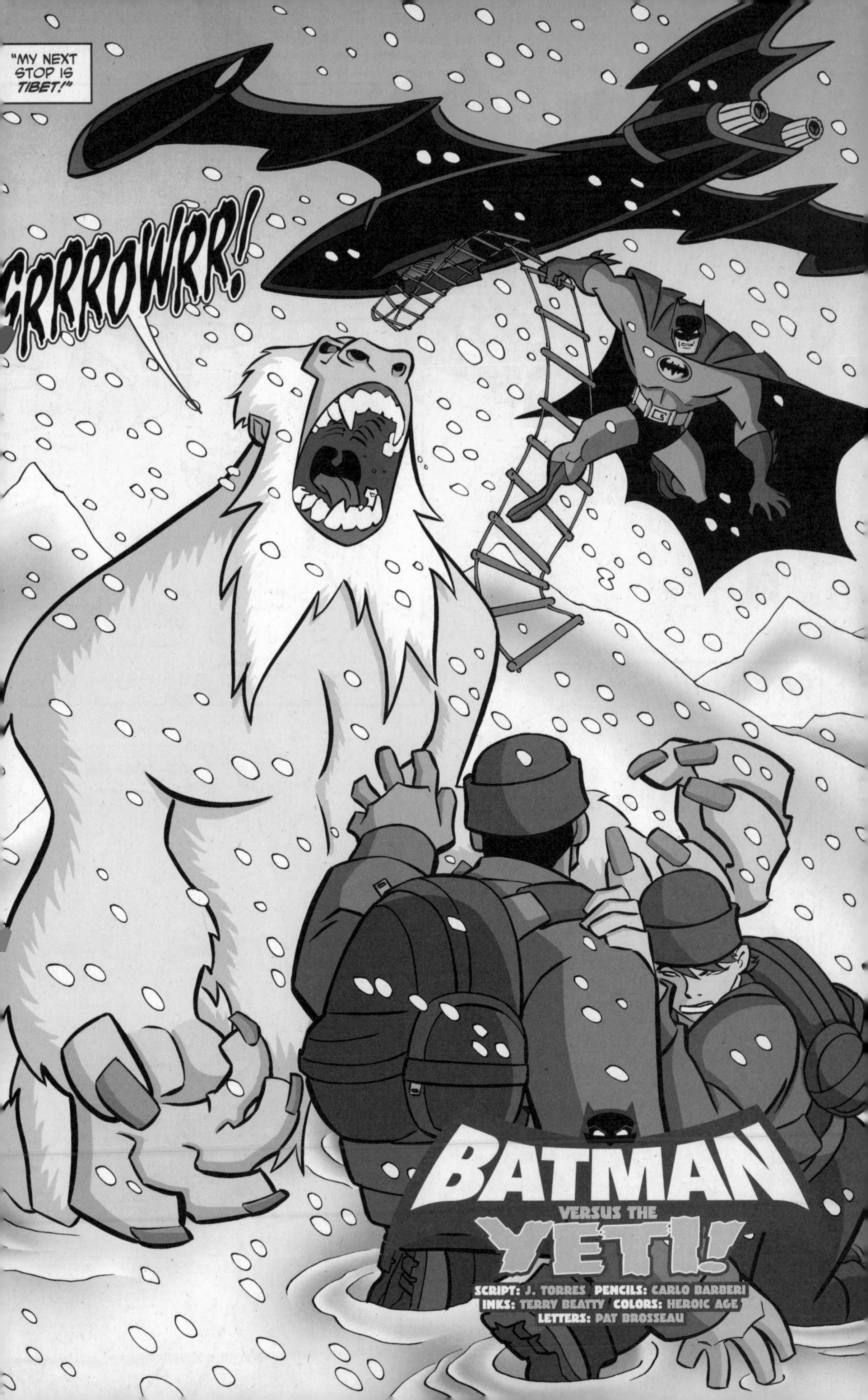
"MY NEXT STOP IS TIBET!"
GRRROWRR!
BATMAN
VERSUS THE
YETI!
SCRIPT: J. TORRES PENCILS: CARLO BARBERI
INKS: TERRY BEATTY COLORS: HEROIC AGE
LETTERS: PAT BROSSEAU

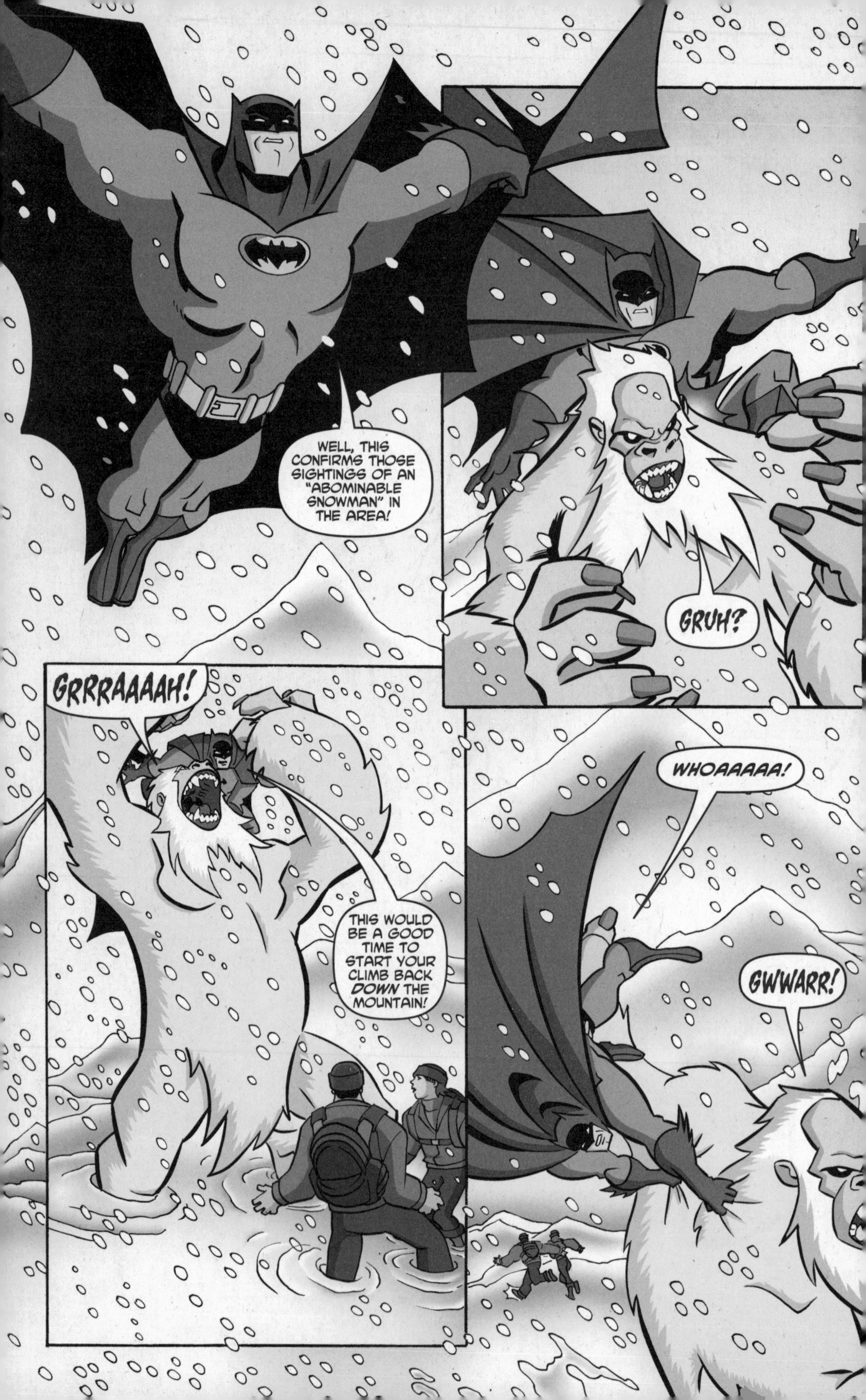
WELL, THIS CONFIRMS THOSE SIGHTINGS OF AN "ABOMINABLE SNOWMAN" IN THE AREA!
GRUH?
GRRRAAAAH!
THIS WOULD BE A GOOD TIME TO START YOUR CLIMB BACK *DOWN* THE MOUNTAIN!
WHOAAAAA!
GWWARR!

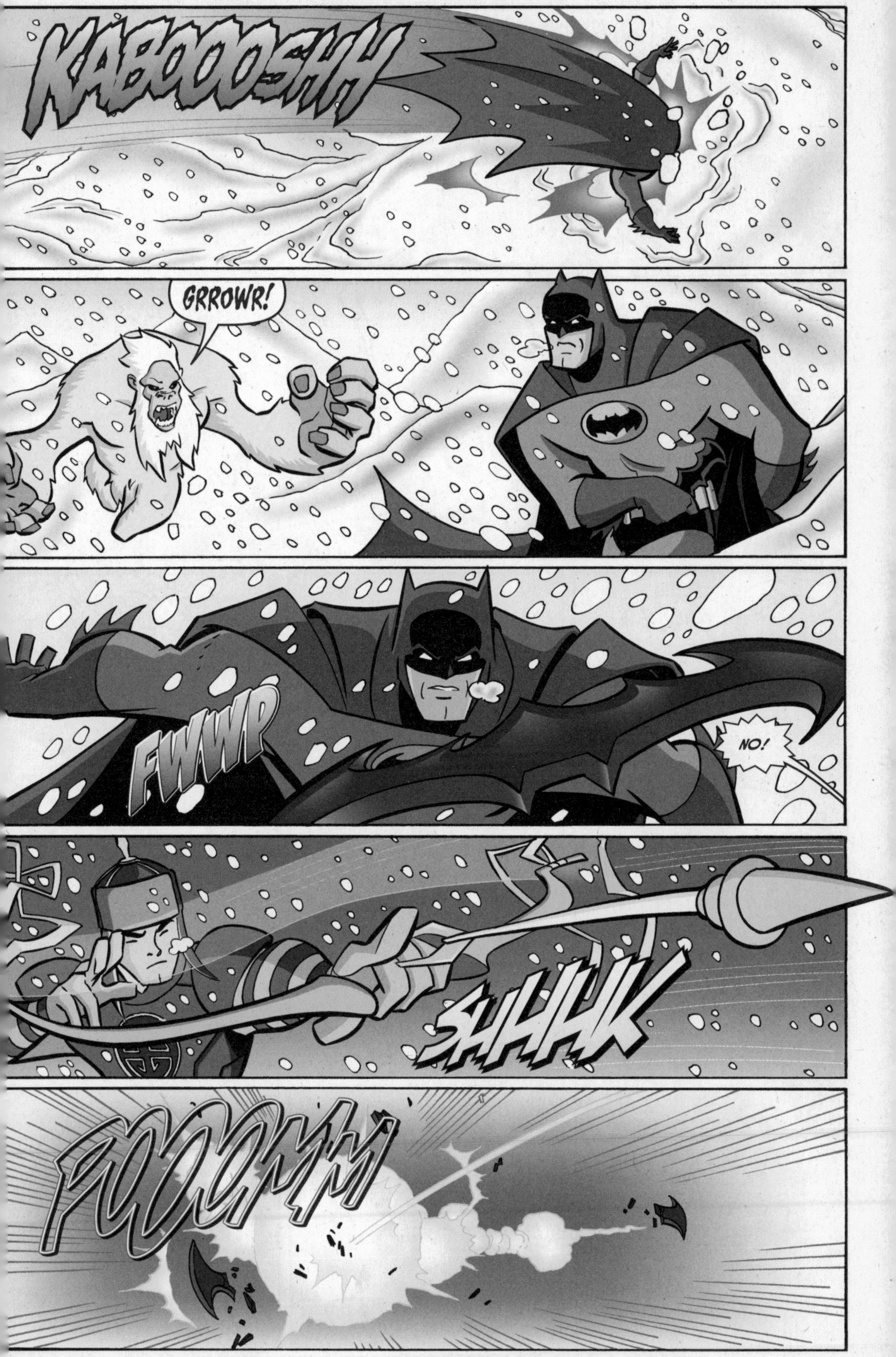
KABOOOSHH
GRRROWR!
FWWP
NO!
SHHHK
FOOOMM

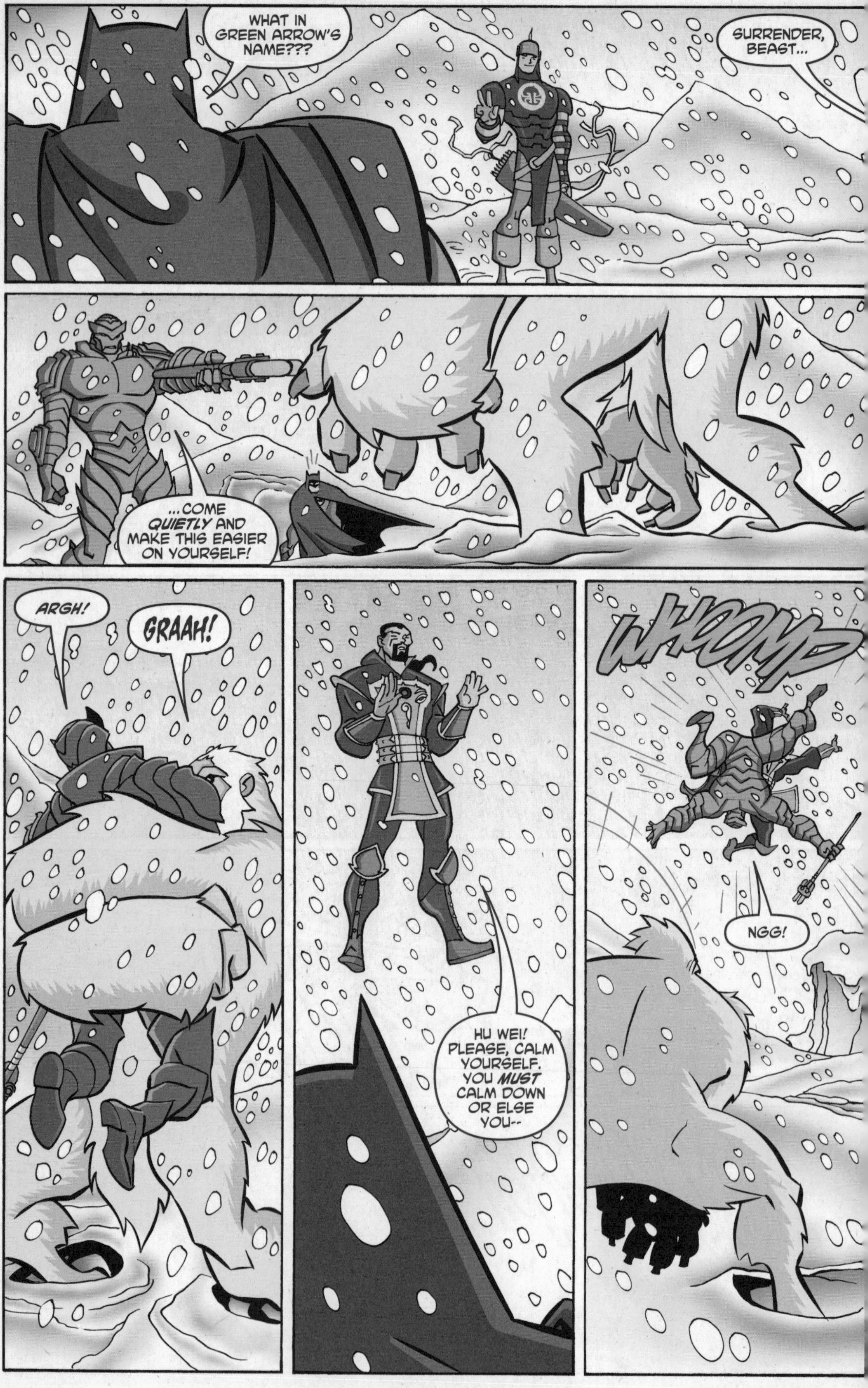
WHAT IN GREEN ARROW'S NAME???
SURRENDER, BEAST...
...COME QUIETLY AND MAKE THIS EASIER ON YOURSELF!
ARGH!
GRAAH!
HU WEI! PLEASE, CALM YOURSELF. YOU MUST CALM DOWN OR ELSE YOU--
WHOOMP
NGG!

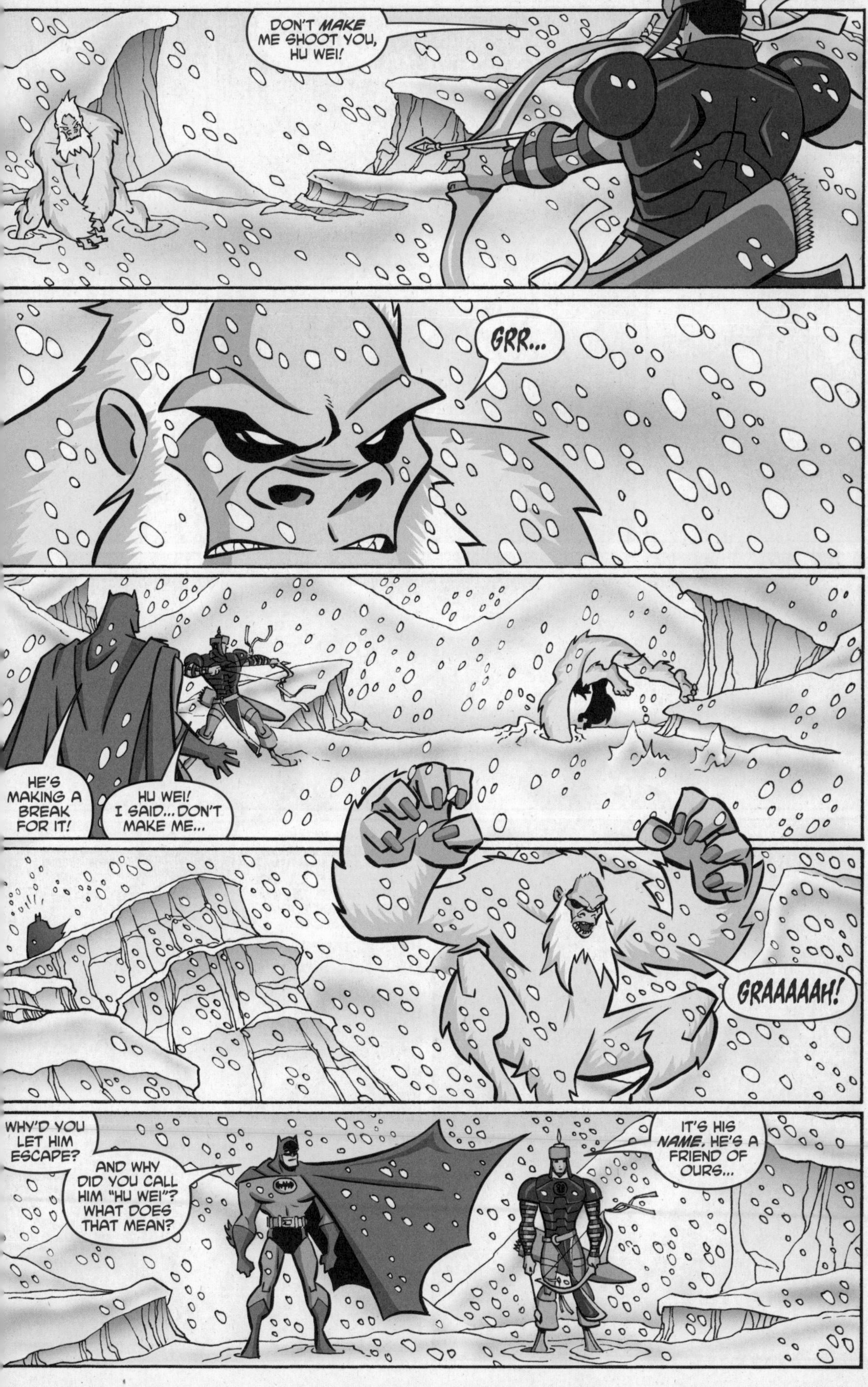
DON'T MAKE ME SHOOT YOU, HU WEI!
GRR...
HE'S MAKING A BREAK FOR IT!
HU WEI! I SAID...DON'T MAKE ME...
GRAAAAAH!
WHY'D YOU LET HIM ESCAPE?
AND WHY DID YOU CALL HIM "HU WEI"? WHAT DOES THAT MEAN?
IT'S HIS NAME. HE'S A FRIEND OF OURS...

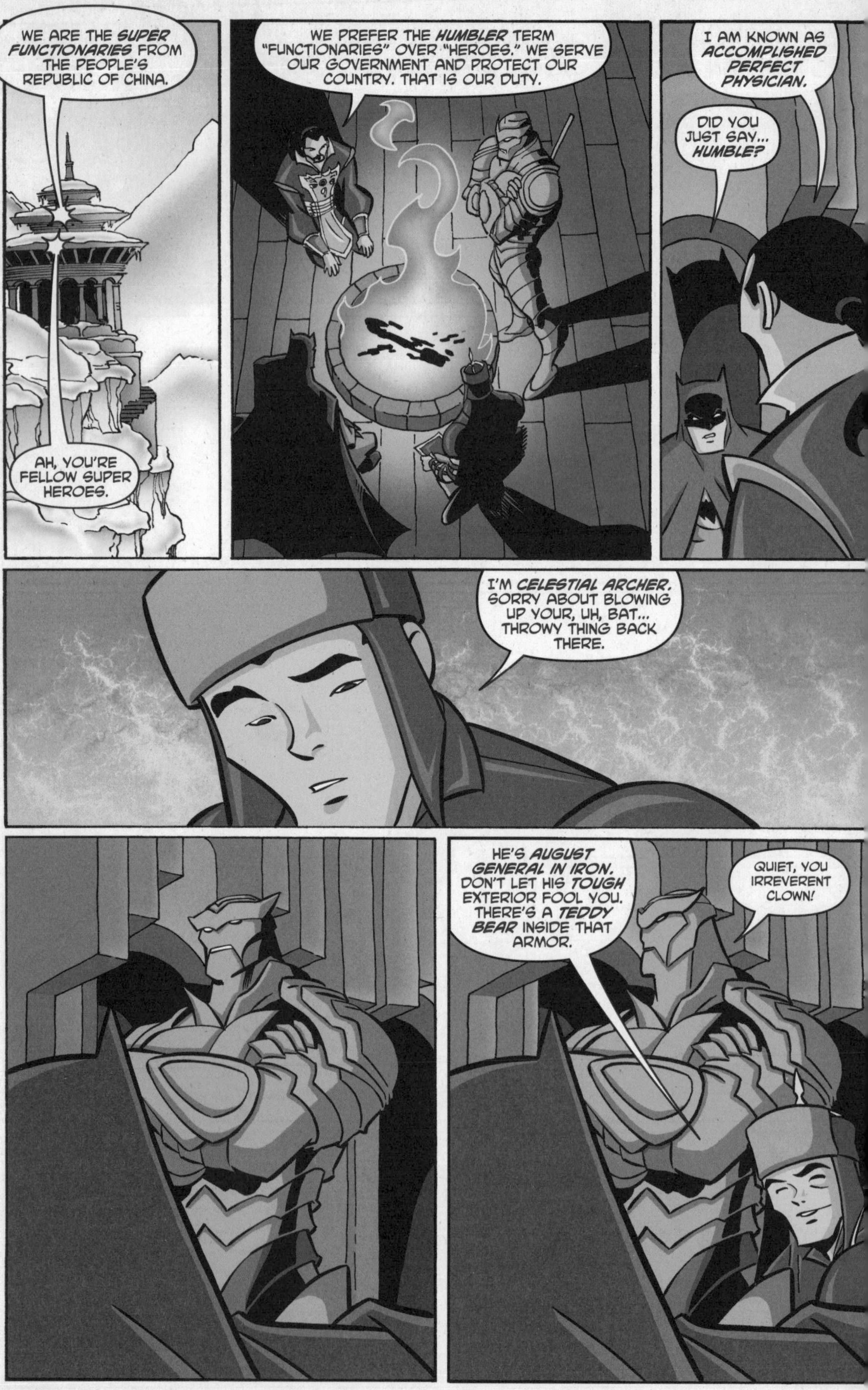
WE ARE THE SUPER FUNCTIONARIES FROM THE PEOPLE'S REPUBLIC OF CHINA.
AH, YOU'RE FELLOW SUPER HEROES.
WE PREFER THE HUMBLER TERM "FUNCTIONARIES" OVER "HEROES." WE SERVE OUR GOVERNMENT AND PROTECT OUR COUNTRY. THAT IS OUR DUTY.
I AM KNOWN AS ACCOMPLISHED PERFECT PHYSICIAN.
DID YOU JUST SAY... HUMBLE?
I'M CELESTIAL ARCHER. SORRY ABOUT BLOWING UP YOUR, UH, BAT... THROWY THING BACK THERE.
HE'S AUGUST GENERAL IN IRON. DON'T LET HIS TOUGH EXTERIOR FOOL YOU. THERE'S A TEDDY BEAR INSIDE THAT ARMOR.
QUIET, YOU IRREVERENT CLOWN!

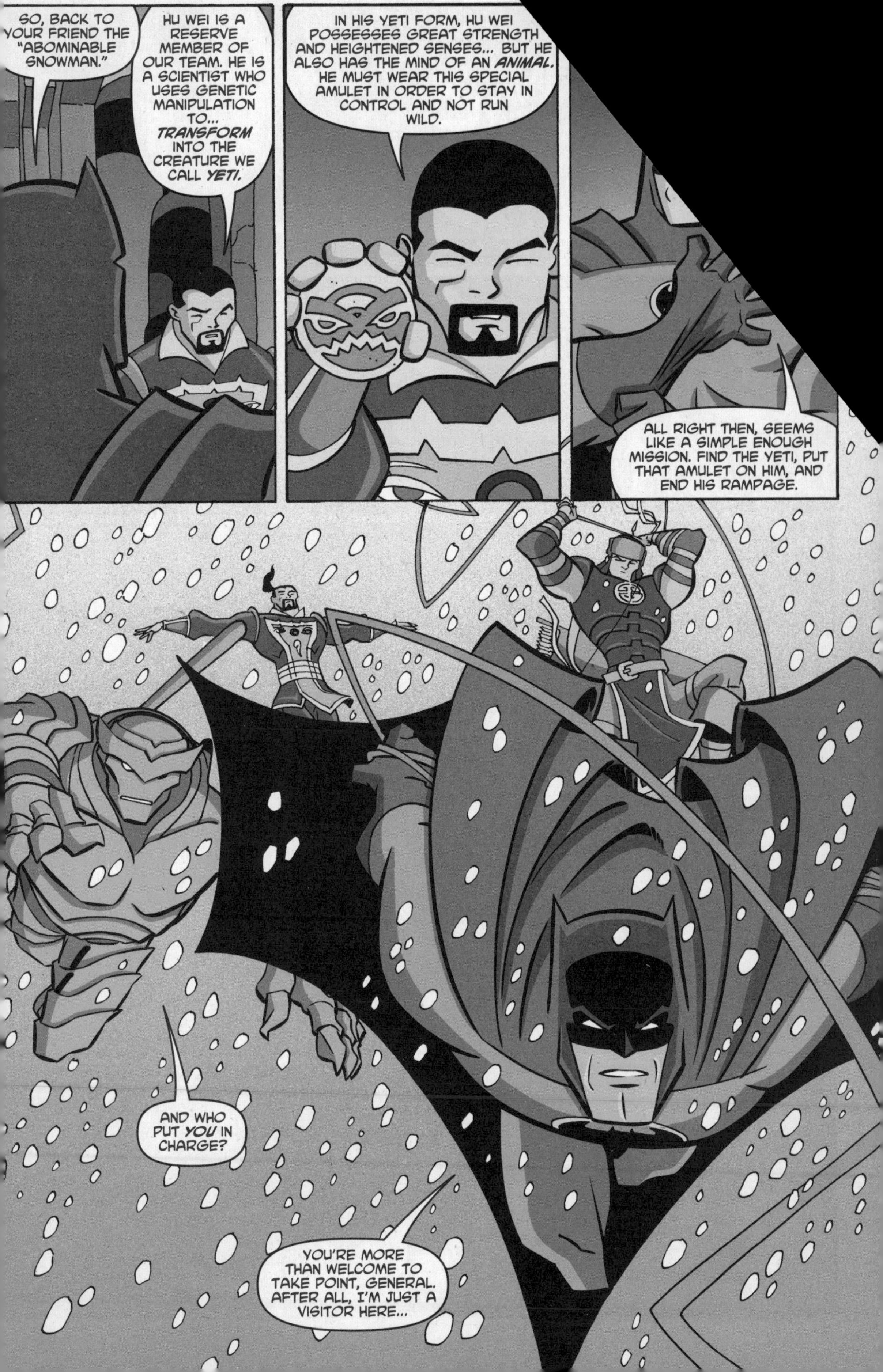
SO, BACK TO YOUR FRIEND THE "ABOMINABLE SNOWMAN."
HU WEI IS A RESERVE MEMBER OF OUR TEAM. HE IS A SCIENTIST WHO USES GENETIC MANIPULATION TO... TRANSFORM INTO THE CREATURE WE CALL YETI.
IN HIS YETI FORM, HU WEI POSSESSES GREAT STRENGTH AND HEIGHTENED SENSES... BUT HE ALSO HAS THE MIND OF AN ANIMAL. HE MUST WEAR THIS SPECIAL AMULET IN ORDER TO STAY IN CONTROL AND NOT RUN WILD.
ALL RIGHT THEN, SEEMS LIKE A SIMPLE ENOUGH MISSION. FIND THE YETI, PUT THAT AMULET ON HIM, AND END HIS RAMPAGE.
AND WHO PUT YOU IN CHARGE?
YOU'RE MORE THAN WELCOME TO TAKE POINT, GENERAL. AFTER ALL, I'M JUST A VISITOR HERE...

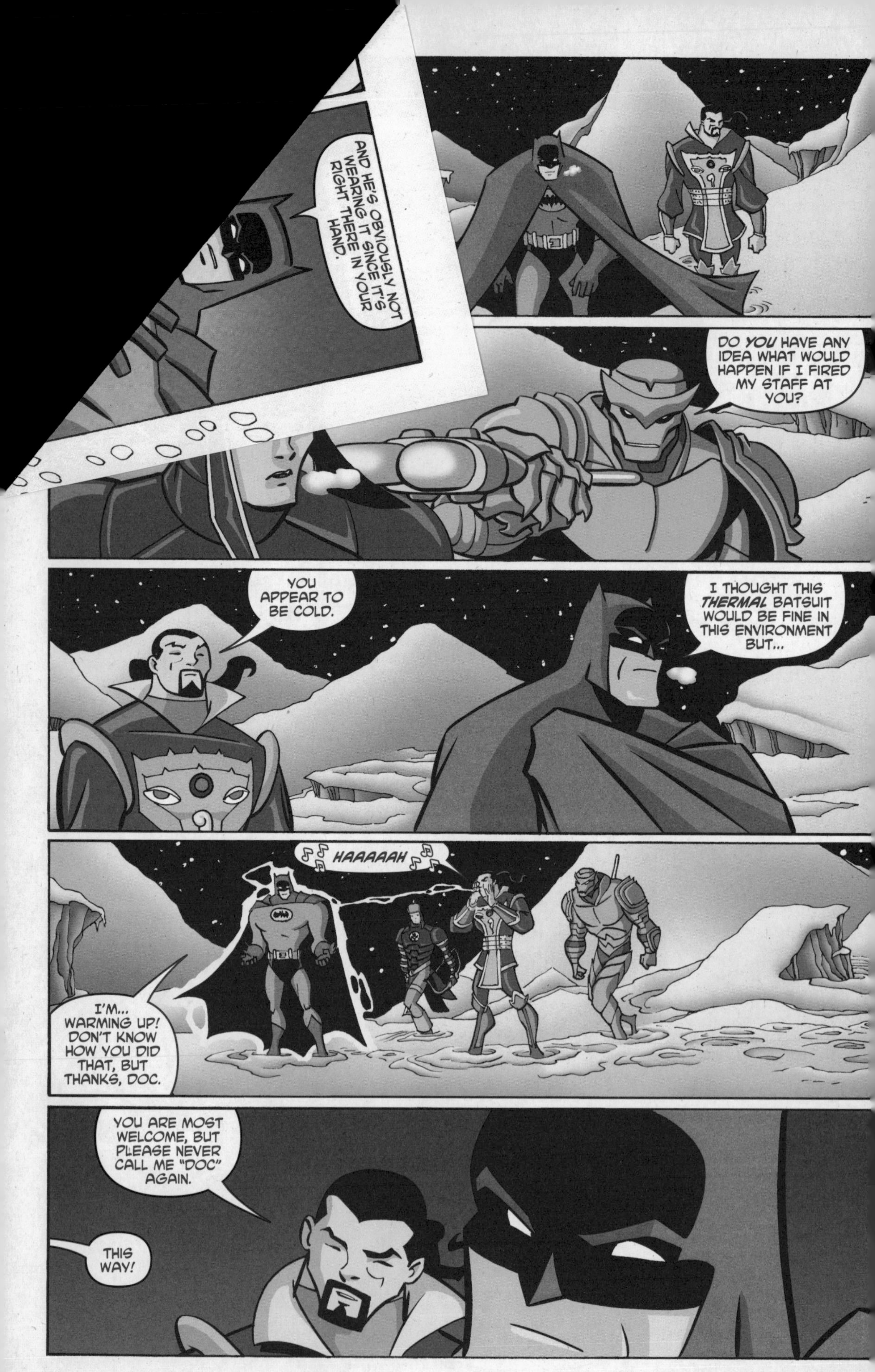
AND HE'S OBVIOUSLY NOT WEARING IT SINCE IT'S RIGHT THERE IN YOUR HAND.
DO *YOU* HAVE ANY IDEA WHAT WOULD HAPPEN IF I FIRED MY STAFF AT YOU?
YOU APPEAR TO BE COLD.
I THOUGHT THIS *THERMAL* BATSUIT WOULD BE FINE IN THIS ENVIRONMENT BUT...
HAAAAAH
I'M... WARMING UP! DON'T KNOW HOW YOU DID THAT, BUT THANKS, DOC.
YOU ARE MOST WELCOME, BUT PLEASE NEVER CALL ME "DOC" AGAIN.
THIS WAY!

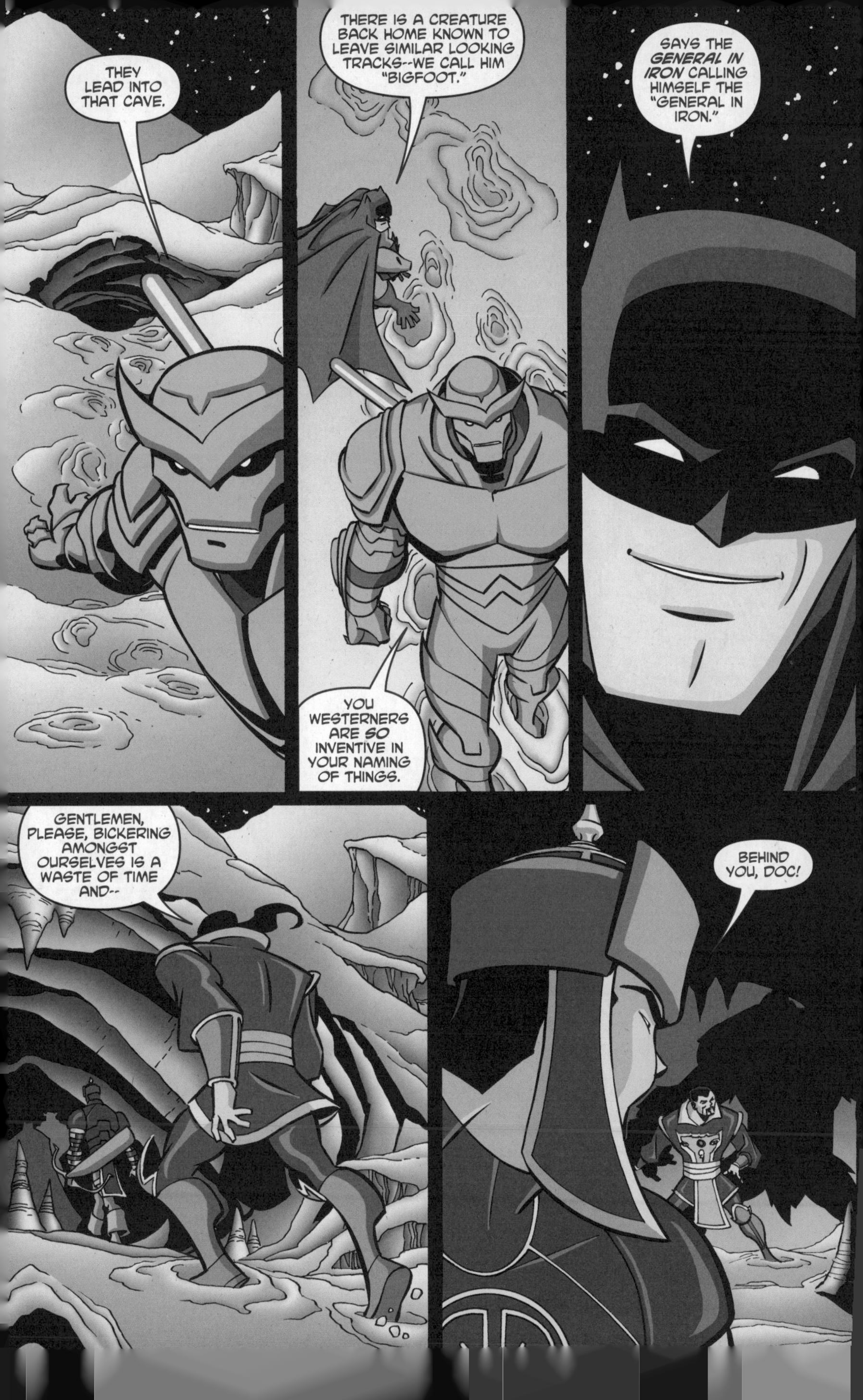
THEY LEAD INTO THAT CAVE.
THERE IS A CREATURE BACK HOME KNOWN TO LEAVE SIMILAR LOOKING TRACKS--WE CALL HIM "BIGFOOT."
YOU WESTERNERS ARE SO INVENTIVE IN YOUR NAMING OF THINGS.
SAYS THE GENERAL IN IRON CALLING HIMSELF THE "GENERAL IN IRON."
GENTLEMEN, PLEASE, BICKERING AMONGST OURSELVES IS A WASTE OF TIME AND--
BEHIND YOU, DOC!

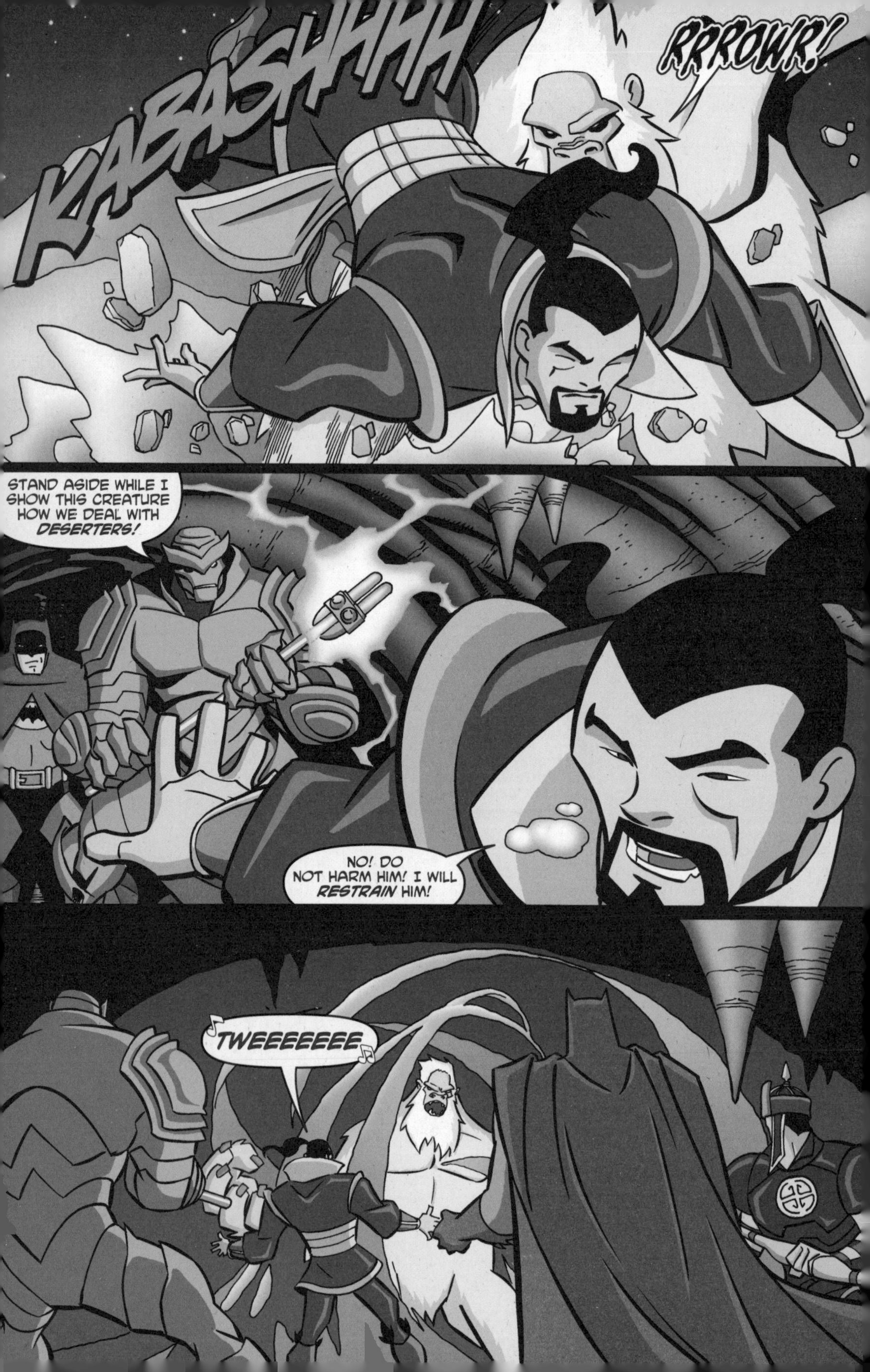
KABASHHHH
RRROWR!
STAND ASIDE WHILE I SHOW THIS CREATURE HOW WE DEAL WITH DESERTERS!
NO! DO NOT HARM HIM! I WILL RESTRAIN HIM!
TWEEEEEEE

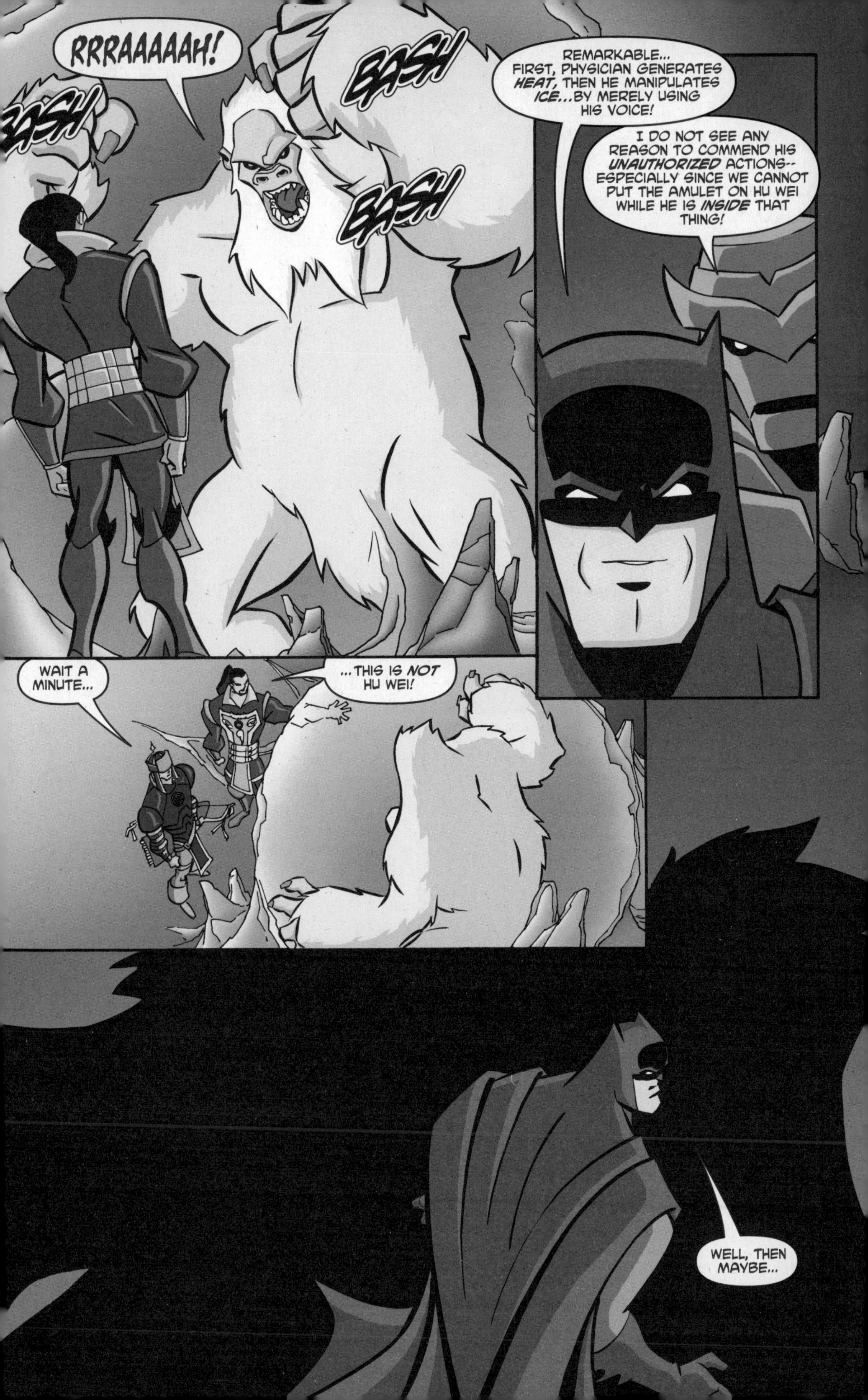
RRRAAAAAH!
BASH
BASH
BASH
REMARKABLE... FIRST, PHYSICIAN GENERATES HEAT, THEN HE MANIPULATES ICE... BY MERELY USING HIS VOICE!
I DO NOT SEE ANY REASON TO COMMEND HIS UNAUTHORIZED ACTIONS-- ESPECIALLY SINCE WE CANNOT PUT THE AMULET ON HU WEI WHILE HE IS INSIDE THAT THING!
WAIT A MINUTE...
...THIS IS NOT HU WEI!
WELL, THEN MAYBE...

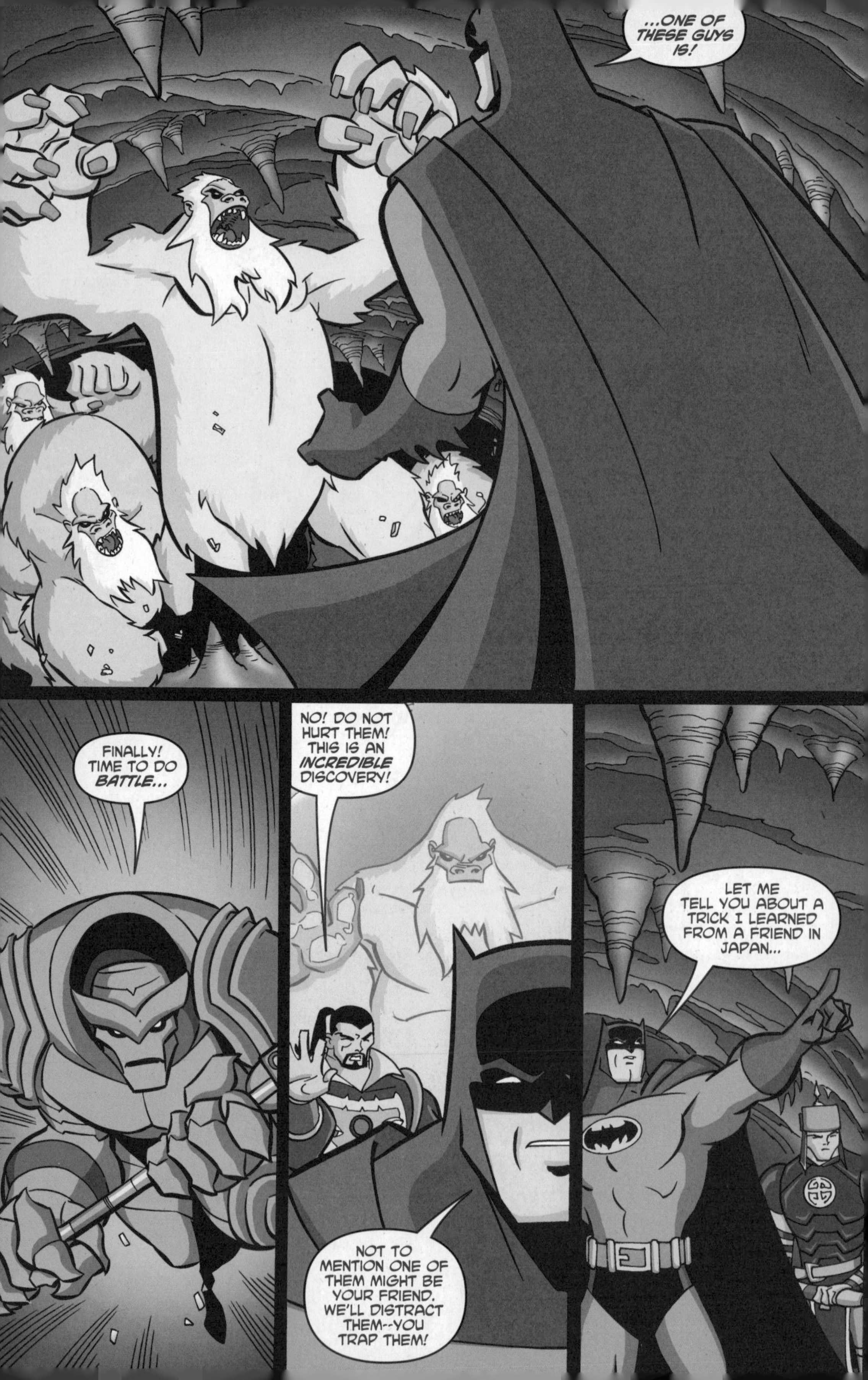
...ONE OF THESE GUYS IS!
FINALLY! TIME TO DO BATTLE...
NO! DO NOT HURT THEM! THIS IS AN INCREDIBLE DISCOVERY!
NOT TO MENTION ONE OF THEM MIGHT BE YOUR FRIEND. WE'LL DISTRACT THEM--YOU TRAP THEM!
LET ME TELL YOU ABOUT A TRICK I LEARNED FROM A FRIEND IN JAPAN...

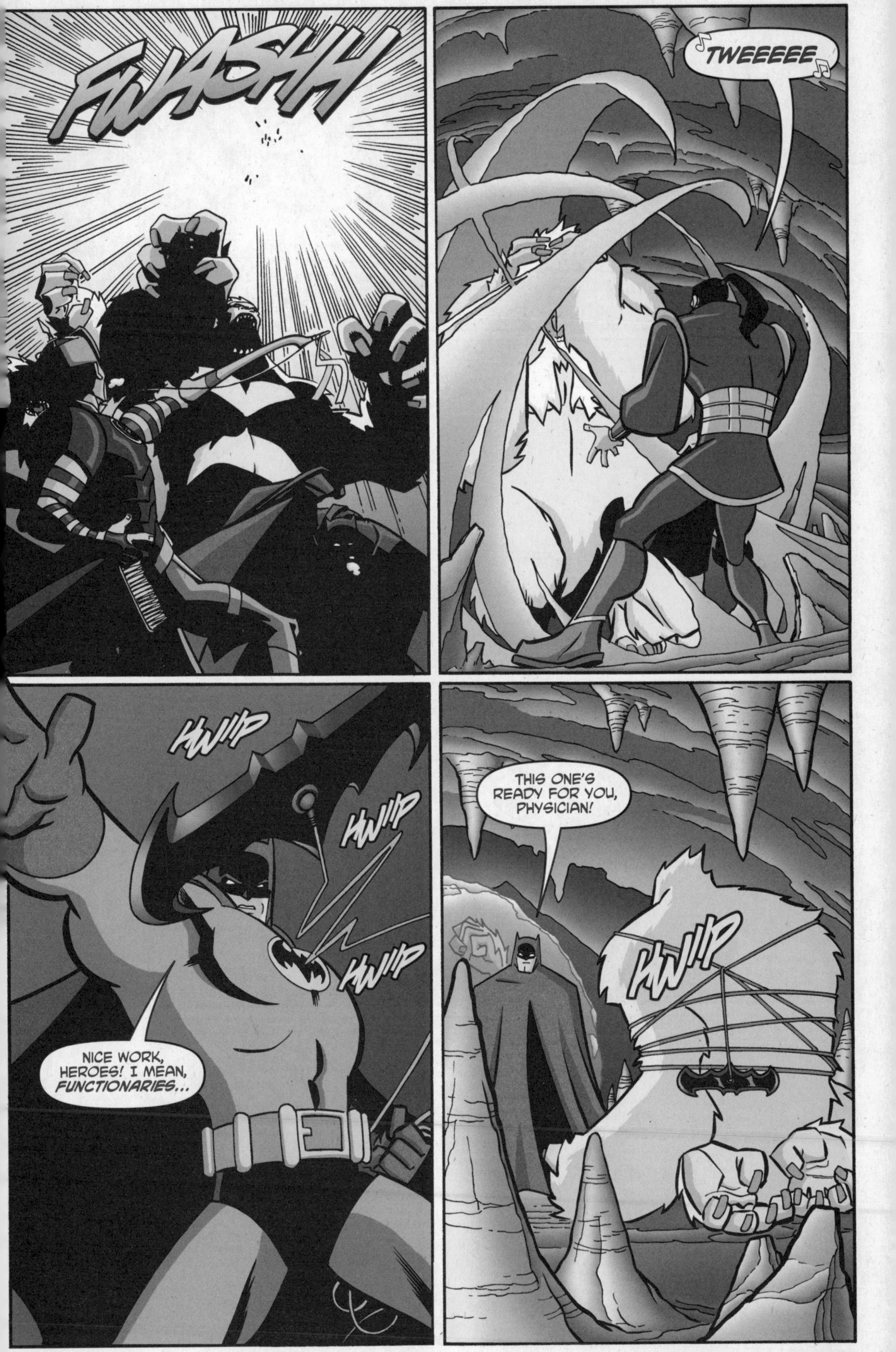
FWASHH
TWEEEEE
KWIIP
KWIIP
KWIIP
NICE WORK, HEROES! I MEAN, FUNCTIONARIES...
THIS ONE'S READY FOR YOU, PHYSICIAN!
KWIIP

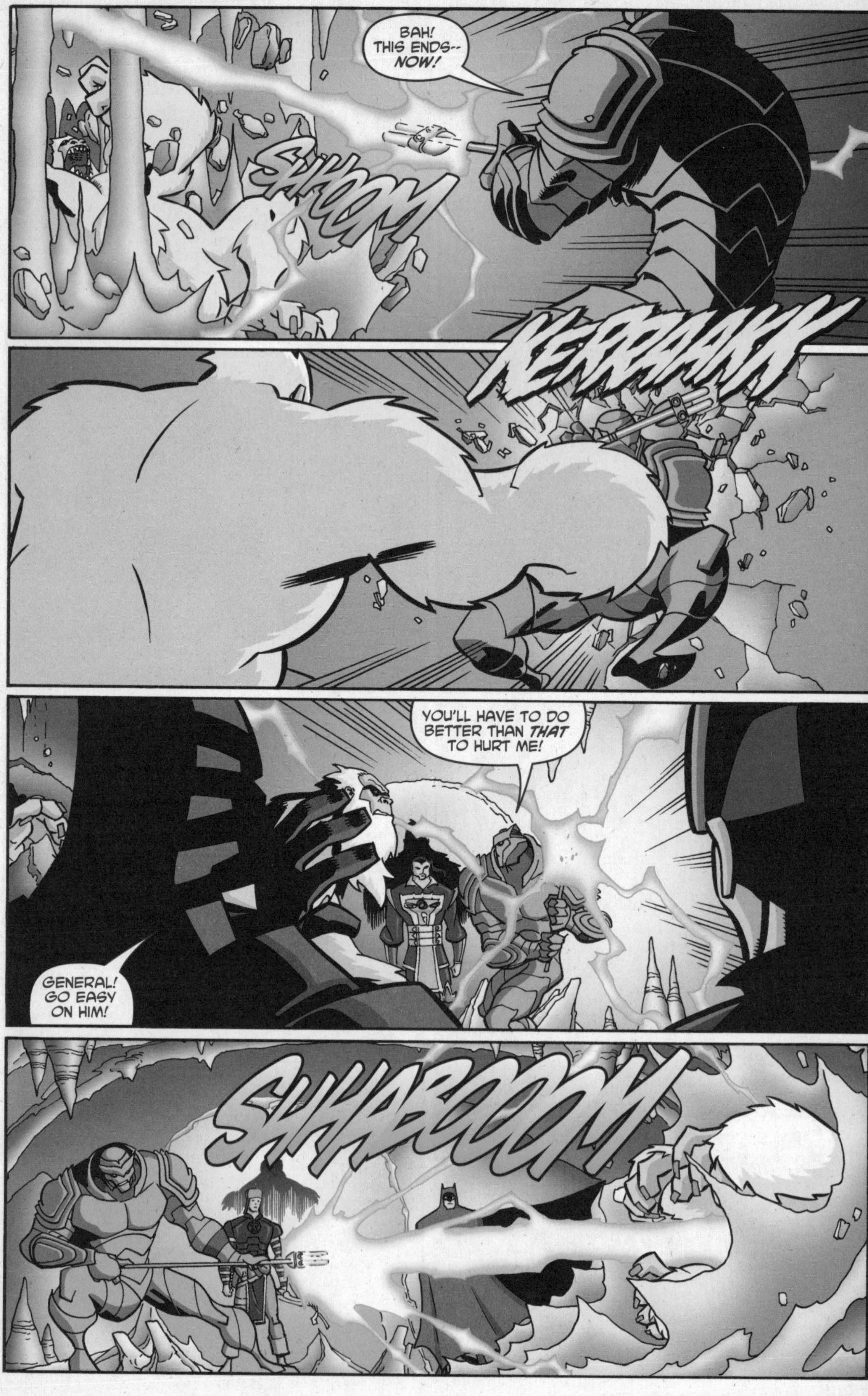
BAH! THIS ENDS-- NOW!
SHHOOM
KERRAAKK
YOU'LL HAVE TO DO BETTER THAN THAT TO HURT ME!
GENERAL! GO EASY ON HIM!
SHHBOOOM

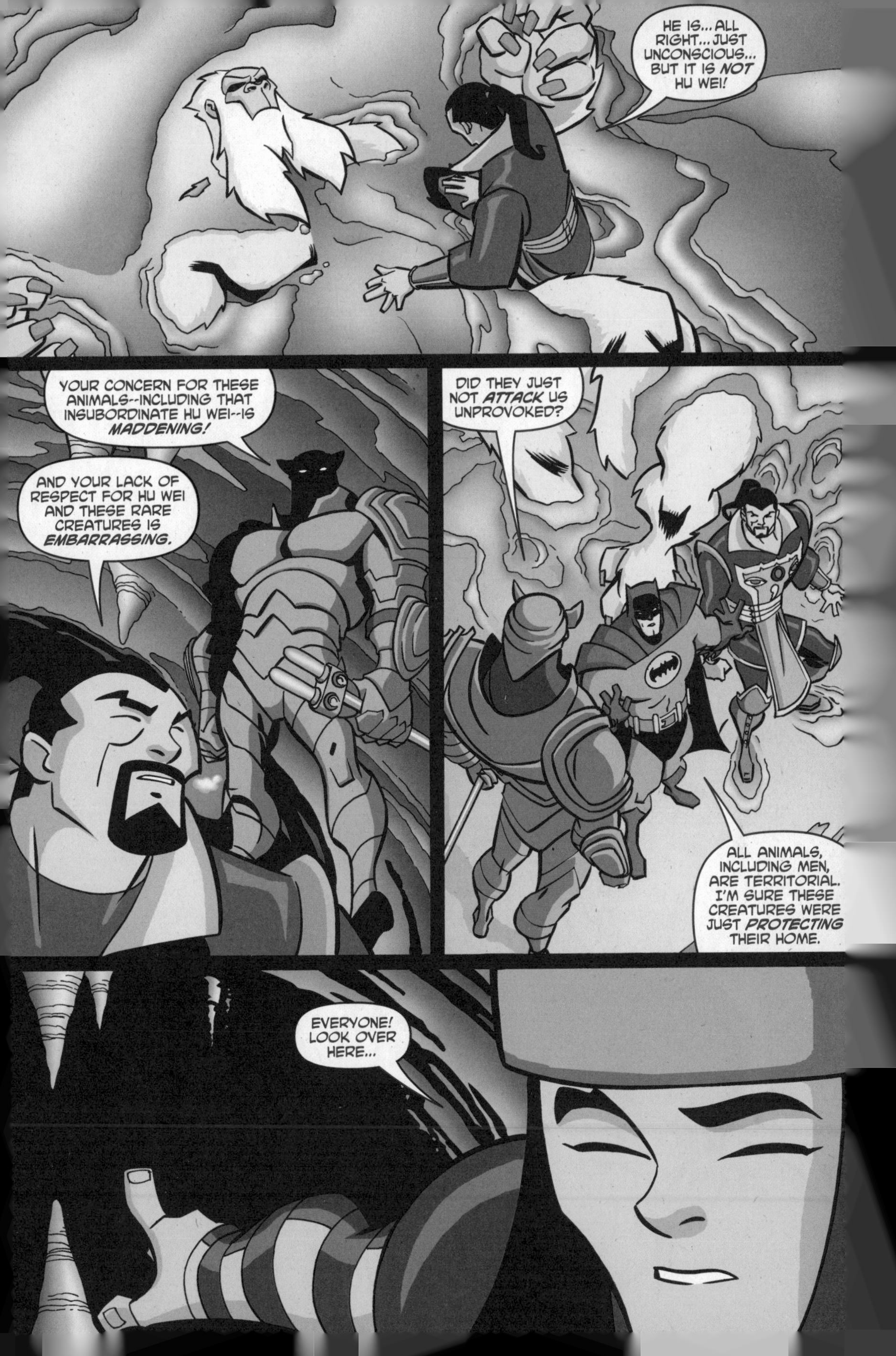
HE IS... ALL RIGHT... JUST UNCONSCIOUS... BUT IT IS *NOT* HU WEI!
YOUR CONCERN FOR THESE ANIMALS--INCLUDING THAT INSUBORDINATE HU WEI--IS *MADDENING!*
AND YOUR LACK OF RESPECT FOR HU WEI AND THESE RARE CREATURES IS *EMBARRASSING.*
DID THEY JUST NOT *ATTACK* US UNPROVOKED?
ALL ANIMALS, INCLUDING MEN, ARE TERRITORIAL. I'M SURE THESE CREATURES WERE JUST *PROTECTING* THEIR HOME.
EVERYONE! LOOK OVER HERE...

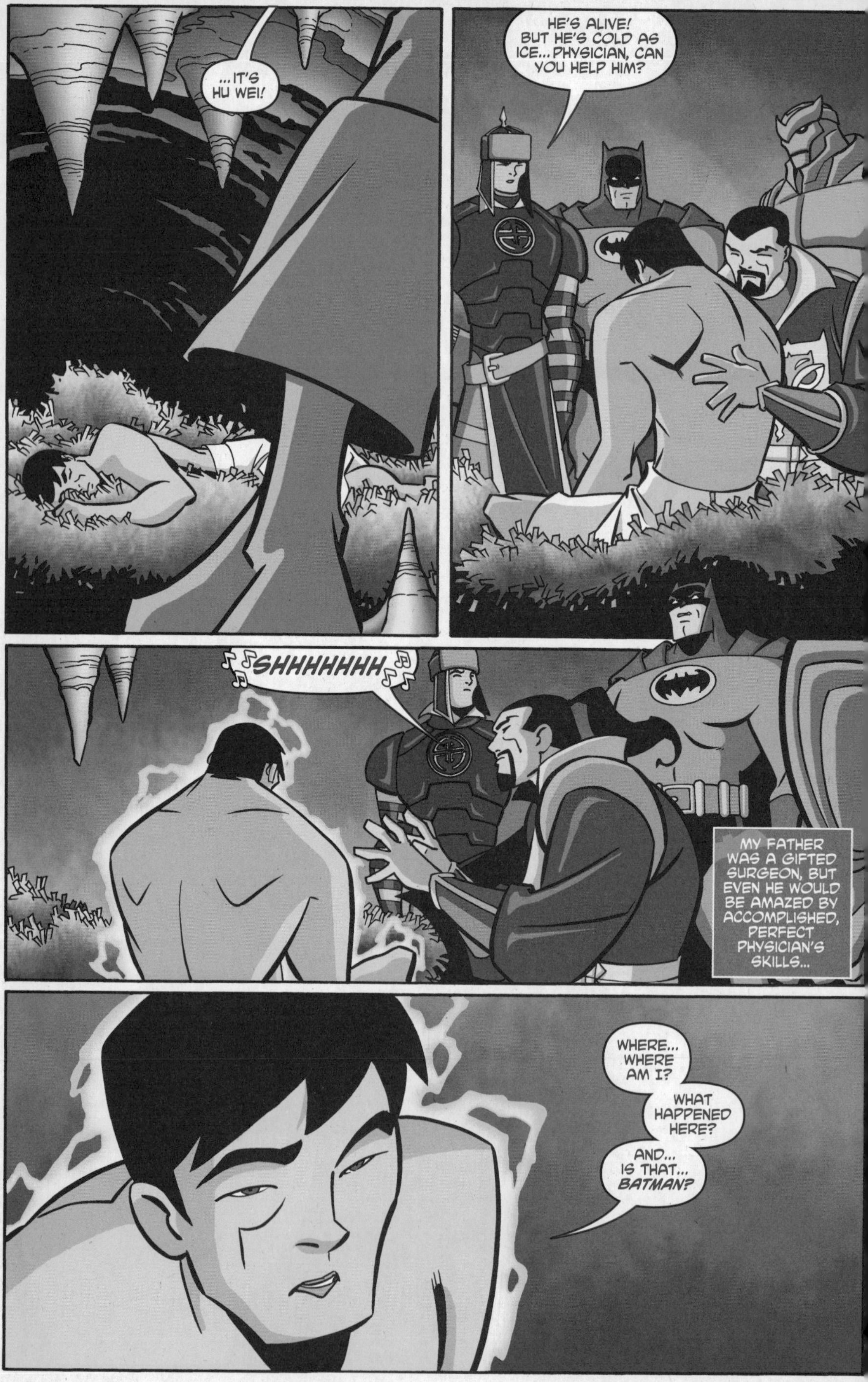
...IT'S HU WEI!
HE'S ALIVE! BUT HE'S COLD AS ICE... PHYSICIAN, CAN YOU HELP HIM?
SHHHHHHH
MY FATHER WAS A GIFTED SURGEON, BUT EVEN HE WOULD BE AMAZED BY ACCOMPLISHED, PERFECT PHYSICIAN'S SKILLS...
WHERE... WHERE AM I?
WHAT HAPPENED HERE?
AND... IS THAT... *BATMAN?*

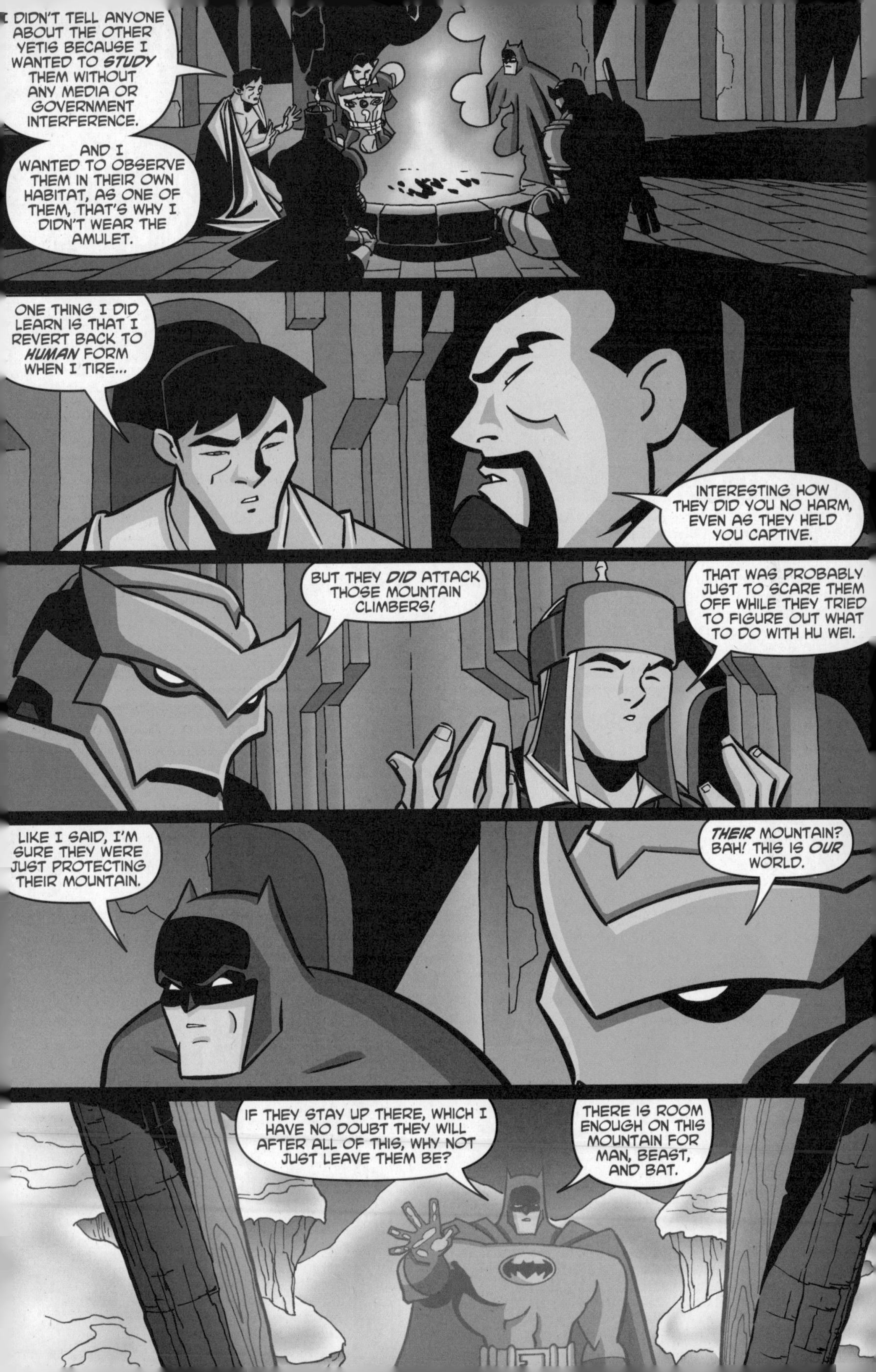
I DIDN'T TELL ANYONE ABOUT THE OTHER YETIS BECAUSE I WANTED TO *STUDY* THEM WITHOUT ANY MEDIA OR GOVERNMENT INTERFERENCE.
AND I WANTED TO OBSERVE THEM IN THEIR OWN HABITAT, AS ONE OF THEM, THAT'S WHY I DIDN'T WEAR THE AMULET.
ONE THING I DID LEARN IS THAT I REVERT BACK TO *HUMAN* FORM WHEN I TIRE...
INTERESTING HOW THEY DID YOU NO HARM, EVEN AS THEY HELD YOU CAPTIVE.
BUT THEY *DID* ATTACK THOSE MOUNTAIN CLIMBERS!
THAT WAS PROBABLY JUST TO SCARE THEM OFF WHILE THEY TRIED TO FIGURE OUT WHAT TO DO WITH HU WEI.
LIKE I SAID, I'M SURE THEY WERE JUST PROTECTING THEIR MOUNTAIN.
THEIR MOUNTAIN? BAH! THIS IS *OUR* WORLD.
IF THEY STAY UP THERE, WHICH I HAVE NO DOUBT THEY WILL AFTER ALL OF THIS, WHY NOT JUST LEAVE THEM BE?
THERE IS ROOM ENOUGH ON THIS MOUNTAIN FOR MAN, BEAST, AND BAT.

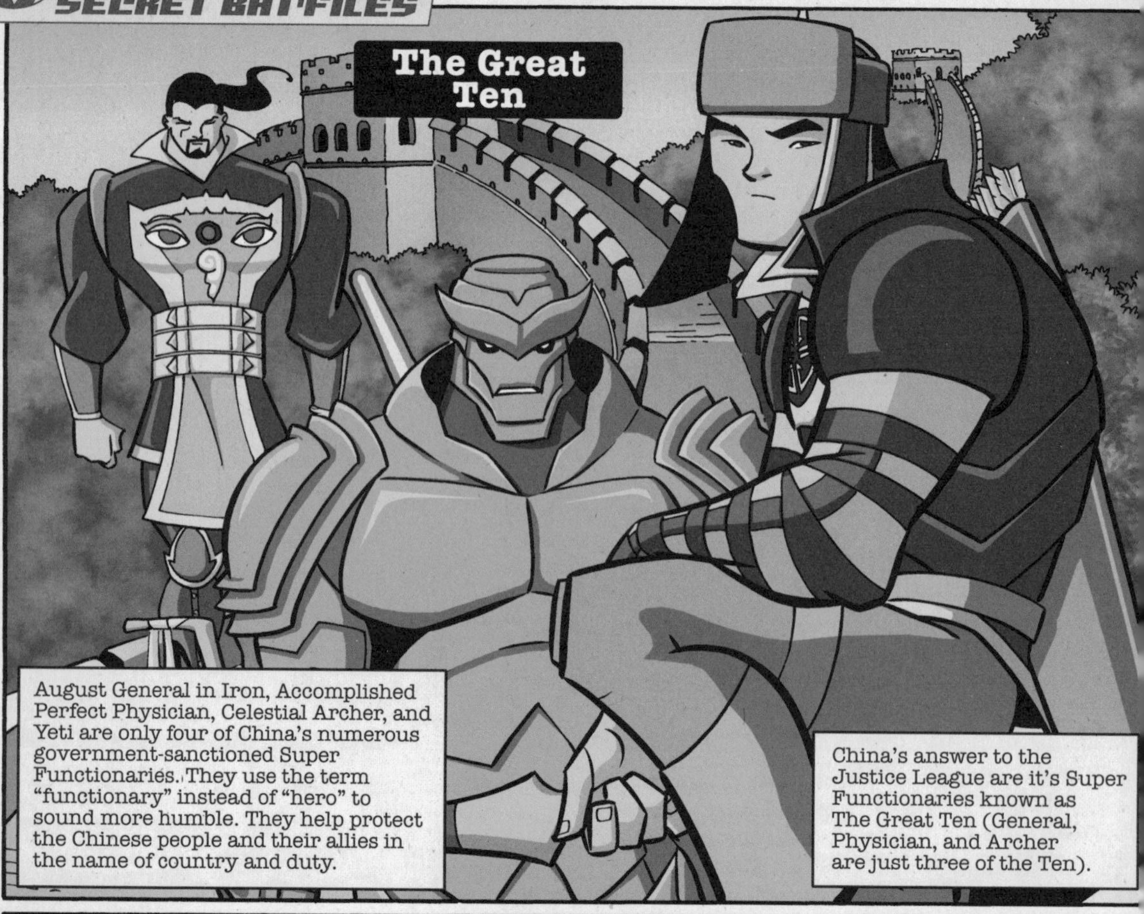
The Great Ten
August General in Iron, Accomplished Perfect Physician, Celestial Archer, and Yeti are only four of China's numerous government-sanctioned Super Functionaries. They use the term "functionary" instead of "hero" to sound more humble. They help protect the Chinese people and their allies in the name of country and duty.
China's answer to the Justice League are it's Super Functionaries known as The Great Ten (General, Physician, and Archer are just three of the Ten).

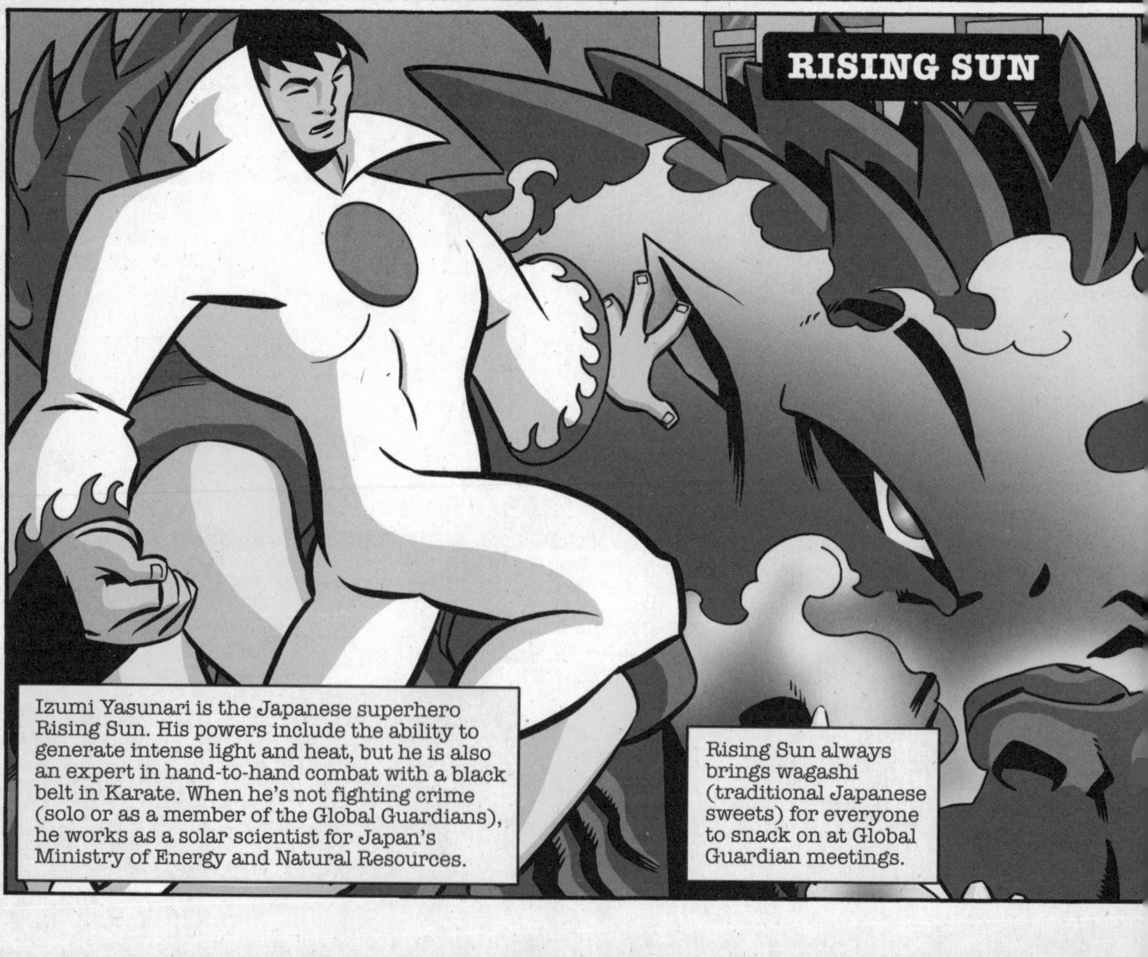
RISING SUN
Izumi Yasunari is the Japanese superhero Rising Sun. His powers include the ability to generate intense light and heat, but he is also an expert in hand-to-hand combat with a black belt in Karate. When he's not fighting crime (solo or as a member of the Global Guardians), he works as a solar scientist for Japan's Ministry of Energy and Natural Resources.
Rising Sun always brings wagashi (traditional Japanese sweets) for everyone to snack on at Global Guardian meetings.

BATMAN: THE BRAVE AND THE BOLD #9
Cover by Eric Jones and Hi-Fi

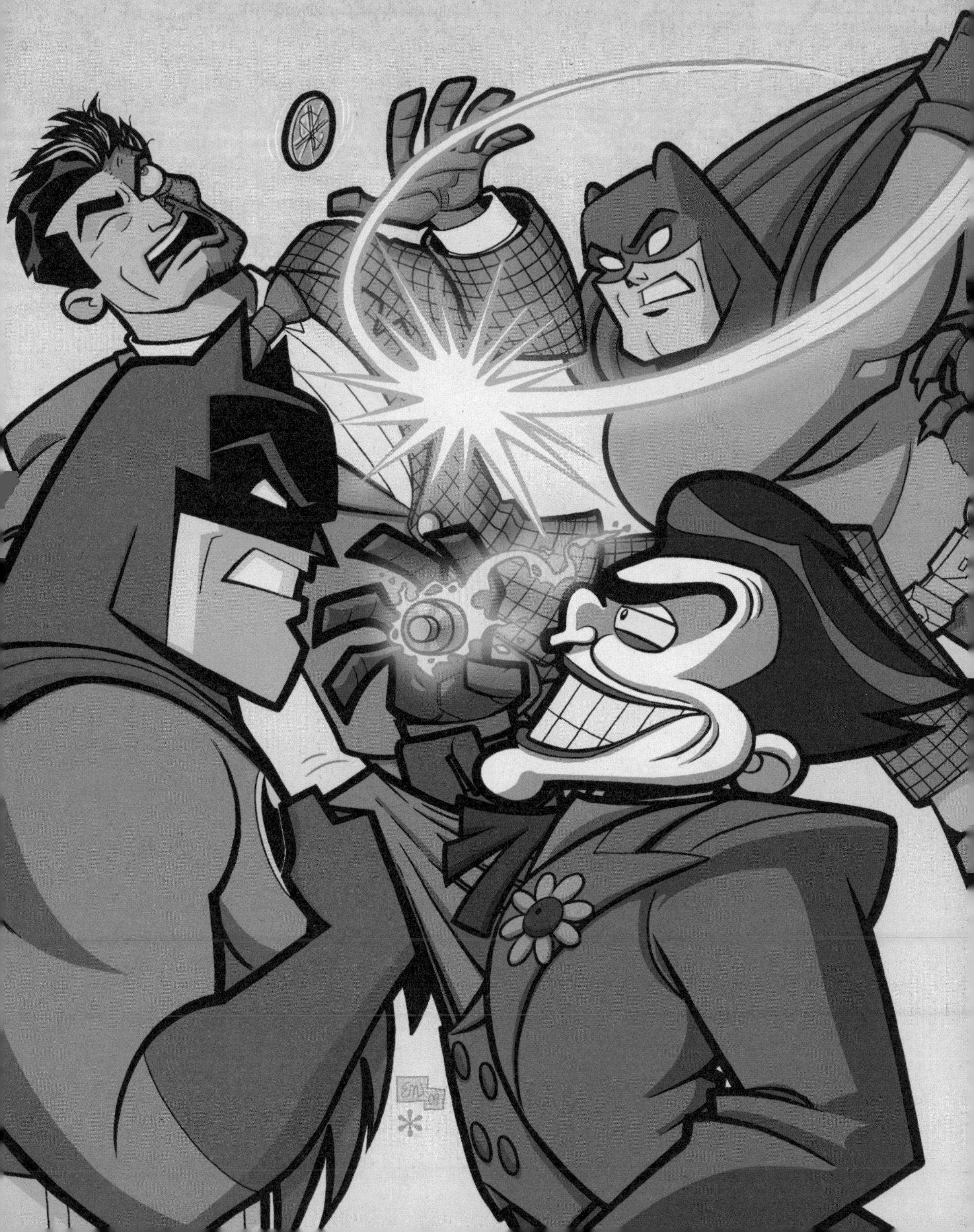

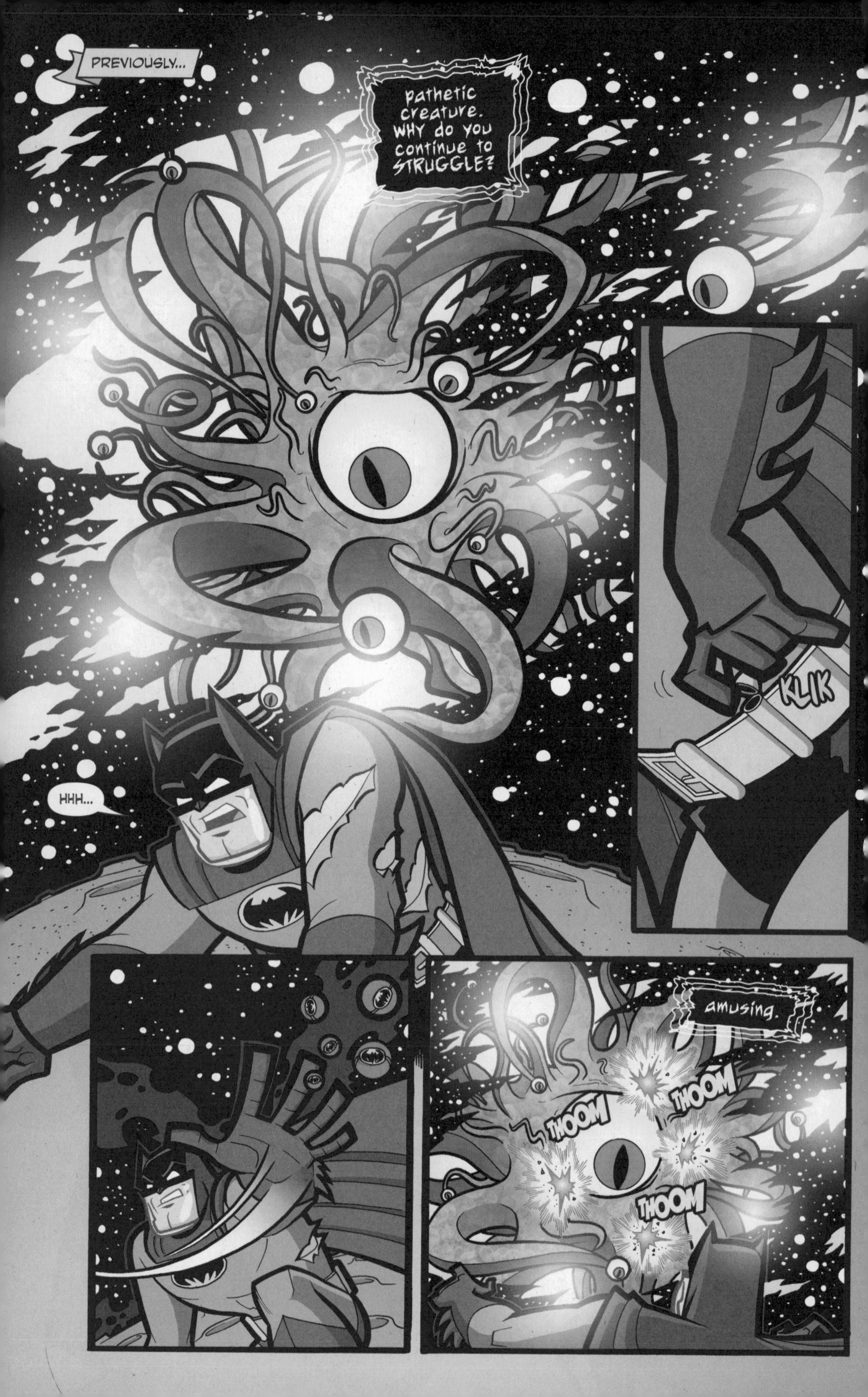
PREVIOUSLY...
pathetic creature. WHY do you continue to STRUGGLE?
HHH...
KLIK
amusing.
THOOM
THOOM
THOOM

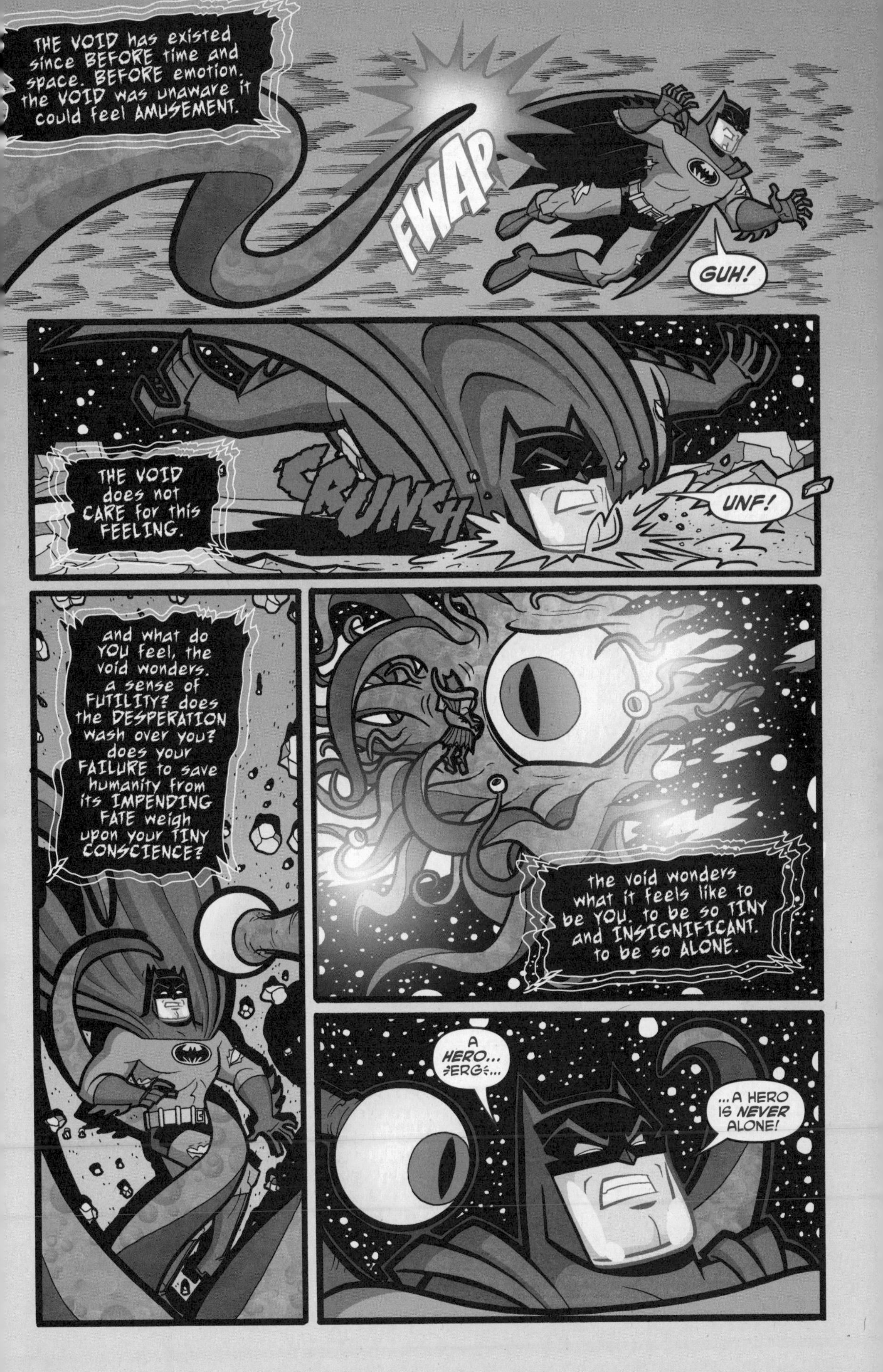
THE VOID has existed since BEFORE time and space. BEFORE emotion, the VOID was unaware it could feel AMUSEMENT.
FWAP
GUH!
THE VOID does not CARE for this FEELING.
CRUNCH
UNF!
and what do YOU feel, the void wonders. a sense of FUTILITY? does the DESPERATION wash over you? does your FAILURE to save humanity from its IMPENDING FATE weigh upon your TINY CONSCIENCE?
the void wonders what it feels like to be YOU. to be so TINY and INSIGNIFICANT. to be so ALONE.
A HERO... ERG...
...A HERO IS NEVER ALONE!

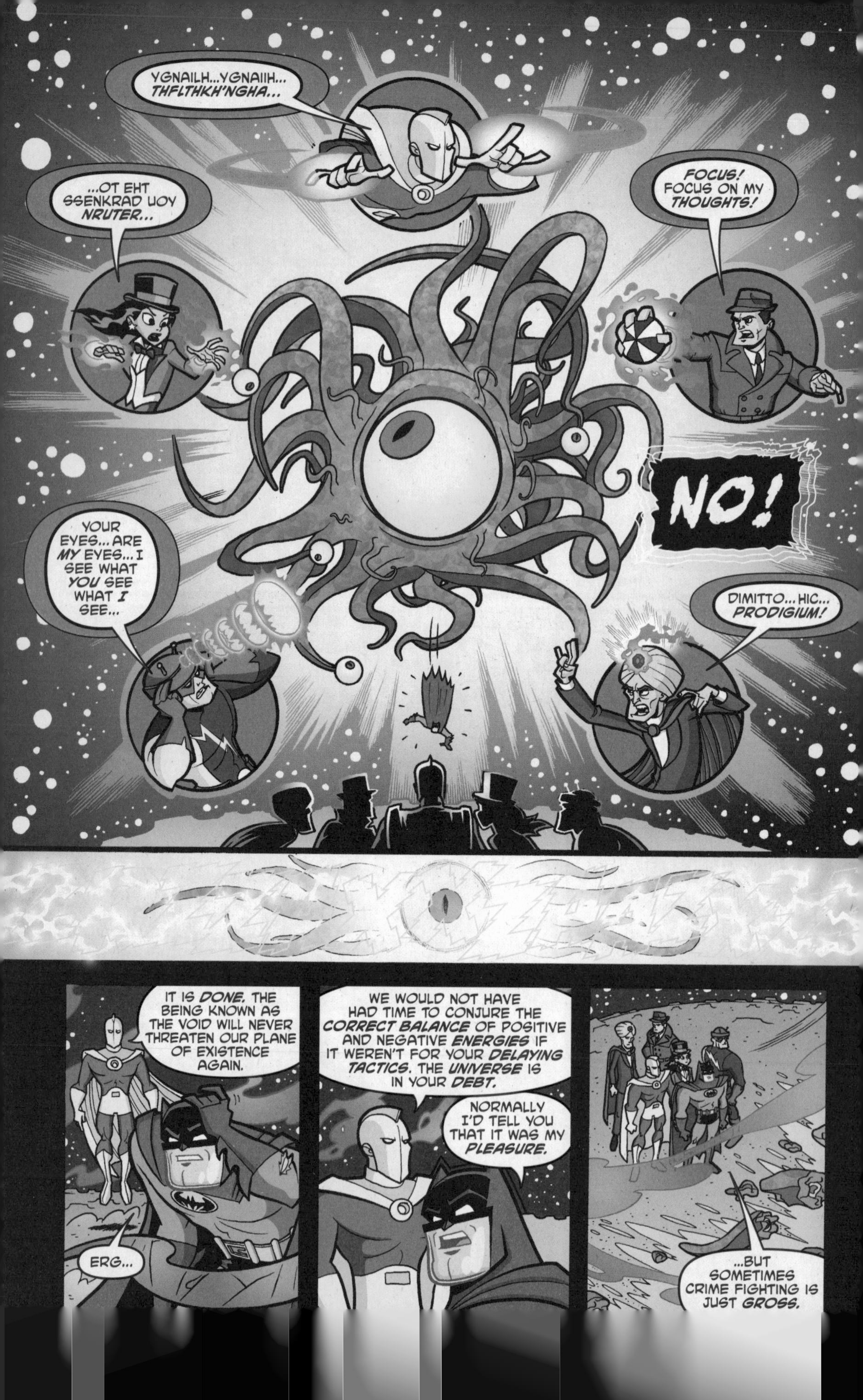

YGNAILH...YGNAIIH... THFLTHKH'NGHA...
...OT EHT SSENKRAD UOY NRUTER...
FOCUS! FOCUS ON MY THOUGHTS!
NO!
YOUR EYES...ARE MY EYES...I SEE WHAT YOU SEE WHAT I SEE...
DIMITTO...HIC... PRODIGIUM!
IT IS DONE. THE BEING KNOWN AS THE VOID WILL NEVER THREATEN OUR PLANE OF EXISTENCE AGAIN.
ERG...
WE WOULD NOT HAVE HAD TIME TO CONJURE THE CORRECT BALANCE OF POSITIVE AND NEGATIVE ENERGIES IF IT WEREN'T FOR YOUR DELAYING TACTICS. THE UNIVERSE IS IN YOUR DEBT.
NORMALLY I'D TELL YOU THAT IT WAS MY PLEASURE.
...BUT SOMETIMES CRIME FIGHTING IS JUST GROSS.

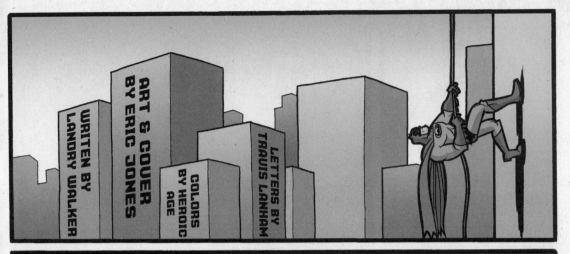

WRITTEN BY LANDRY WALKER

ART & COVER BY ERIC JONES

COLORS BY HEROIC AGE

LETTERS BY TRAVIS LANHAM

THE TALE OF THE CATMAN!

GOTHAM CITY.

MY HOME.

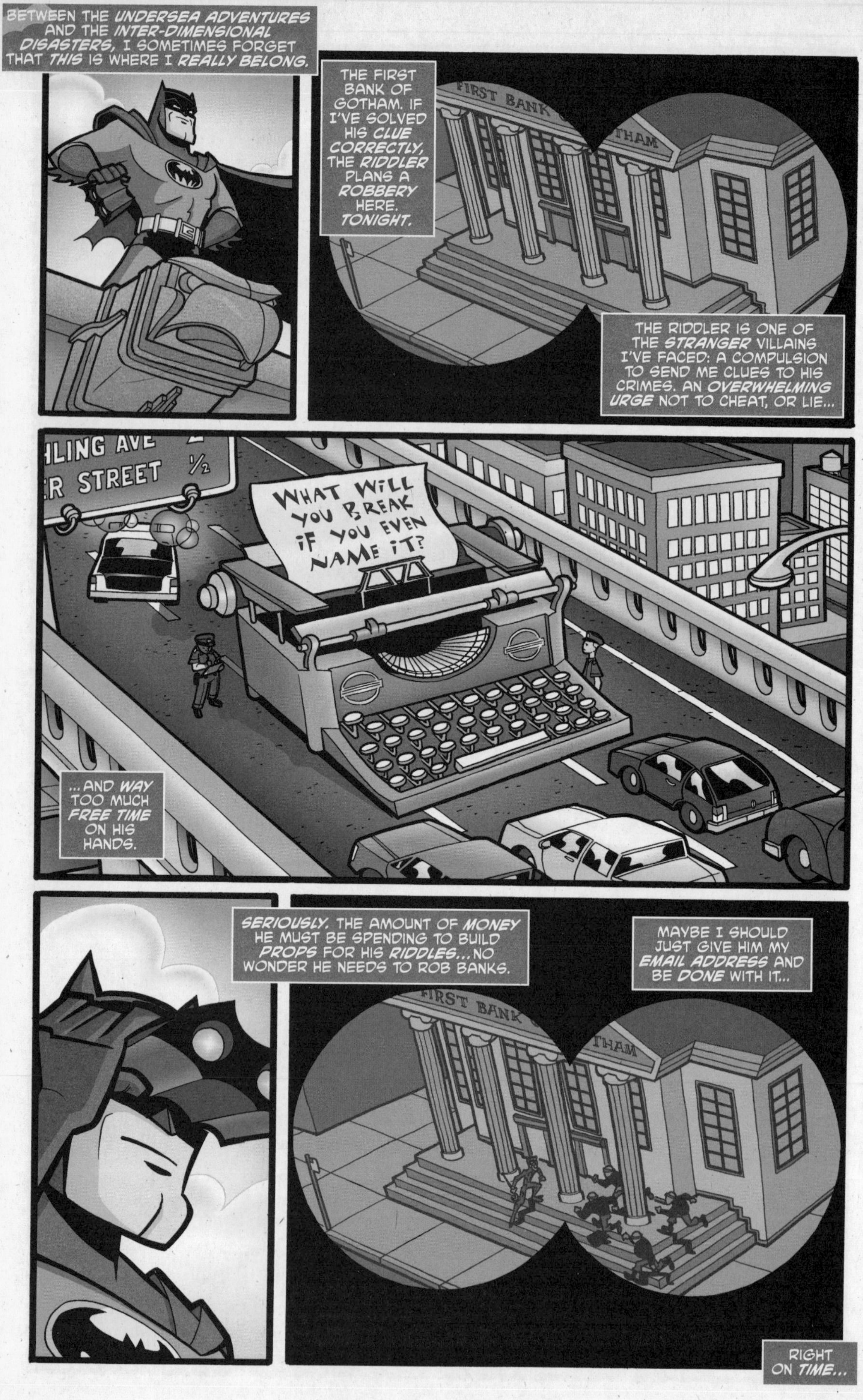
BETWEEN THE UNDERSEA ADVENTURES AND THE INTER-DIMENSIONAL DISASTERS, I SOMETIMES FORGET THAT THIS IS WHERE I REALLY BELONG.
THE FIRST BANK OF GOTHAM. IF I'VE SOLVED HIS CLUE CORRECTLY, THE RIDDLER PLANS A ROBBERY HERE. TONIGHT.
FIRST BANK
THAM
THE RIDDLER IS ONE OF THE STRANGER VILLAINS I'VE FACED: A COMPULSION TO SEND ME CLUES TO HIS CRIMES. AN OVERWHELMING URGE NOT TO CHEAT, OR LIE...
HLING AVE
ER STREET
1/2
WHAT WILL YOU BREAK IF YOU EVEN NAME IT?
...AND WAY TOO MUCH FREE TIME ON HIS HANDS.
SERIOUSLY. THE AMOUNT OF MONEY HE MUST BE SPENDING TO BUILD PROPS FOR HIS RIDDLES... NO WONDER HE NEEDS TO ROB BANKS.
MAYBE I SHOULD JUST GIVE HIM MY EMAIL ADDRESS AND BE DONE WITH IT...
FIRST BANK
THAM
RIGHT ON TIME...

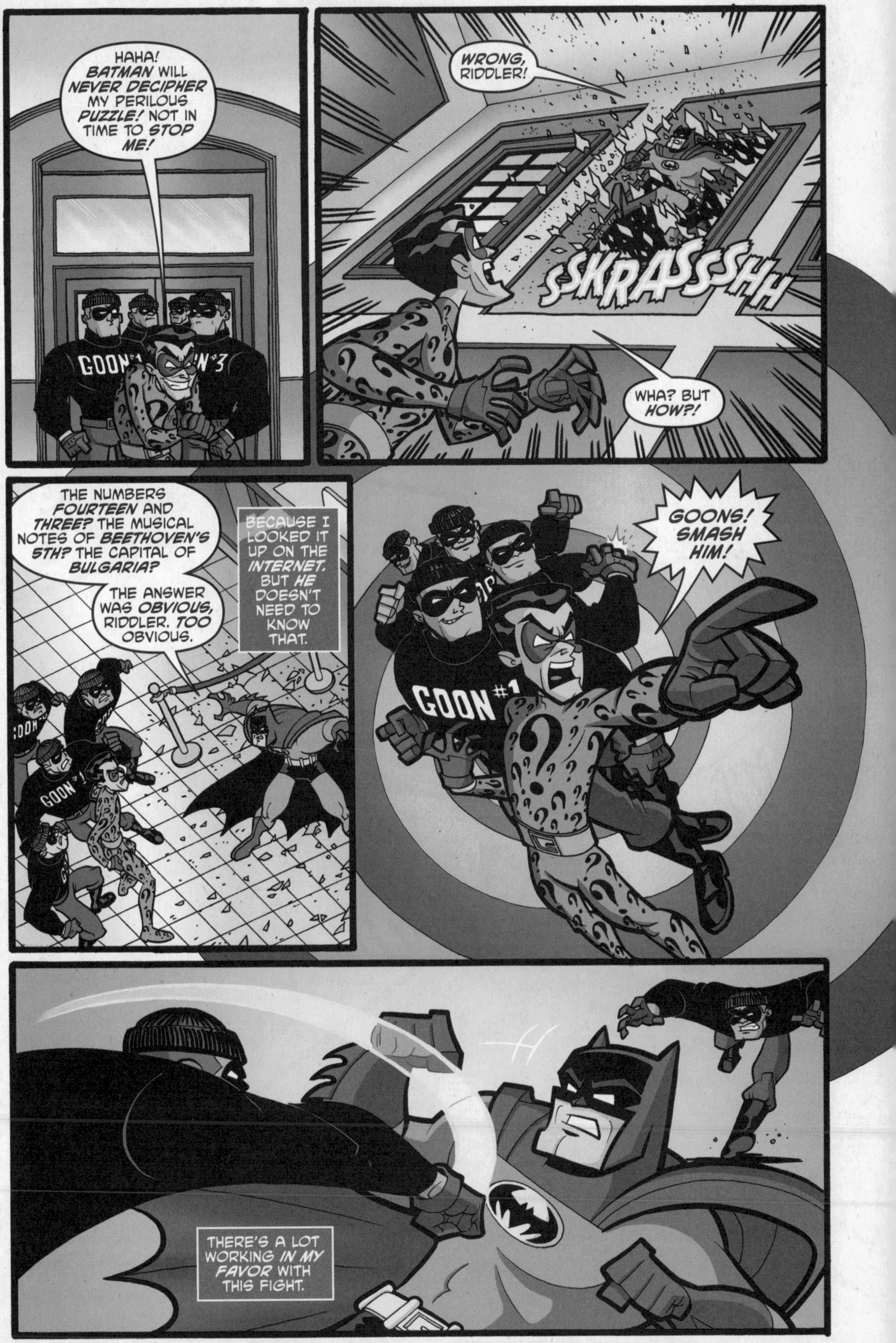
HAHA! BATMAN WILL NEVER DECIPHER MY PERILOUS PUZZLE! NOT IN TIME TO STOP ME!
GOON #1
N #3
WRONG, RIDDLER!
SSKRASSSHH
WHA? BUT HOW?!
THE NUMBERS FOURTEEN AND THREE? THE MUSICAL NOTES OF BEETHOVEN'S 5TH? THE CAPITAL OF BULGARIA?
THE ANSWER WAS OBVIOUS, RIDDLER. TOO OBVIOUS.
BECAUSE I LOOKED IT UP ON THE INTERNET. BUT HE DOESN'T NEED TO KNOW THAT.
GOONS! SMASH HIM!
GOON #1
THERE'S A LOT WORKING IN MY FAVOR WITH THIS FIGHT.

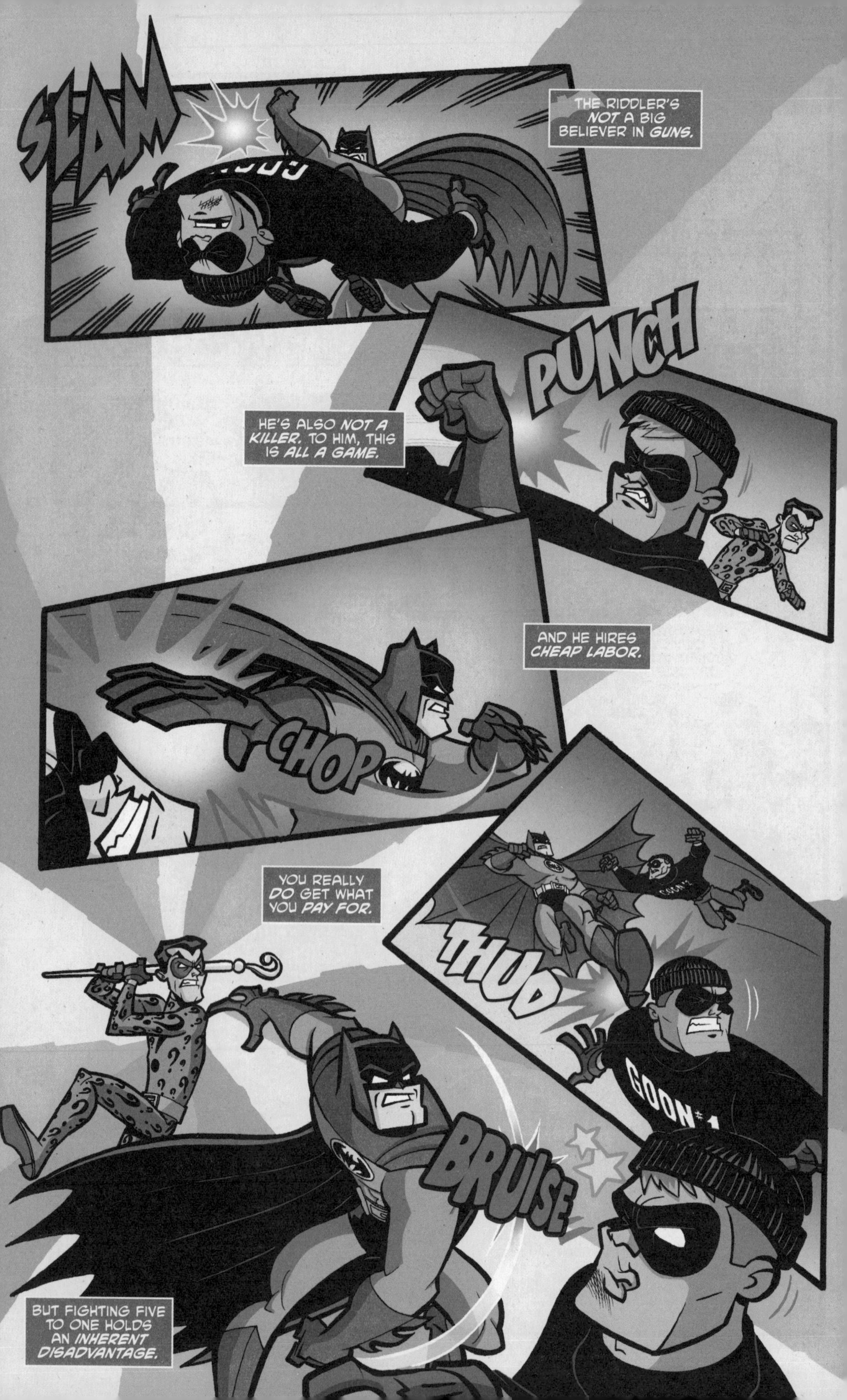
SLAM
THE RIDDLER'S NOT A BIG BELIEVER IN GUNS.
PUNCH
HE'S ALSO NOT A KILLER. TO HIM, THIS IS ALL A GAME.
AND HE HIRES CHEAP LABOR.
CHOP
YOU REALLY DO GET WHAT YOU PAY FOR.
THUD
GOON #1
BRUISE
BUT FIGHTING FIVE TO ONE HOLDS AN INHERENT DISADVANTAGE.

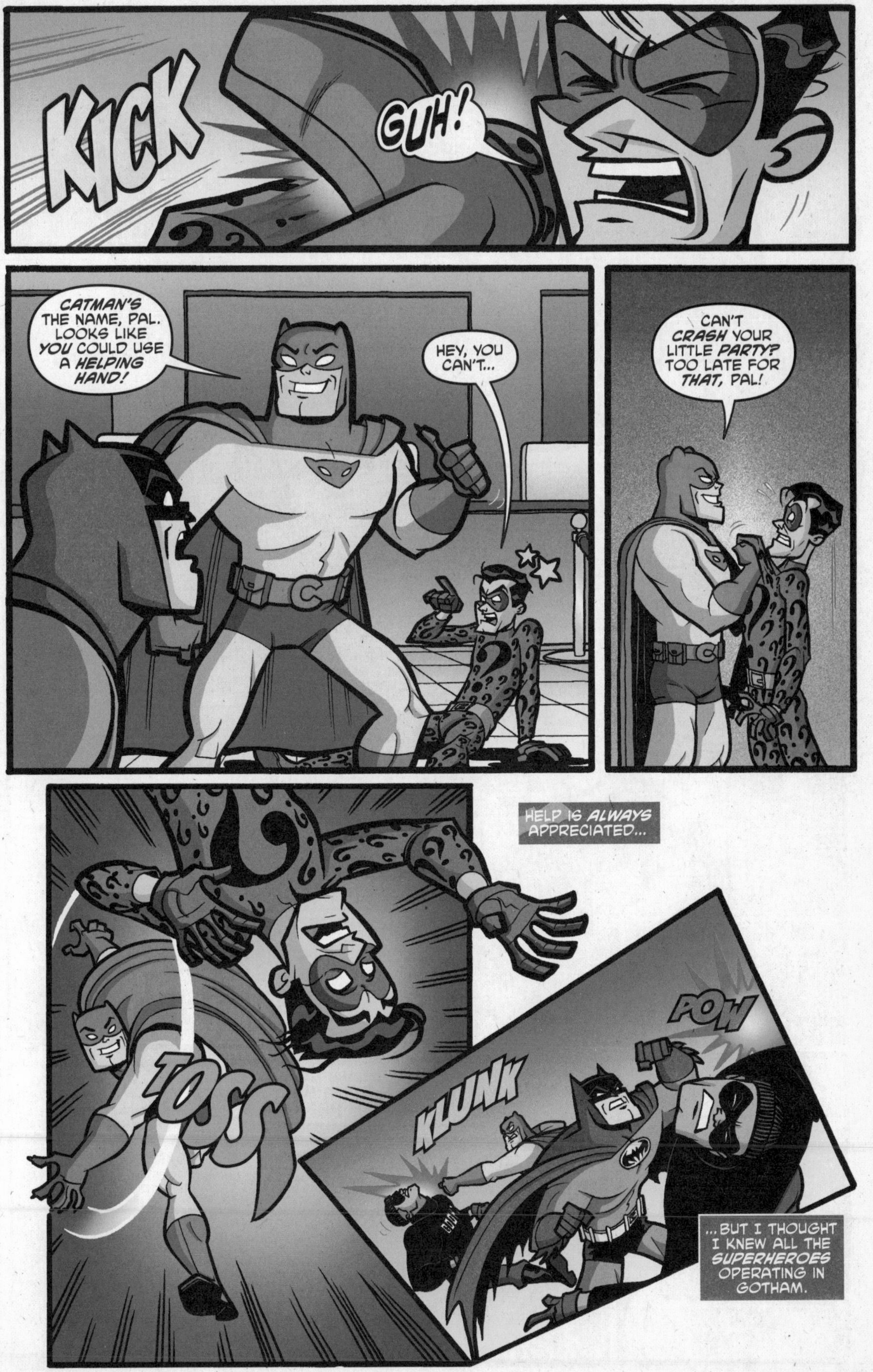
KICK
GUH!
CATMAN'S THE NAME, PAL. LOOKS LIKE YOU COULD USE A HELPING HAND!
HEY, YOU CAN'T...
CAN'T CRASH YOUR LITTLE PARTY? TOO LATE FOR THAT, PAL!
HELP IS ALWAYS APPRECIATED...
TOSS
POW
KLUNK
...BUT I THOUGHT I KNEW ALL THE SUPERHEROES OPERATING IN GOTHAM.

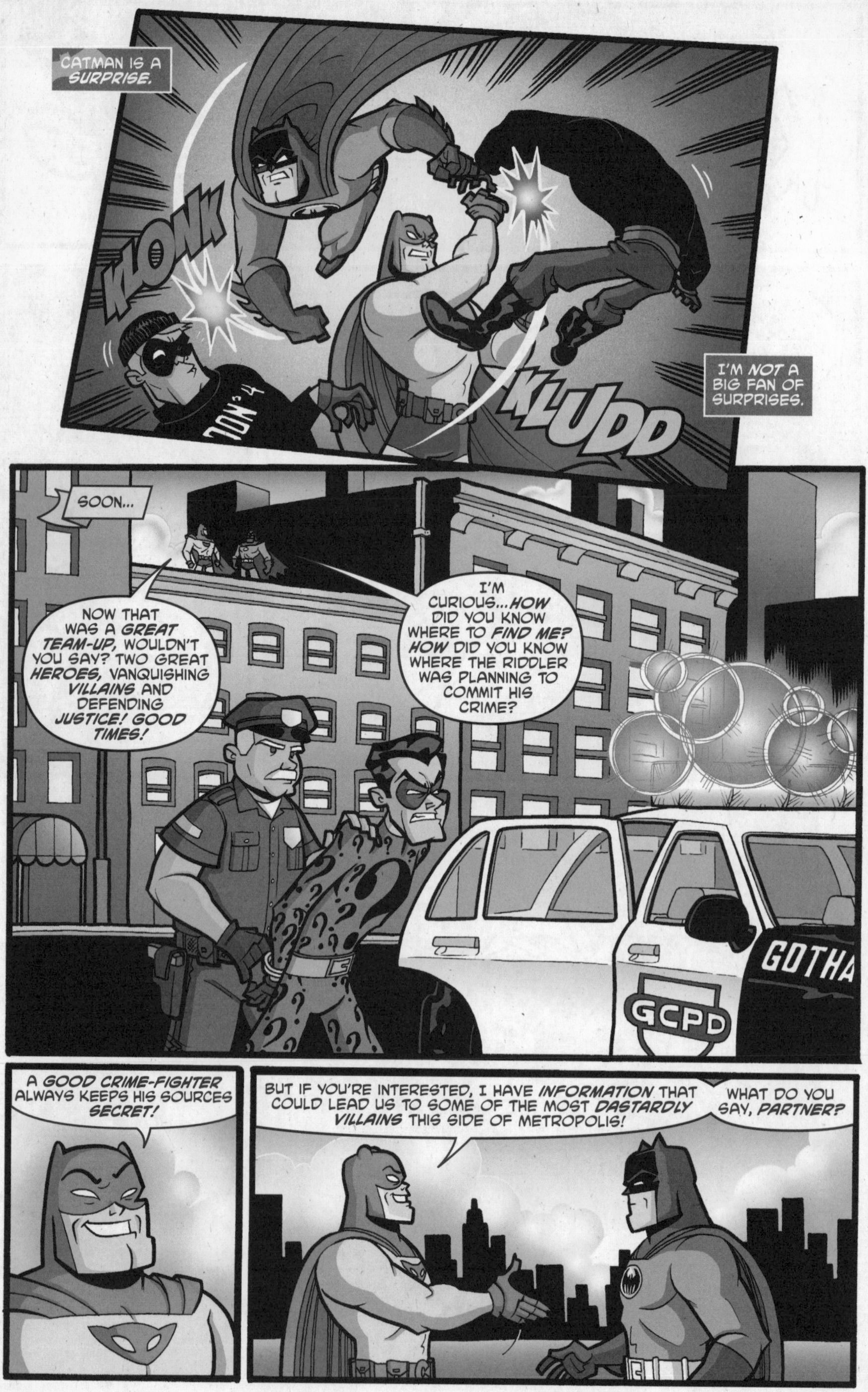
CATMAN IS A SURPRISE.
KLONK
KLUDD
I'M NOT A BIG FAN OF SURPRISES.
SOON...
NOW THAT WAS A GREAT TEAM-UP, WOULDN'T YOU SAY? TWO GREAT HEROES, VANQUISHING VILLAINS AND DEFENDING JUSTICE! GOOD TIMES!
I'M CURIOUS...HOW DID YOU KNOW WHERE TO FIND ME? HOW DID YOU KNOW WHERE THE RIDDLER WAS PLANNING TO COMMIT HIS CRIME?
GOTHA
GCPD
A GOOD CRIME-FIGHTER ALWAYS KEEPS HIS SOURCES SECRET!
BUT IF YOU'RE INTERESTED, I HAVE INFORMATION THAT COULD LEAD US TO SOME OF THE MOST DASTARDLY VILLAINS THIS SIDE OF METROPOLIS!
WHAT DO YOU SAY, PARTNER?

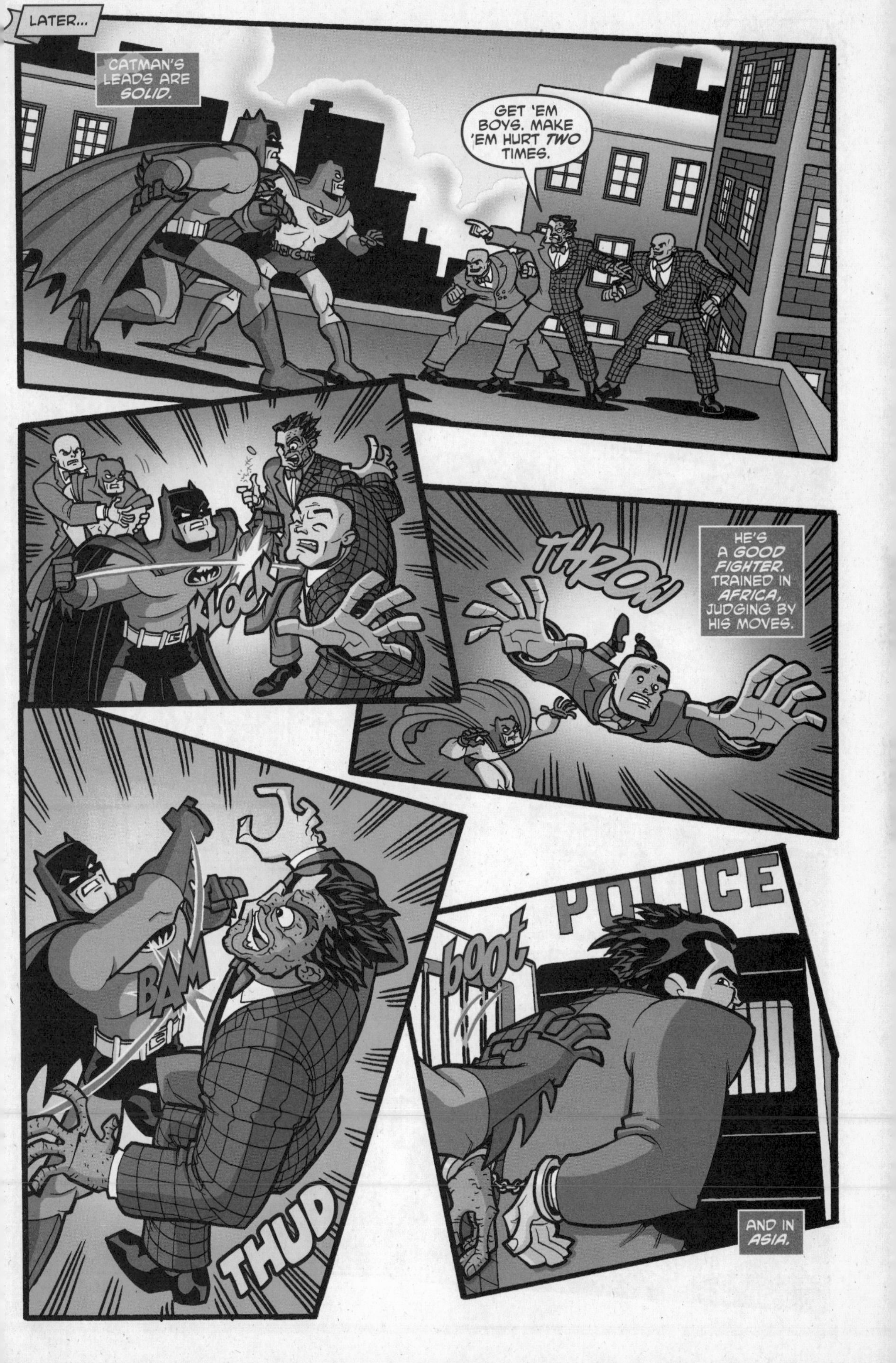
LATER...
CATMAN'S LEADS ARE SOLID.
GET 'EM BOYS. MAKE 'EM HURT TWO TIMES.
KLOCK
THROW
HE'S A GOOD FIGHTER. TRAINED IN AFRICA, JUDGING BY HIS MOVES.
BAM
THUD
POLICE
boot
AND IN ASIA.

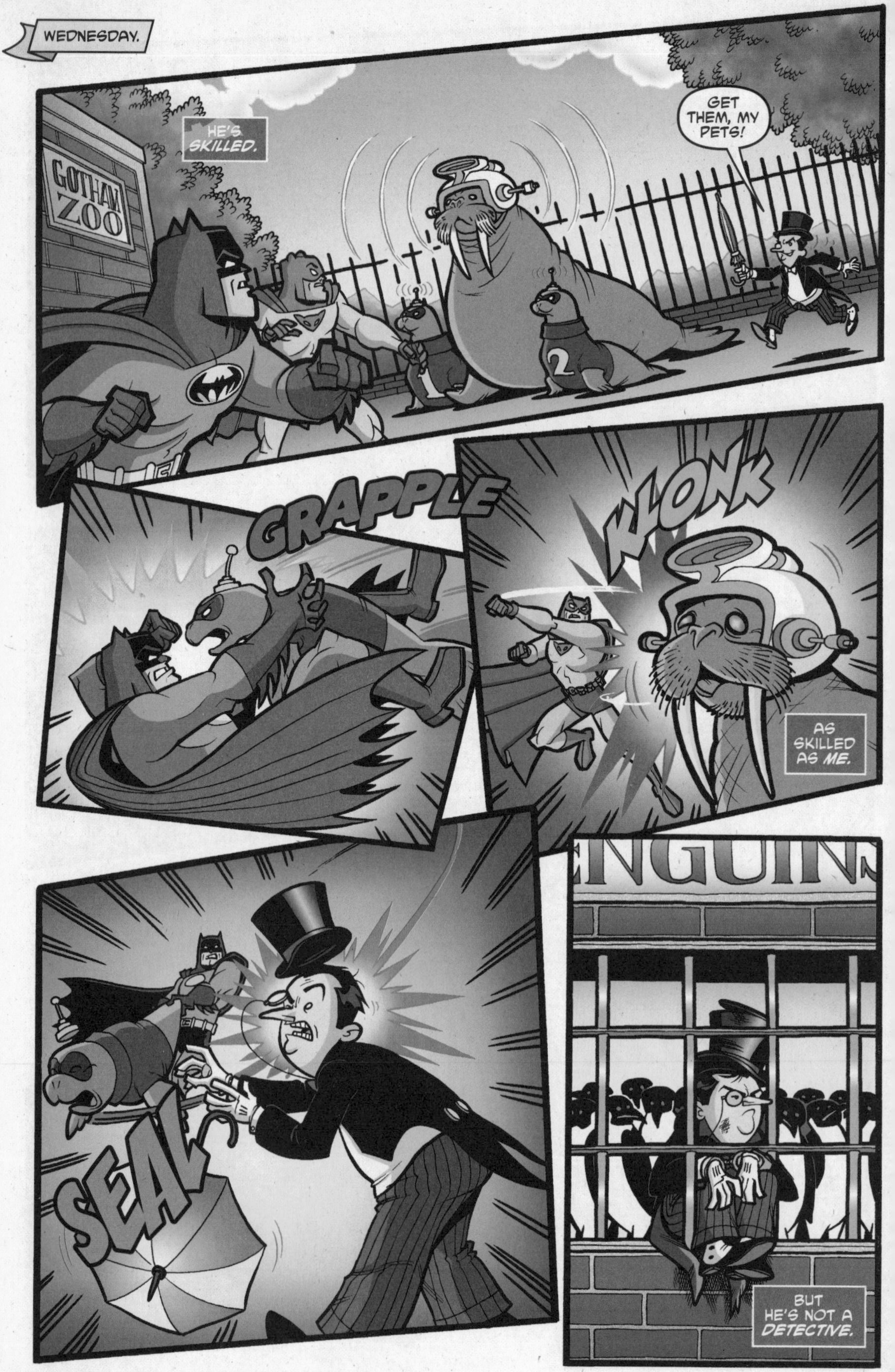
WEDNESDAY.
GOTHAM ZOO
HE'S *SKILLED.*
GET THEM, MY PETS!
GRAPPLE
KLONK
AS SKILLED AS *ME.*
SEAL
ENGUIN
BUT HE'S NOT A *DETECTIVE.*

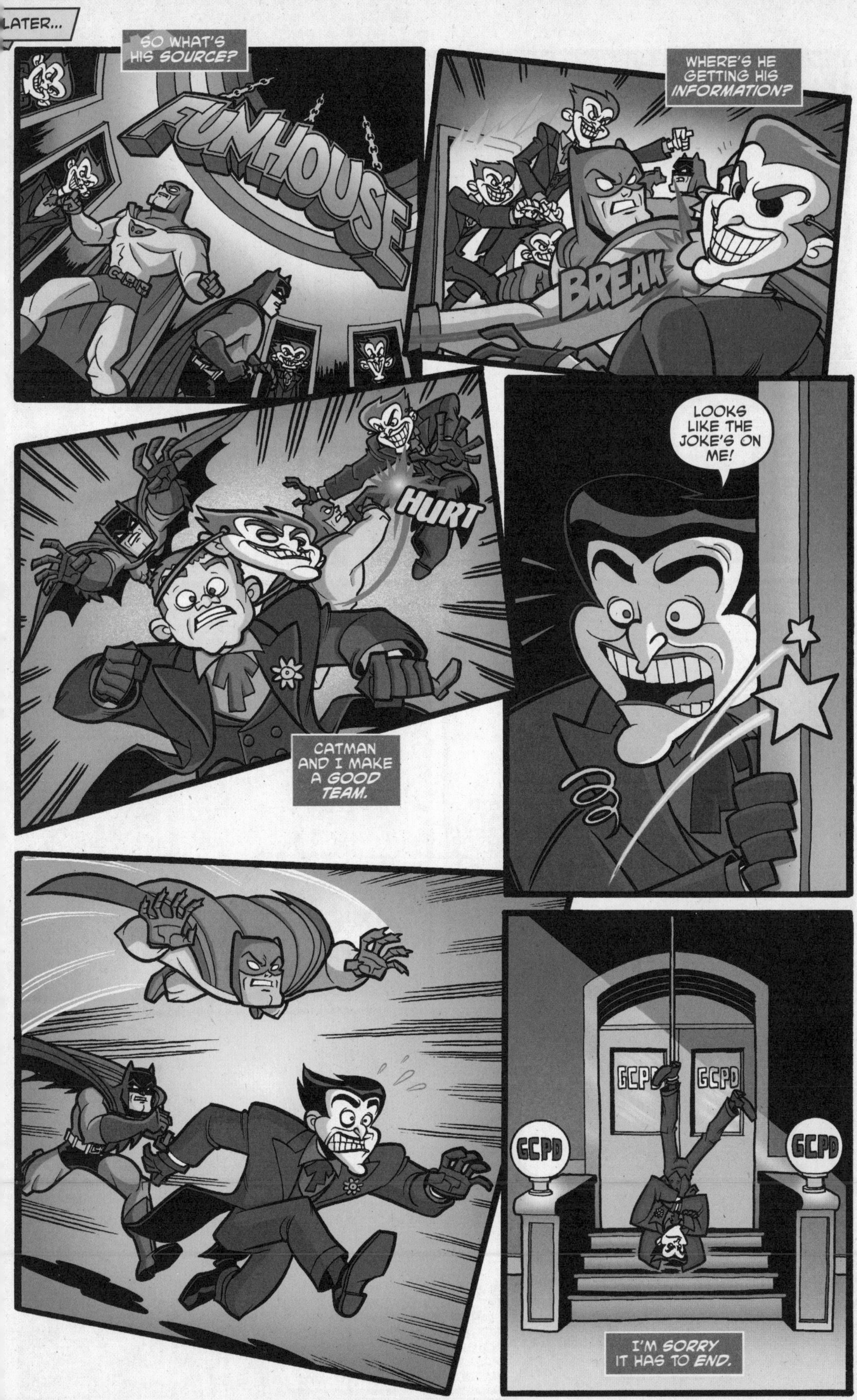
LATER...
SO WHAT'S HIS SOURCE?
FUNHOUSE
WHERE'S HE GETTING HIS INFORMATION?
BREAK
HURT
CATMAN AND I MAKE A GOOD TEAM.
LOOKS LIKE THE JOKE'S ON ME!
GCPD
GCPD
GCPD
GCPD
I'M SORRY IT HAS TO END.

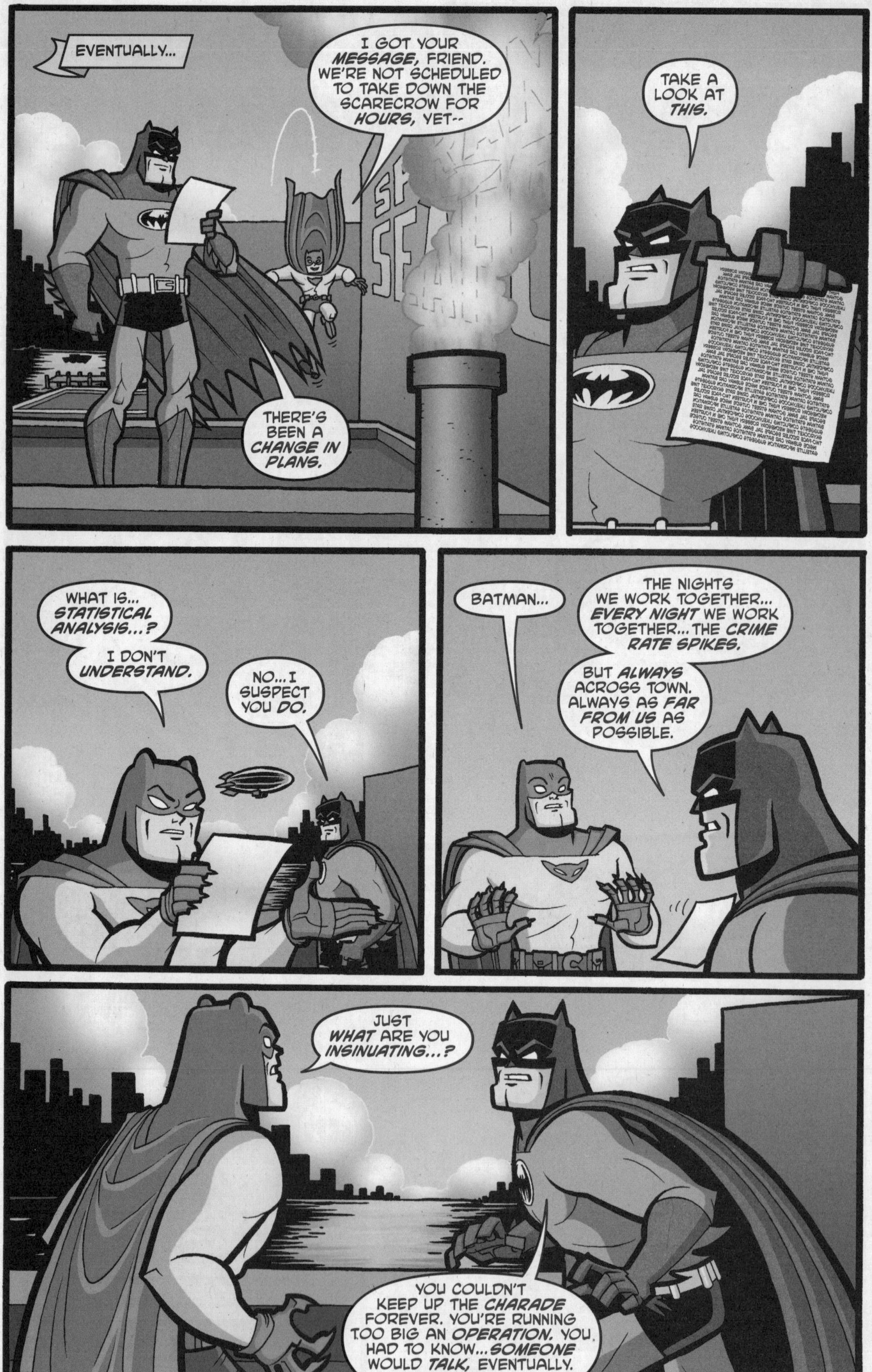
EVENTUALLY...
I GOT YOUR MESSAGE, FRIEND. WE'RE NOT SCHEDULED TO TAKE DOWN THE SCARECROW FOR HOURS, YET--
THERE'S BEEN A CHANGE IN PLANS.
TAKE A LOOK AT THIS.
WHAT IS... STATISTICAL ANALYSIS...?
I DON'T UNDERSTAND.
NO... I SUSPECT YOU DO.
BATMAN...
THE NIGHTS WE WORK TOGETHER... EVERY NIGHT WE WORK TOGETHER... THE CRIME RATE SPIKES.
BUT ALWAYS ACROSS TOWN. ALWAYS AS FAR FROM US AS POSSIBLE.
JUST WHAT ARE YOU INSINUATING...?
YOU COULDN'T KEEP UP THE CHARADE FOREVER. YOU'RE RUNNING TOO BIG AN OPERATION. YOU HAD TO KNOW... SOMEONE WOULD TALK, EVENTUALLY.

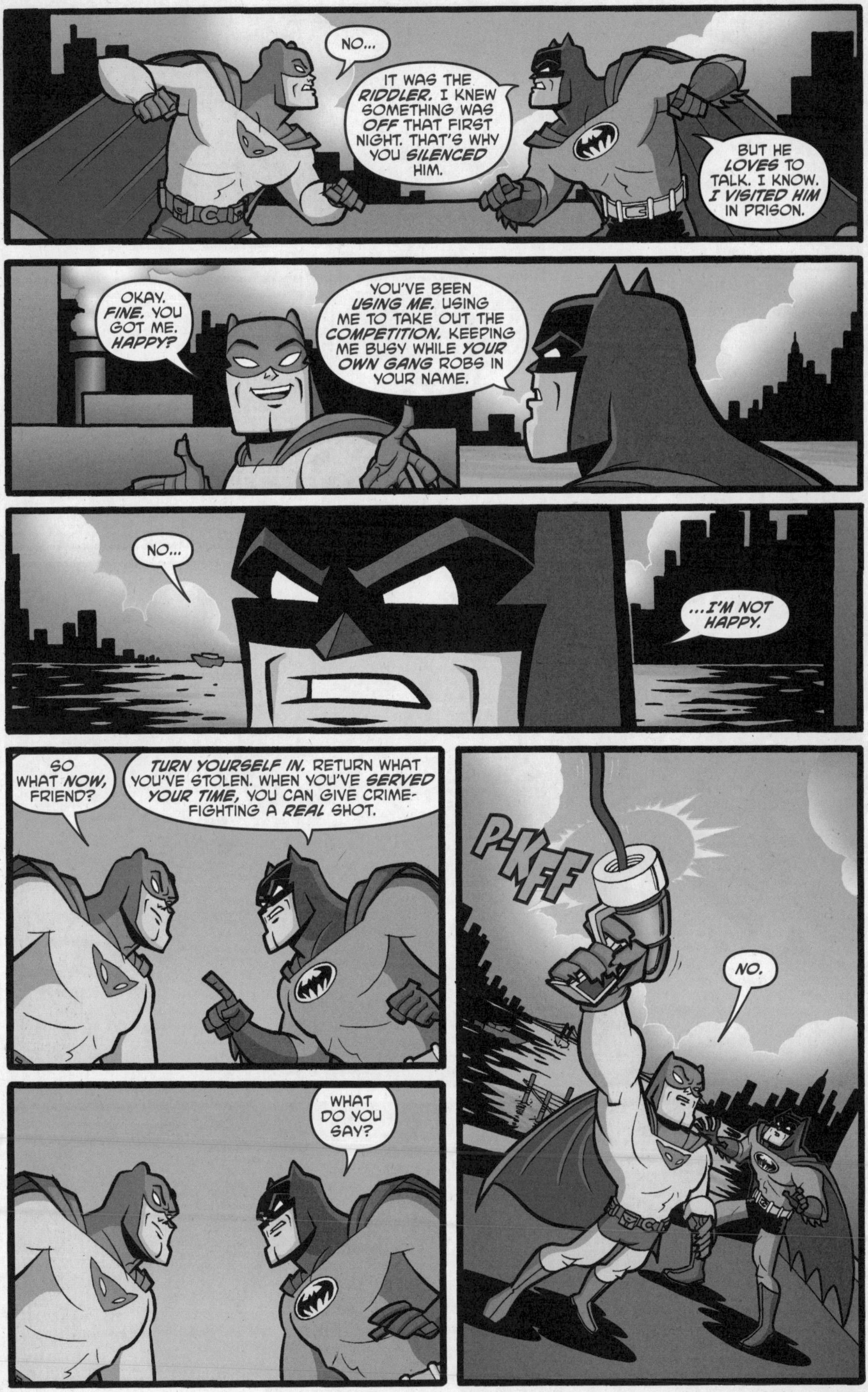
NO...
IT WAS THE RIDDLER. I KNEW SOMETHING WAS OFF THAT FIRST NIGHT. THAT'S WHY YOU SILENCED HIM.
BUT HE LOVES TO TALK. I KNOW. I VISITED HIM IN PRISON.
OKAY. FINE. YOU GOT ME. HAPPY?
YOU'VE BEEN USING ME. USING ME TO TAKE OUT THE COMPETITION. KEEPING ME BUSY WHILE YOUR OWN GANG ROBS IN YOUR NAME.
NO...
...I'M NOT HAPPY.
SO WHAT NOW, FRIEND?
TURN YOURSELF IN. RETURN WHAT YOU'VE STOLEN. WHEN YOU'VE SERVED YOUR TIME, YOU CAN GIVE CRIME-FIGHTING A REAL SHOT.
WHAT DO YOU SAY?
P-KFF
NO.

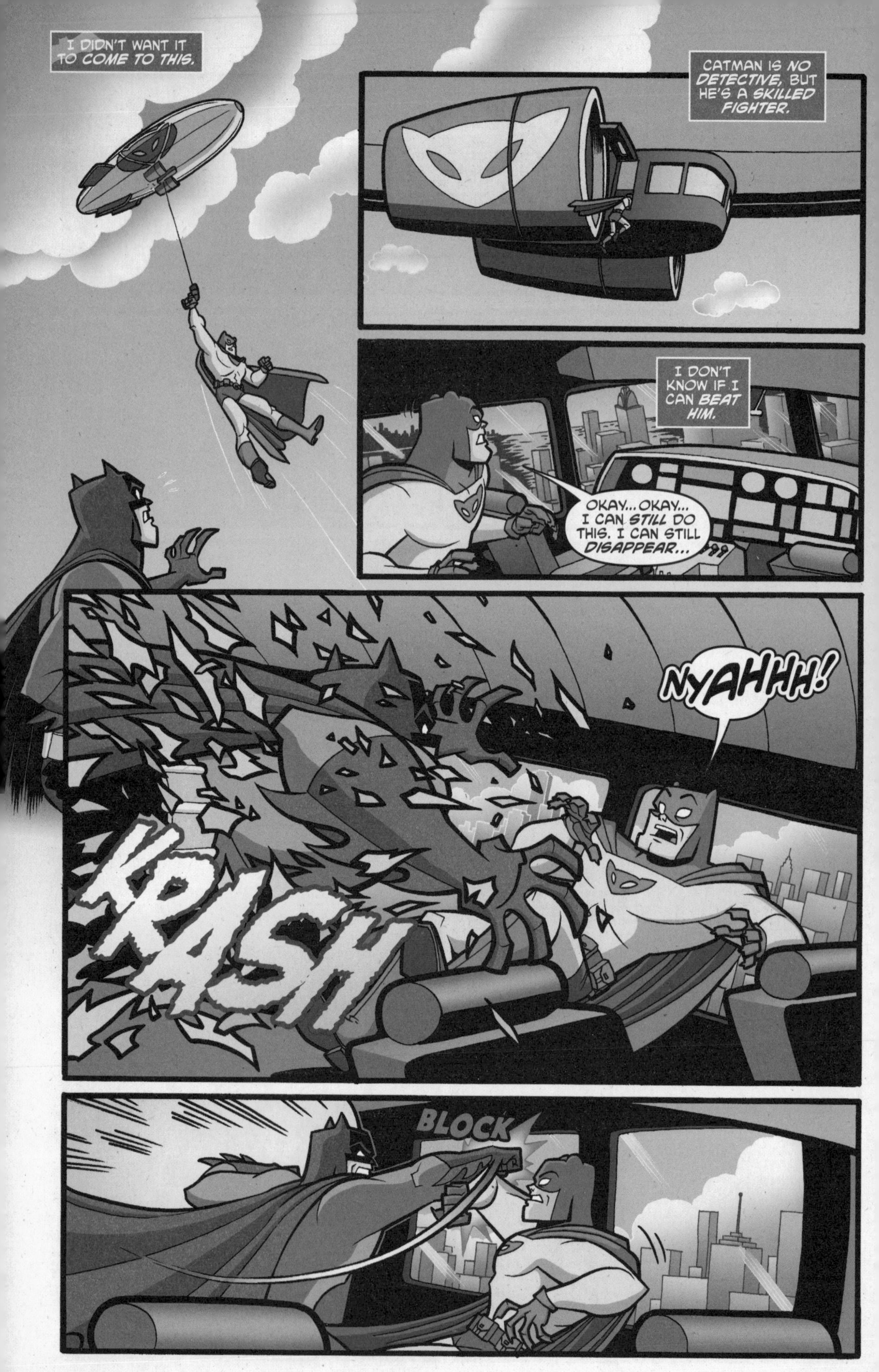
I DIDN'T WANT IT TO COME TO THIS.
CATMAN IS NO DETECTIVE, BUT HE'S A SKILLED FIGHTER.
I DON'T KNOW IF I CAN BEAT HIM.
OKAY... OKAY... I CAN STILL DO THIS. I CAN STILL DISAPPEAR...
NYAHHH!
KRASH
BLOCK

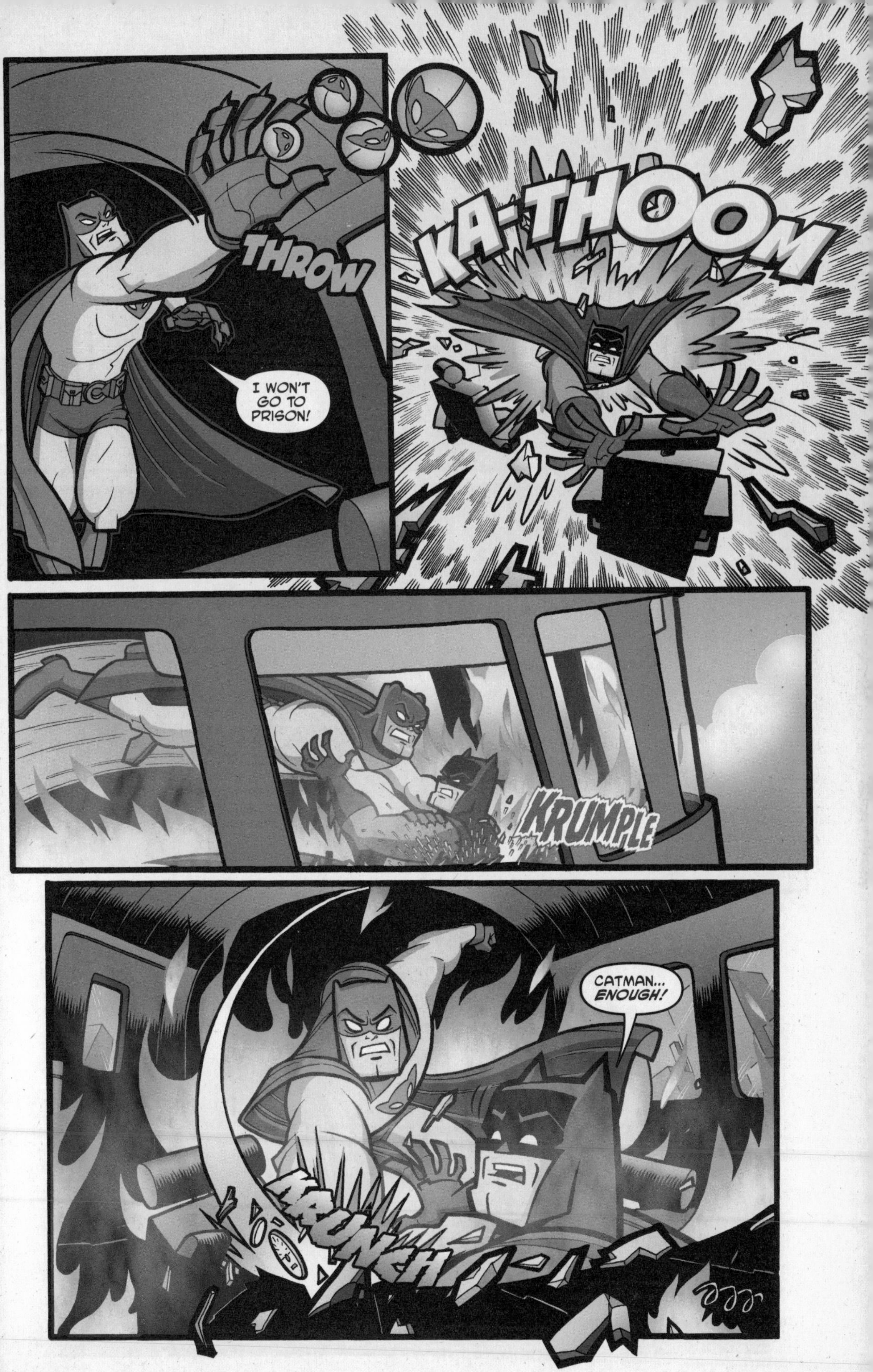
THROW
I WON'T GO TO PRISON!
KA-THOOM
KRUMPLE
CATMAN... ENOUGH!
KRUNCH

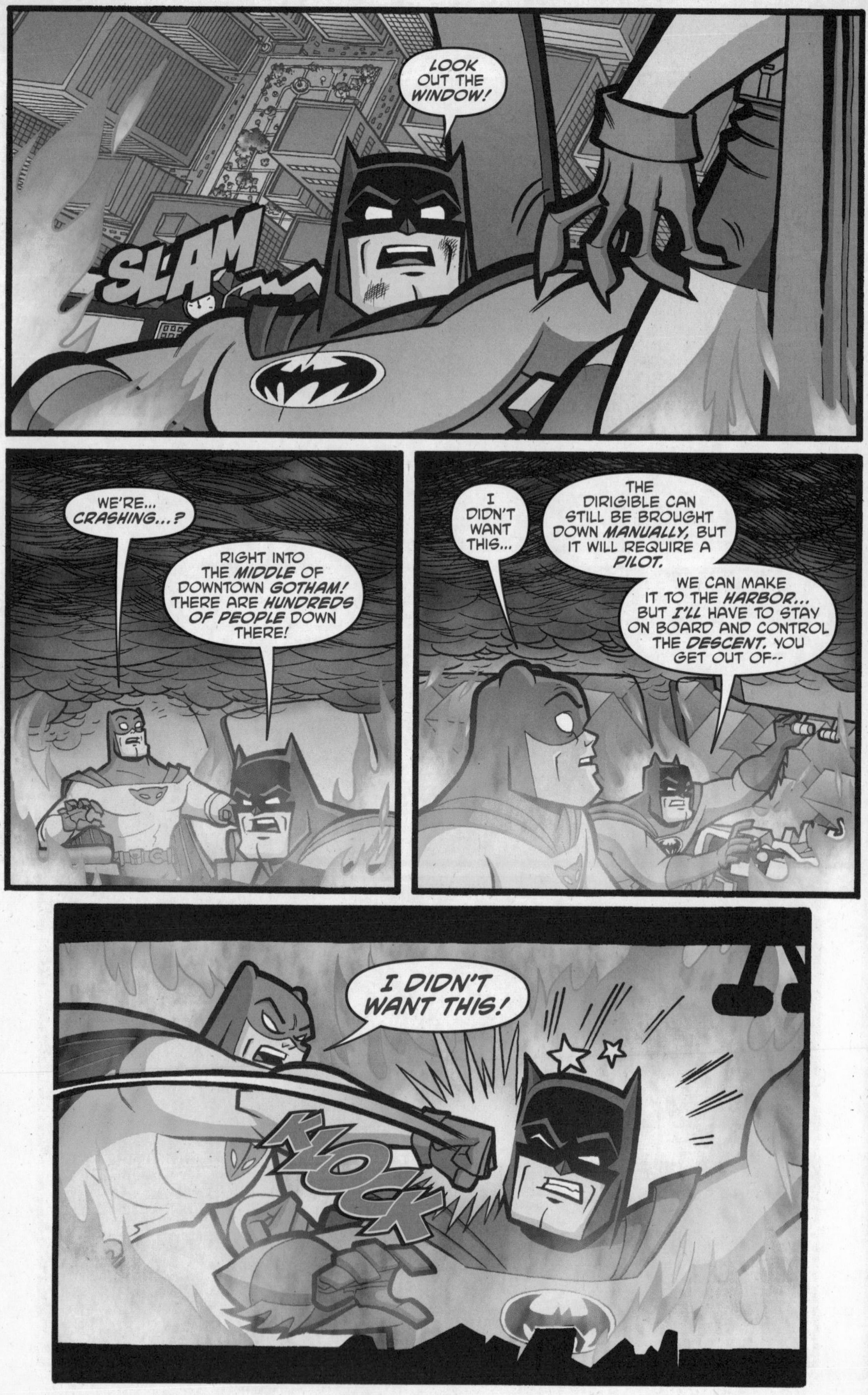
LOOK OUT THE WINDOW!
SLAM
WE'RE... CRASHING...?
RIGHT INTO THE MIDDLE OF DOWNTOWN GOTHAM! THERE ARE HUNDREDS OF PEOPLE DOWN THERE!
I DIDN'T WANT THIS...
THE DIRIGIBLE CAN STILL BE BROUGHT DOWN MANUALLY, BUT IT WILL REQUIRE A PILOT.
WE CAN MAKE IT TO THE HARBOR... BUT I'LL HAVE TO STAY ON BOARD AND CONTROL THE DESCENT. YOU GET OUT OF--
I DIDN'T WANT THIS!
KLOCK

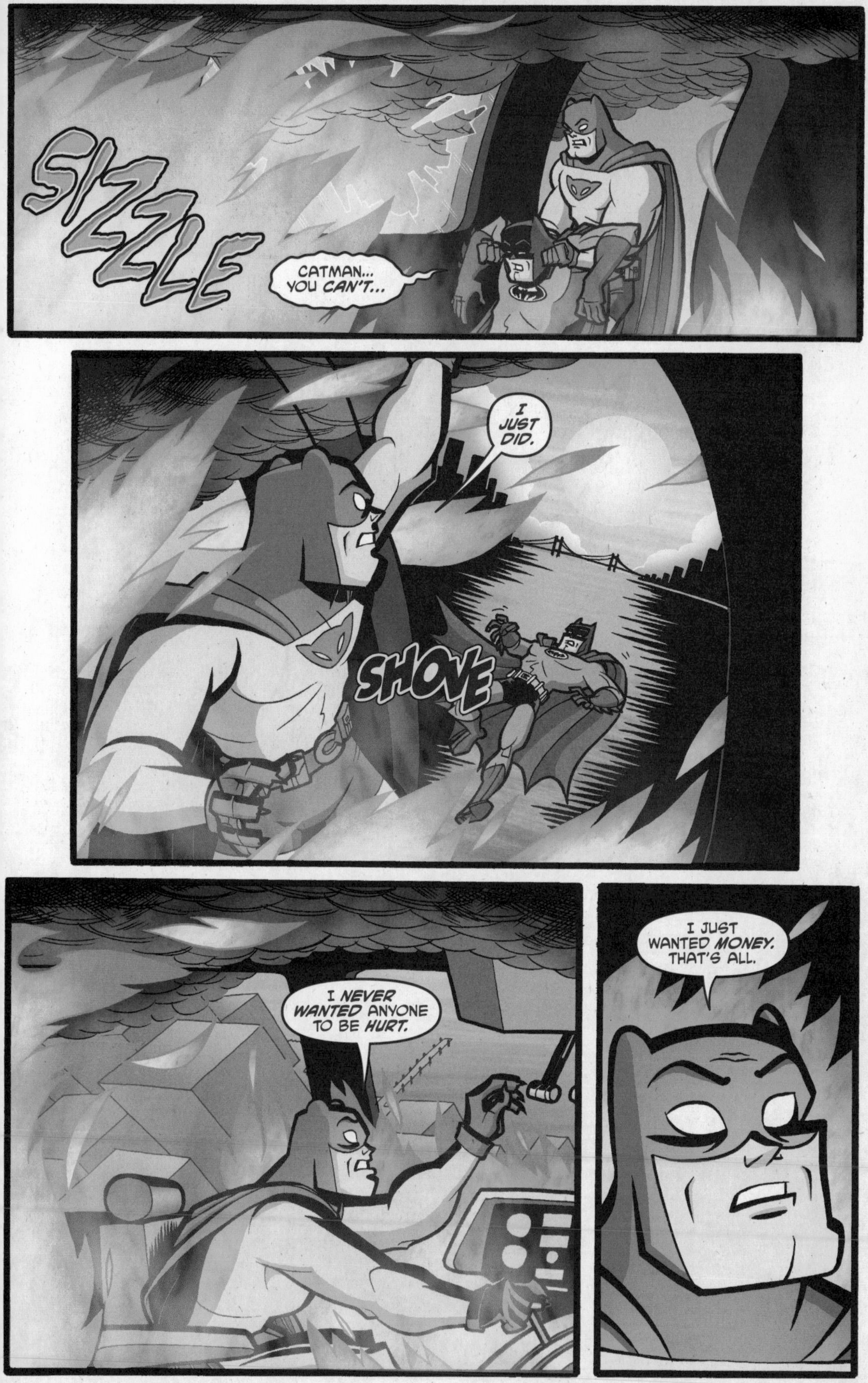
SIZZLE
CATMAN... YOU CAN'T...
I JUST DID.
SHOVE
I NEVER WANTED ANYONE TO BE HURT.
I JUST WANTED MONEY. THAT'S ALL.

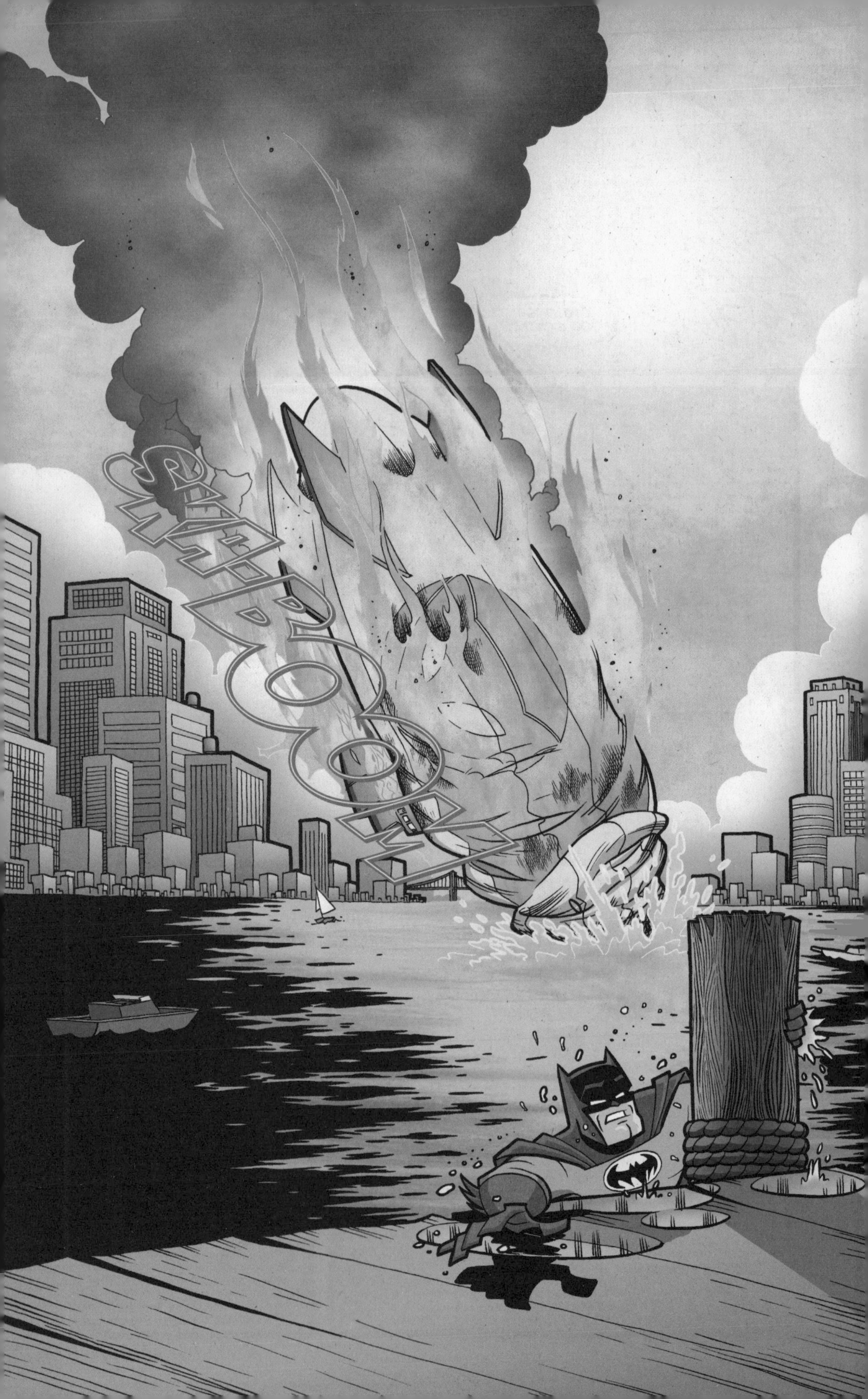
SPLABOOOM

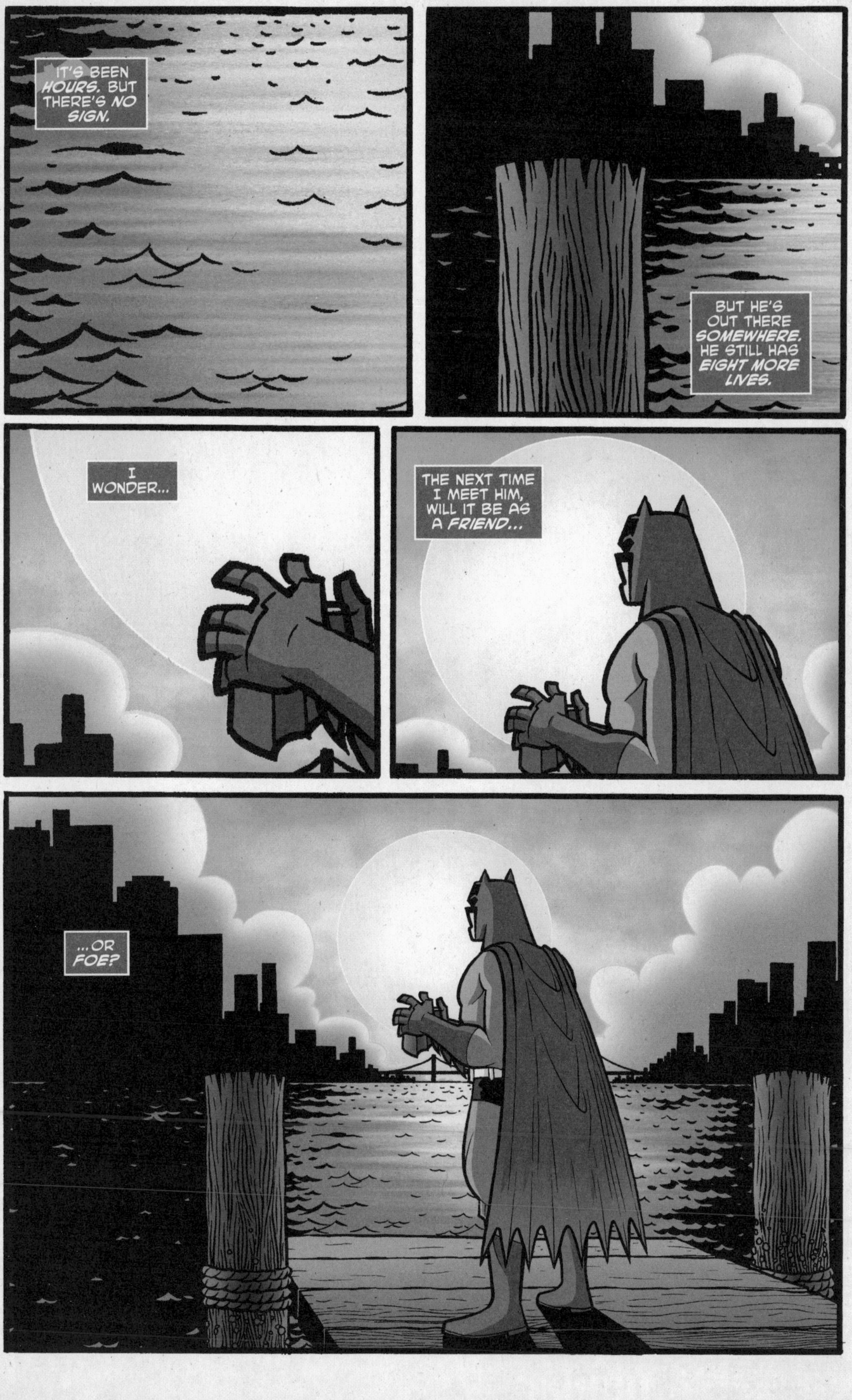
IT'S BEEN HOURS. BUT THERE'S NO SIGN.
BUT HE'S OUT THERE SOMEWHERE. HE STILL HAS EIGHT MORE LIVES.
I WONDER...
THE NEXT TIME I MEET HIM, WILL IT BE AS A FRIEND...
...OR FOE?

BATMAN: THE BRAVE AND THE BOLD #10

Cover by Eric Jones and Hi-Fi

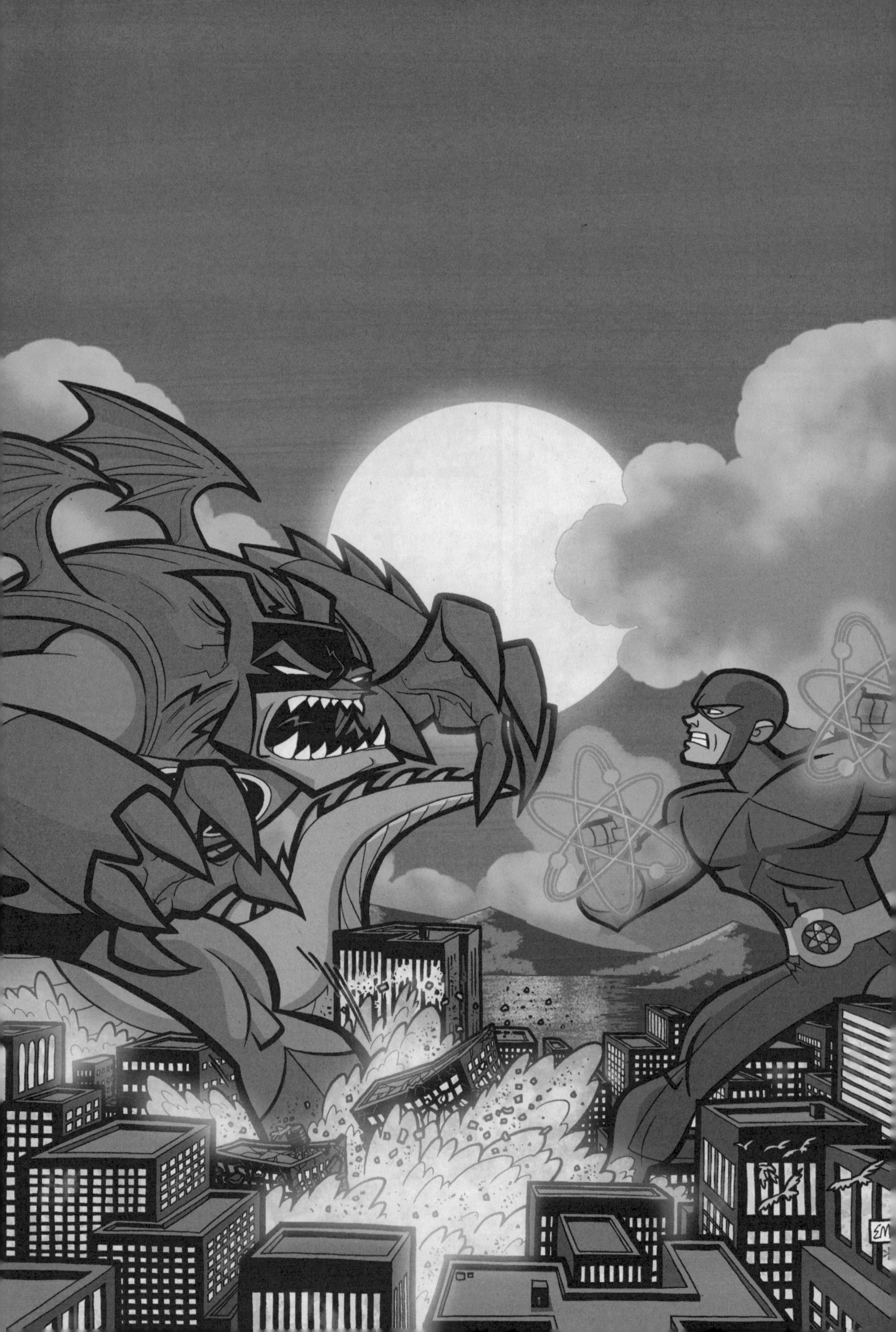

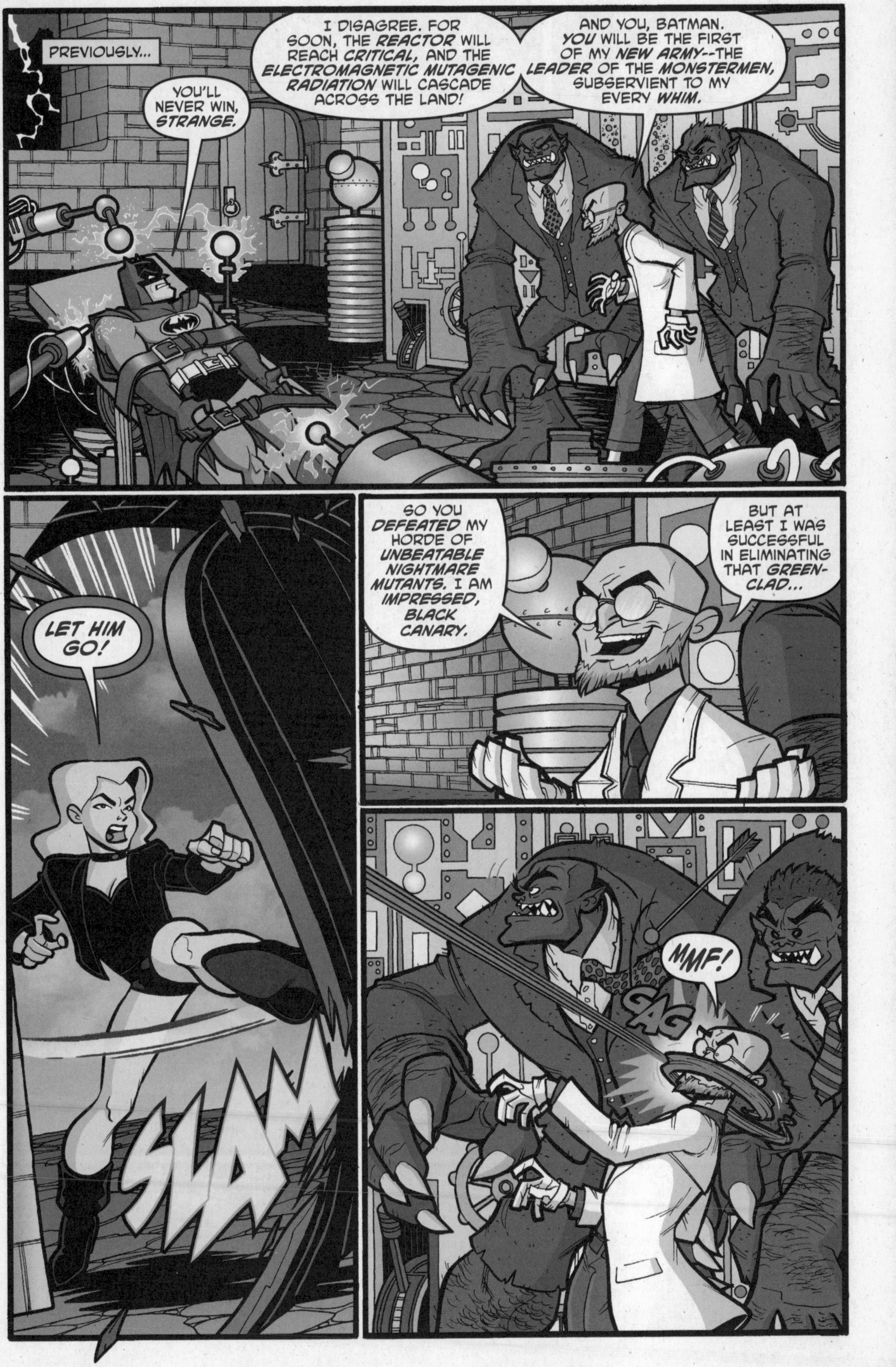
PREVIOUSLY...
YOU'LL NEVER WIN, STRANGE.
I DISAGREE. FOR SOON, THE REACTOR WILL REACH CRITICAL, AND THE ELECTROMAGNETIC MUTAGENIC RADIATION WILL CASCADE ACROSS THE LAND!
AND YOU, BATMAN. YOU WILL BE THE FIRST OF MY NEW ARMY--THE LEADER OF THE MONSTERMEN, SUBSERVIENT TO MY EVERY WHIM.
LET HIM GO!
SLAM
SO YOU DEFEATED MY HORDE OF UNBEATABLE NIGHTMARE MUTANTS. I AM IMPRESSED, BLACK CANARY.
BUT AT LEAST I WAS SUCCESSFUL IN ELIMINATING THAT GREEN-CLAD...
MMF!
GAG

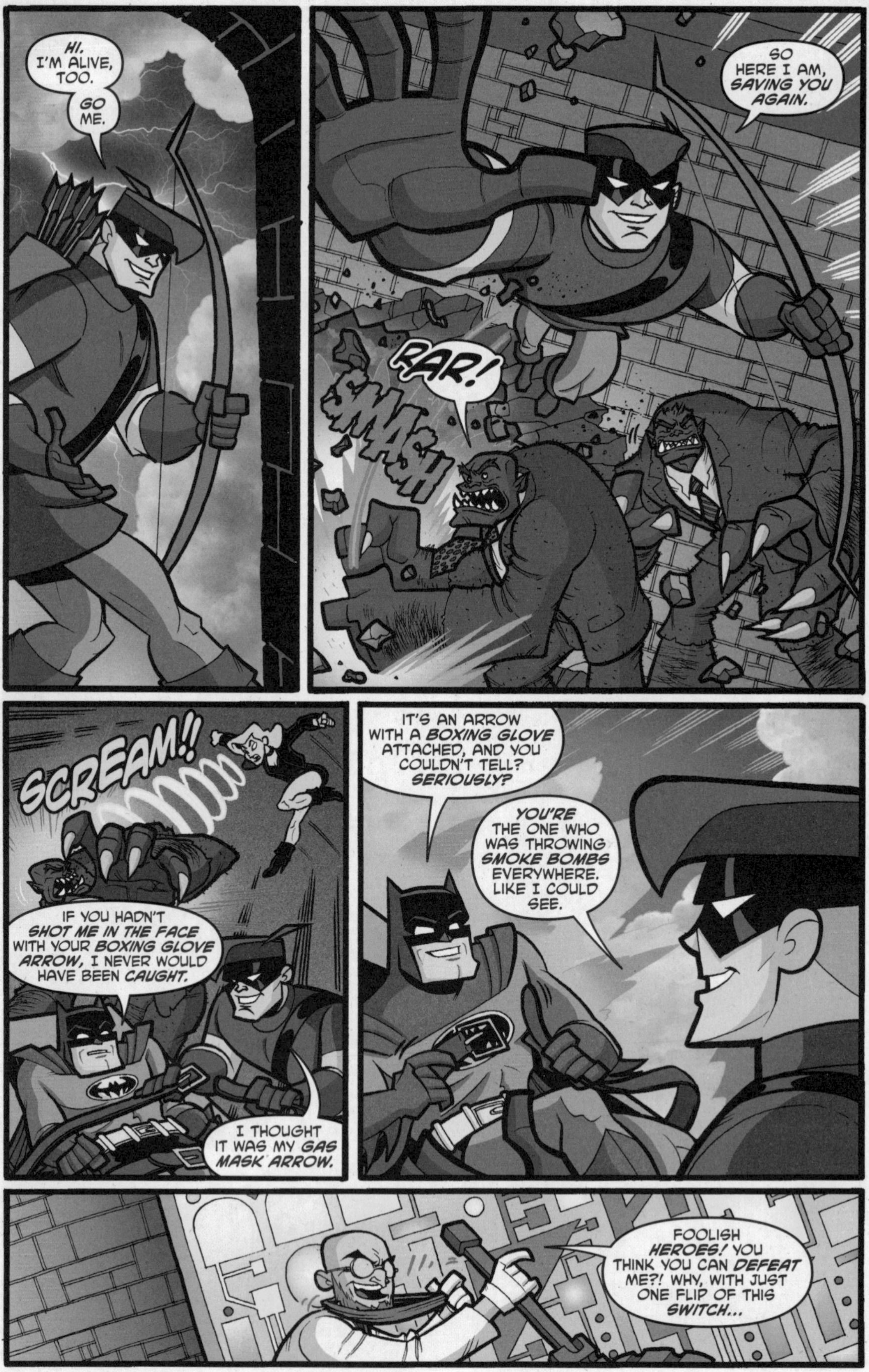
HI. I'M ALIVE, TOO.
GO ME.
SO HERE I AM, SAVING YOU AGAIN.
RAR!
SMASH
SCREAM!!
IF YOU HADN'T SHOT ME IN THE FACE WITH YOUR BOXING GLOVE ARROW, I NEVER WOULD HAVE BEEN CAUGHT.
I THOUGHT IT WAS MY GAS MASK ARROW.
IT'S AN ARROW WITH A BOXING GLOVE ATTACHED, AND YOU COULDN'T TELL? SERIOUSLY?
YOU'RE THE ONE WHO WAS THROWING SMOKE BOMBS EVERYWHERE. LIKE I COULD SEE.
FOOLISH HEROES! YOU THINK YOU CAN DEFEAT ME?! WHY, WITH JUST ONE FLIP OF THIS SWITCH...

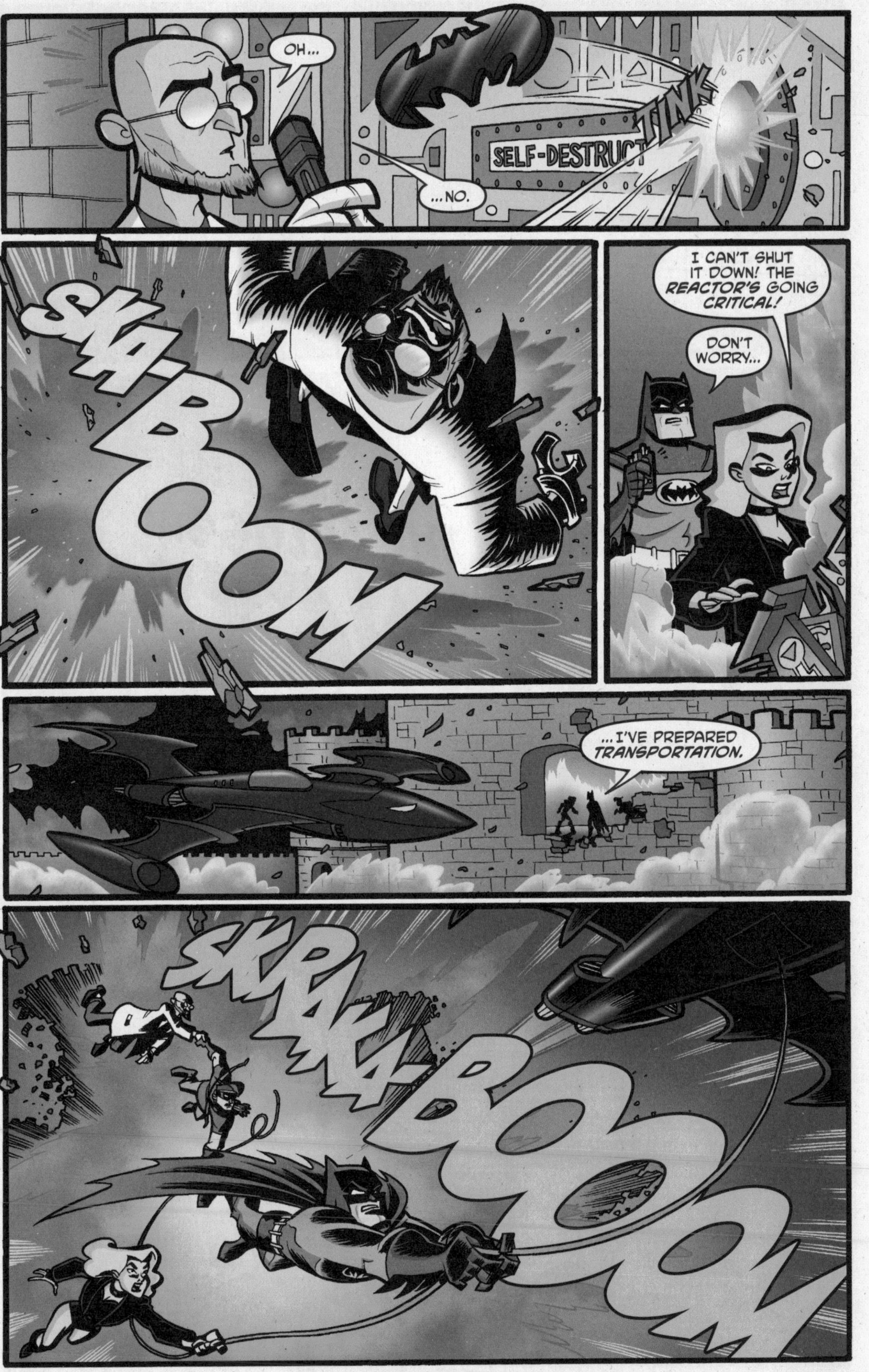
OH...
SELF-DESTRUCT
TINK
...NO.
SKA-BOOM
I CAN'T SHUT IT DOWN! THE *REACTOR'S* GOING *CRITICAL!*
DON'T WORRY...
...I'VE PREPARED *TRANSPORTATION.*
SKRAKA-BOOM

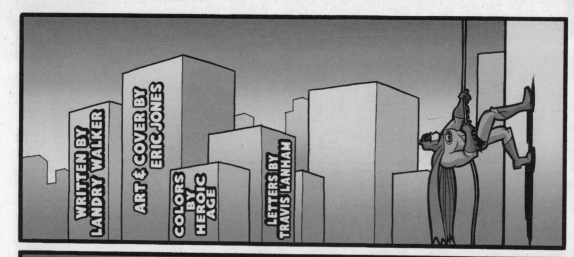

WRITTEN BY LANDRY WALKER

ART & COVER BY ERIC JONES

COLORS BY HEROIC AGE

LETTERS BY TRAVIS LANHAM

ATTACK OF THE COLOSSAL BAT-MONSTER!

IT HAD BEEN DAYS SINCE GREEN ARROW, BLACK CANARY AND I DEFEATED *HUGO STRANGE*.

HIS CASTLE LABORATORY WAS IN *RUINS*. HIS MUTANT MONSTERS ACCOUNTED FOR AND HIS HENCHMEN *ARRESTED*.

THE CASE WAS *CLOSED*.

BUT AS USUAL, SOME NEW EVIL WAS WAITING *RIGHT AROUND THE CORNER*.

GOTHAM MUSEUM

SEE THE MOON EXHIBIT!

SSKRASH

THE EARTH'S MOON

THE MOON GANG. STANDARD THEME-VILLAINS. BUBBLE HELMETS AND RAY GUNS.

THEIR TARGET: THE GOTHAM MUSEUM'S LUNAR ARTIFACTS DISPLAY. AND TONIGHT IS THE FIRST NIGHT OF THE FULL MOON.

PUNCH

THROW

AND EVER SINCE THE MOON ROSE, I AD BEEN FEELING... OFF, JUMPY...

ALMOST... TINGLY.

I SHOULD HAVE KNOWN SOMETHING WAS WRONG.

KICK

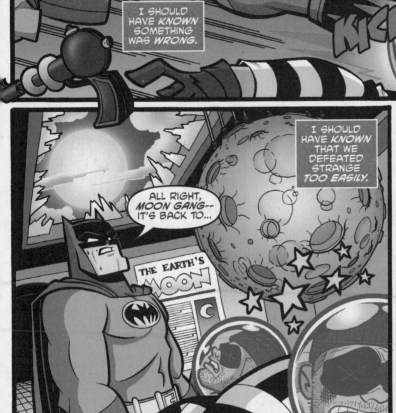

I SHOULD HAVE KNOWN THAT WE DEFEATED STRANGE TOO EASILY.

ALL RIGHT, MOON GANG-- IT'S BACK TO...

THE EARTH'S MOON

BACK... BACK TO...

ARG!!
RROOOAR!
AAAH!
MERCIFUL MOONBEAMS!
RETREAT! RETREAT TO THE SAFETY OF THE MOON!
GROW
RAARRR!

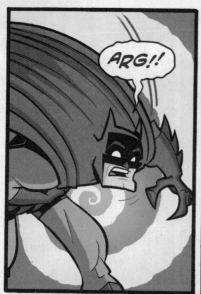

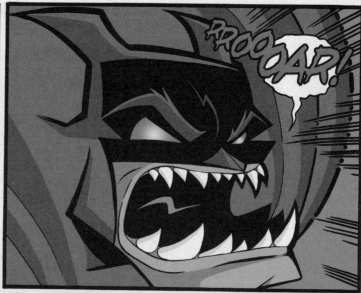

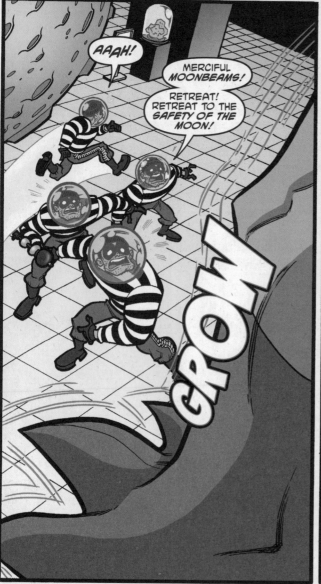

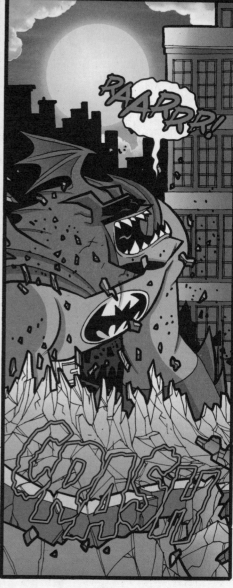

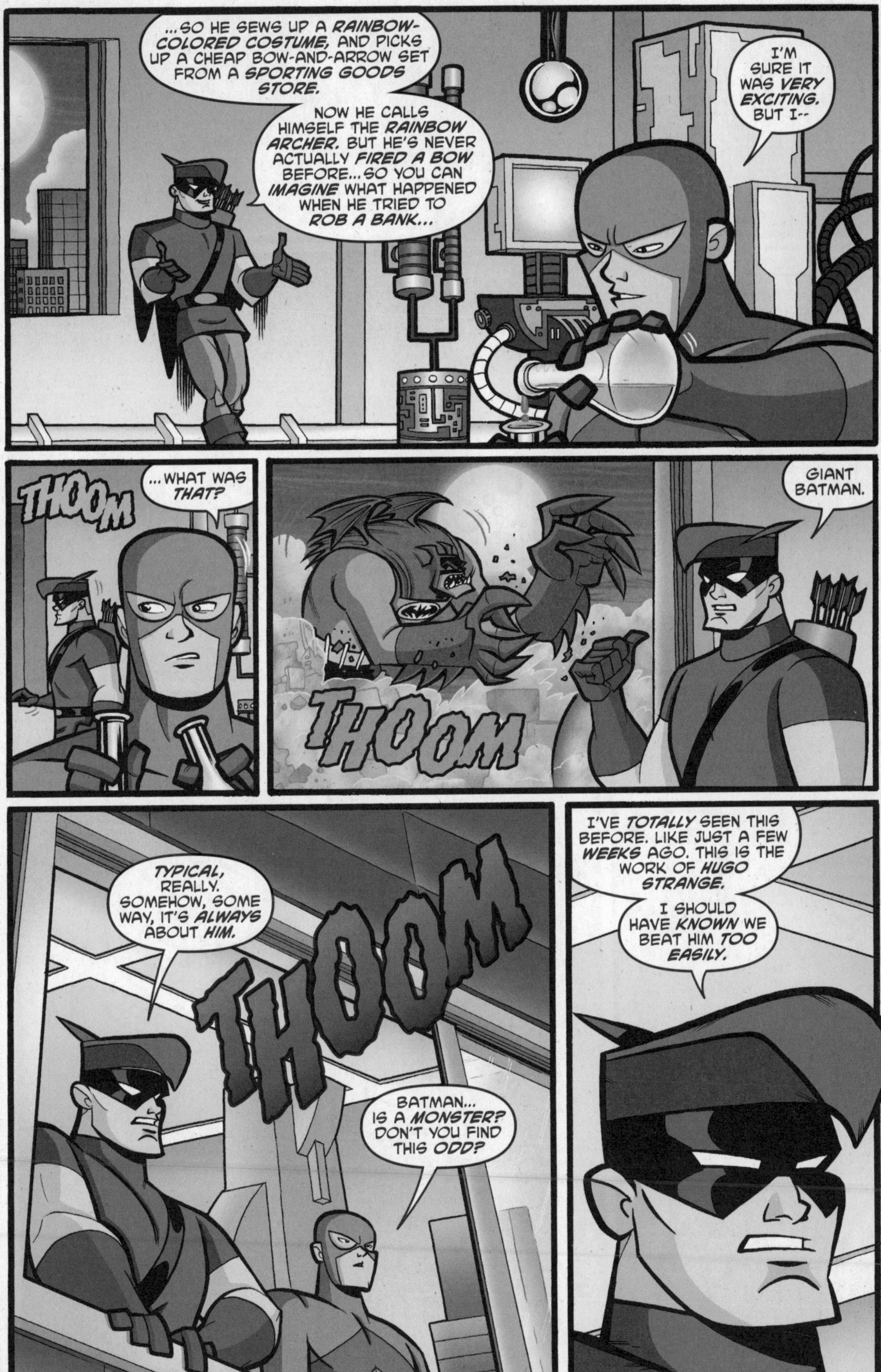
...SO HE SEWS UP A RAINBOW-COLORED COSTUME, AND PICKS UP A CHEAP BOW-AND-ARROW SET FROM A SPORTING GOODS STORE.
NOW HE CALLS HIMSELF THE RAINBOW ARCHER. BUT HE'S NEVER ACTUALLY FIRED A BOW BEFORE... SO YOU CAN IMAGINE WHAT HAPPENED WHEN HE TRIED TO ROB A BANK...
I'M SURE IT WAS VERY EXCITING. BUT I--
THOOM
...WHAT WAS THAT?
THOOM
GIANT BATMAN.
TYPICAL, REALLY. SOMEHOW, SOME WAY, IT'S ALWAYS ABOUT HIM.
THOOM
BATMAN... IS A MONSTER? DON'T YOU FIND THIS ODD?
I'VE TOTALLY SEEN THIS BEFORE. LIKE JUST A FEW WEEKS AGO. THIS IS THE WORK OF HUGO STRANGE.
I SHOULD HAVE KNOWN WE BEAT HIM TOO EASILY.

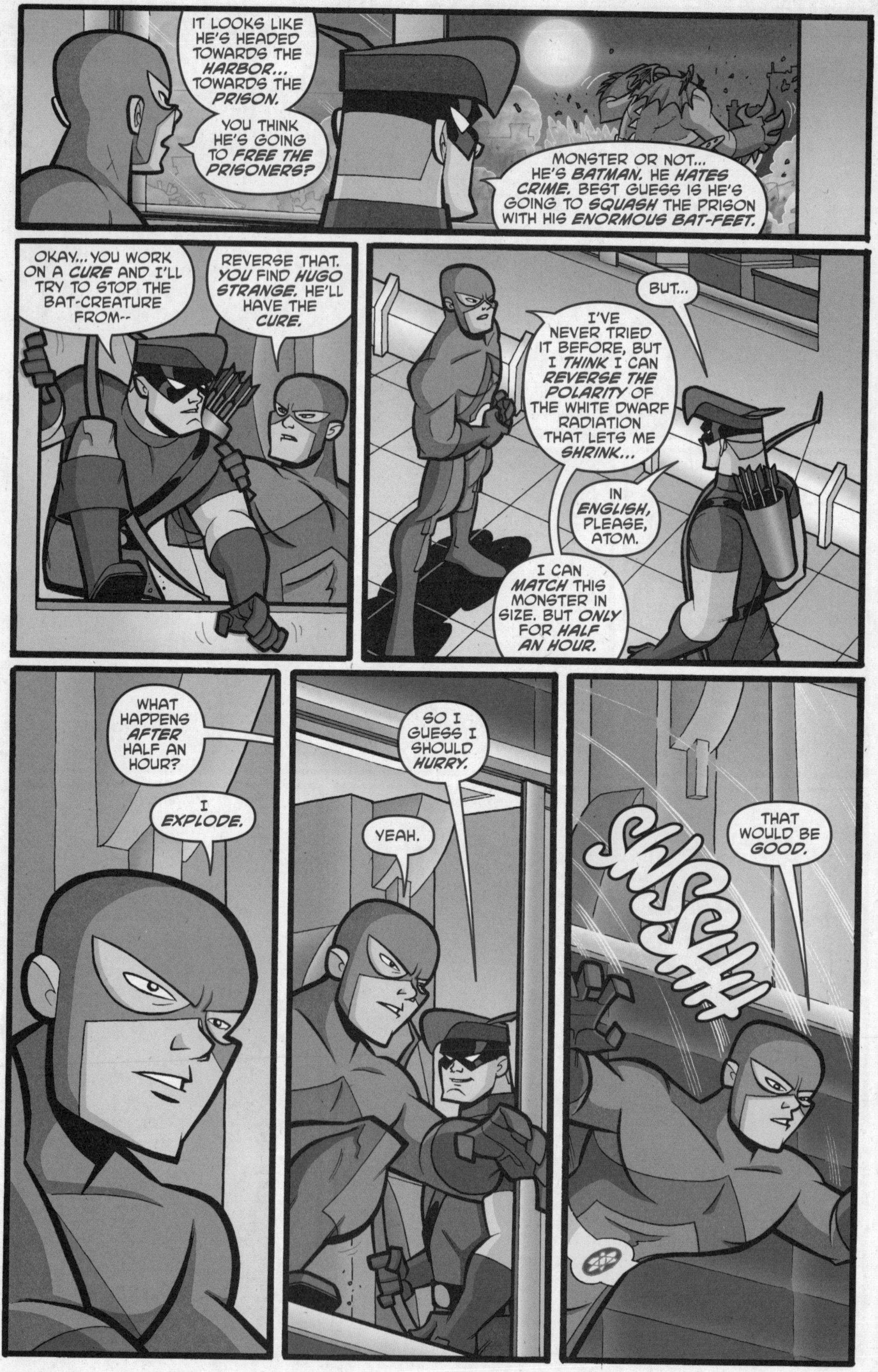
IT LOOKS LIKE HE'S HEADED TOWARDS THE HARBOR... TOWARDS THE PRISON.
YOU THINK HE'S GOING TO FREE THE PRISONERS?
MONSTER OR NOT... HE'S BATMAN. HE HATES CRIME. BEST GUESS IS HE'S GOING TO SQUASH THE PRISON WITH HIS ENORMOUS BAT-FEET.
OKAY... YOU WORK ON A CURE AND I'LL TRY TO STOP THE BAT-CREATURE FROM--
REVERSE THAT. YOU FIND HUGO STRANGE. HE'LL HAVE THE CURE.
BUT...
I'VE NEVER TRIED IT BEFORE, BUT I THINK I CAN REVERSE THE POLARITY OF THE WHITE DWARF RADIATION THAT LETS ME SHRINK...
IN ENGLISH, PLEASE, ATOM.
I CAN MATCH THIS MONSTER IN SIZE. BUT ONLY FOR HALF AN HOUR.
WHAT HAPPENS AFTER HALF AN HOUR?
I EXPLODE.
SO I GUESS I SHOULD HURRY.
YEAH.
SWSSHH!
THAT WOULD BE GOOD.

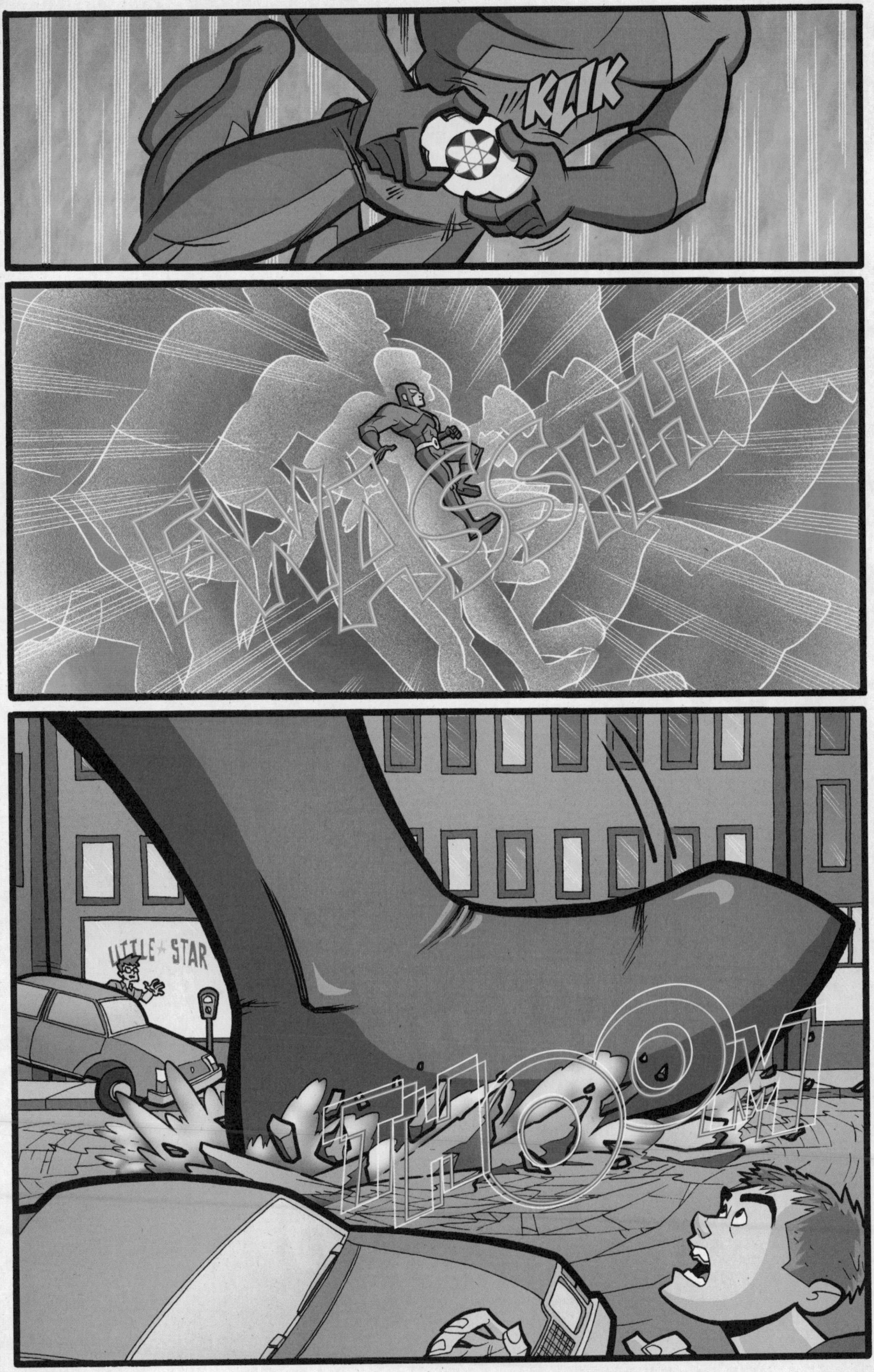
KLIK
FWASSHH
LITTLE STAR
THOOM

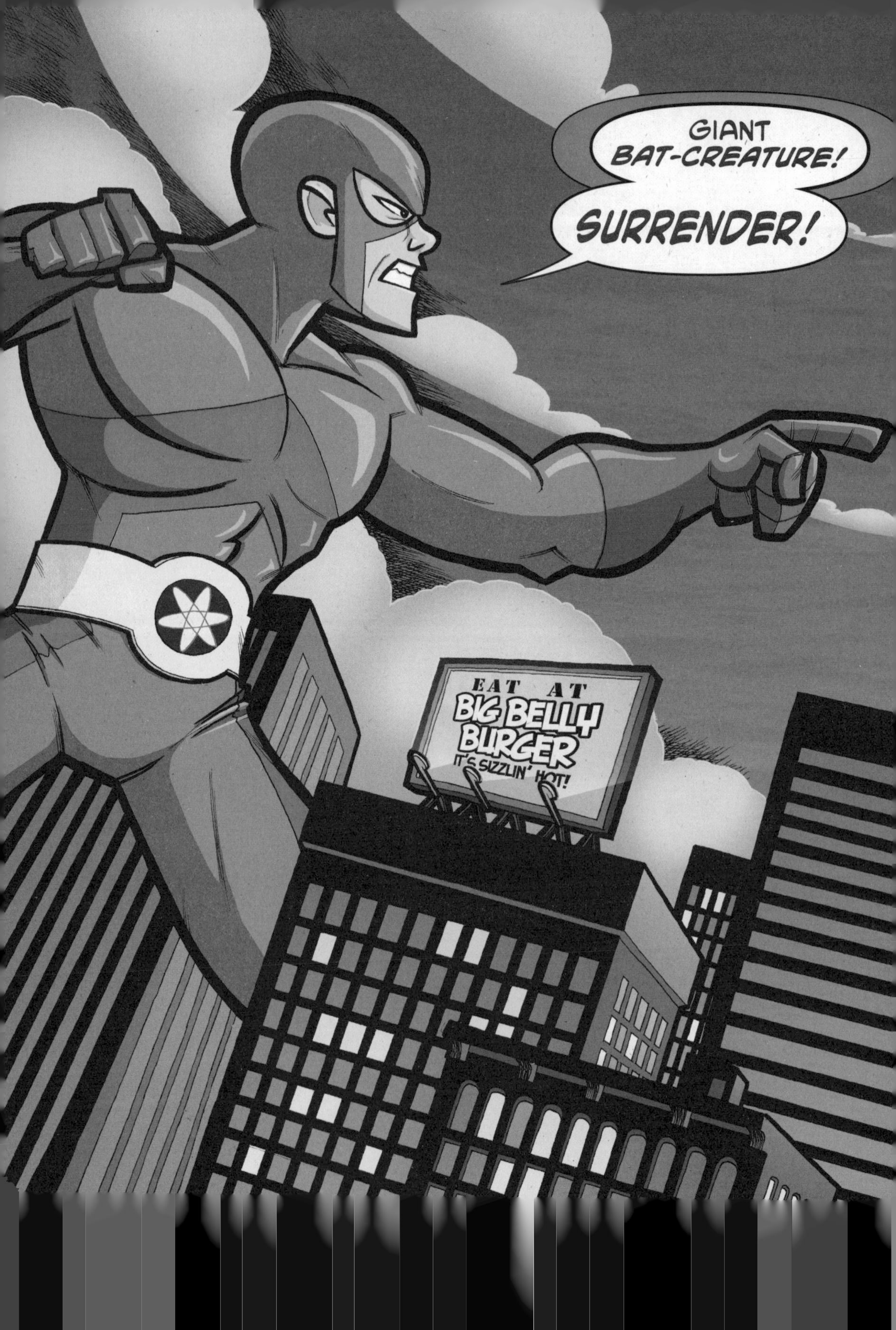
GIANT BAT-CREATURE!
SURRENDER!
EAT AT
BIG BELLY BURGER
IT'S SIZZLIN' HOT!

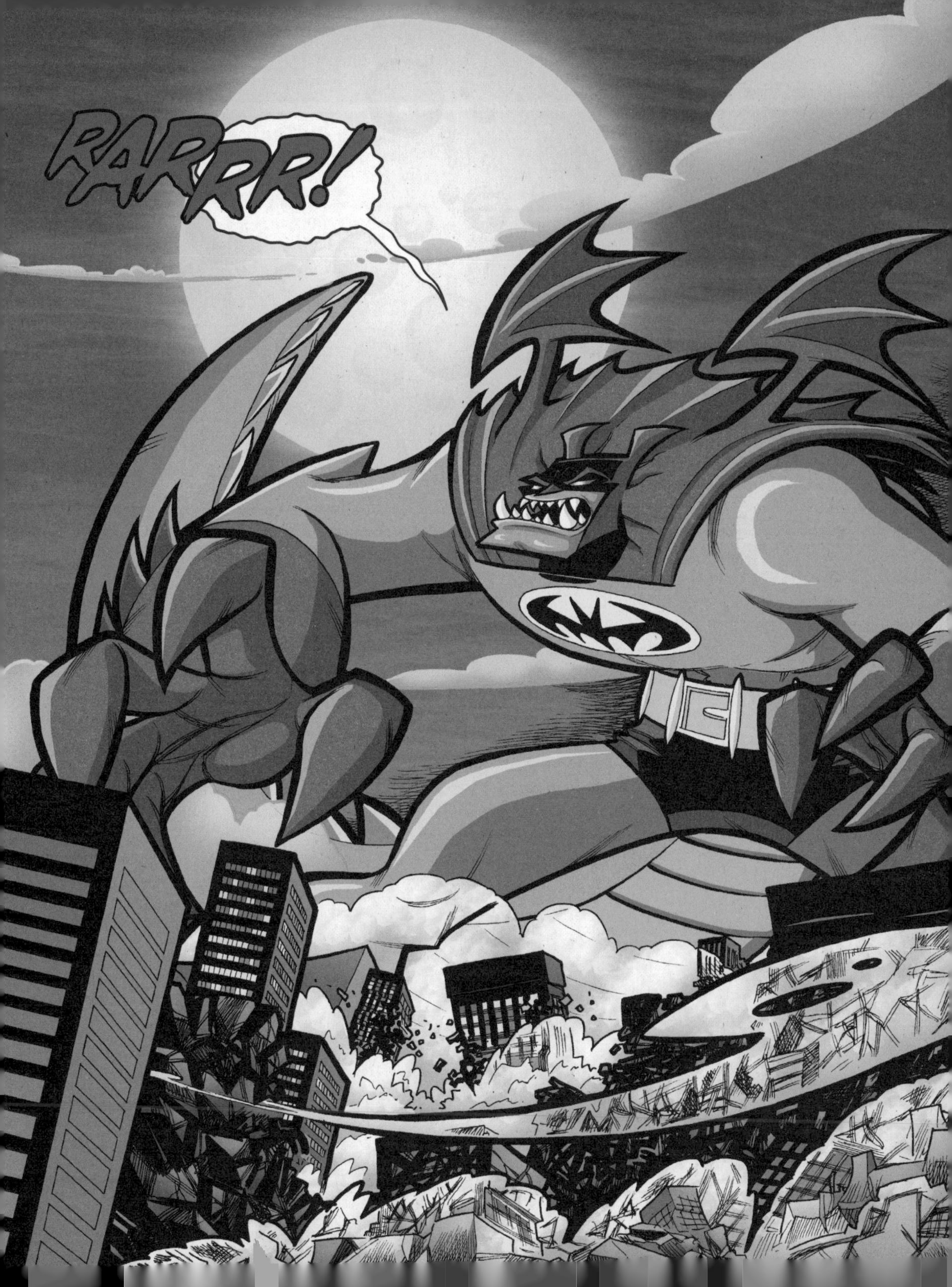
RARRR!

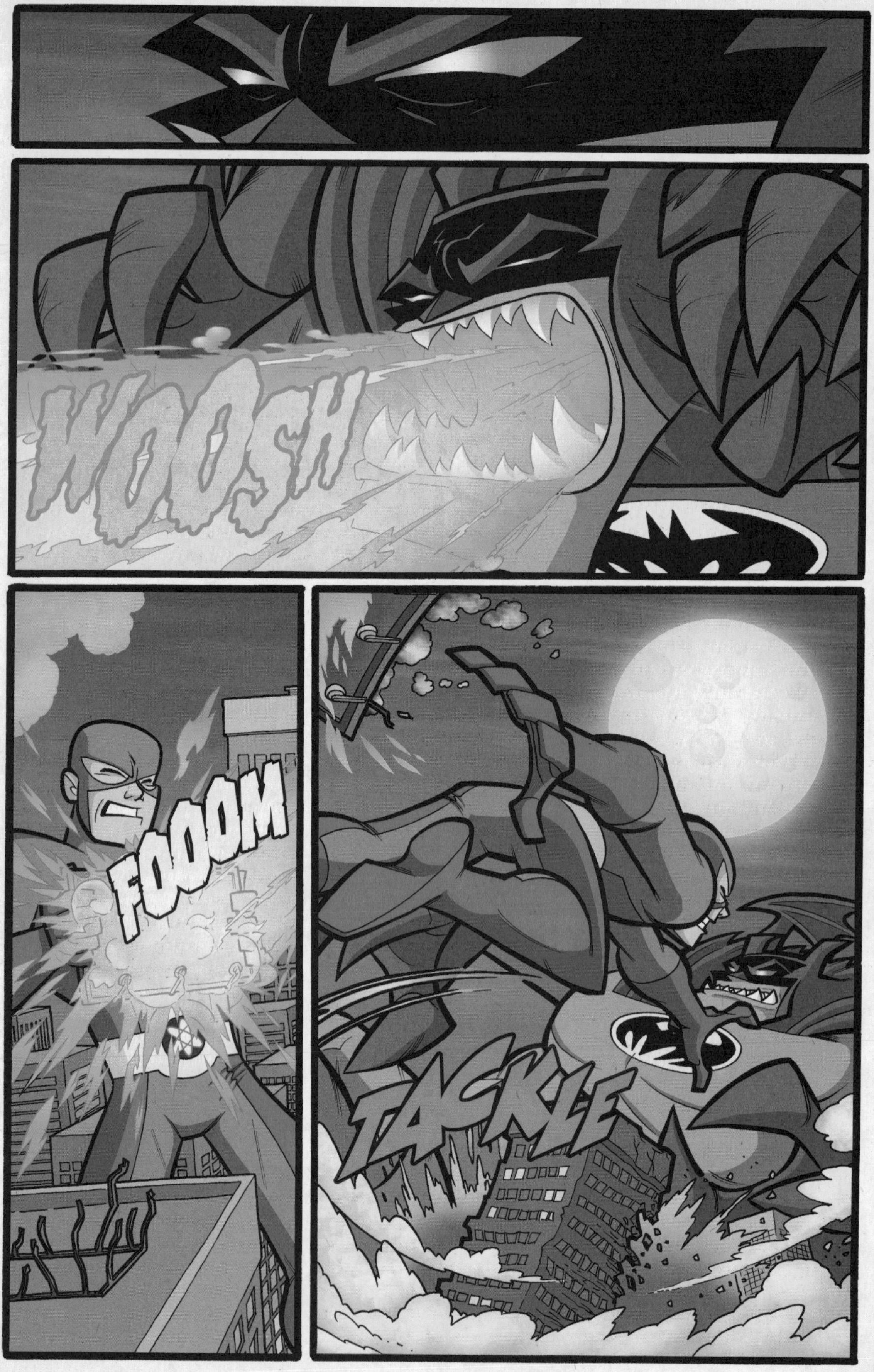
WOOSH
FOOOM
TACKLE

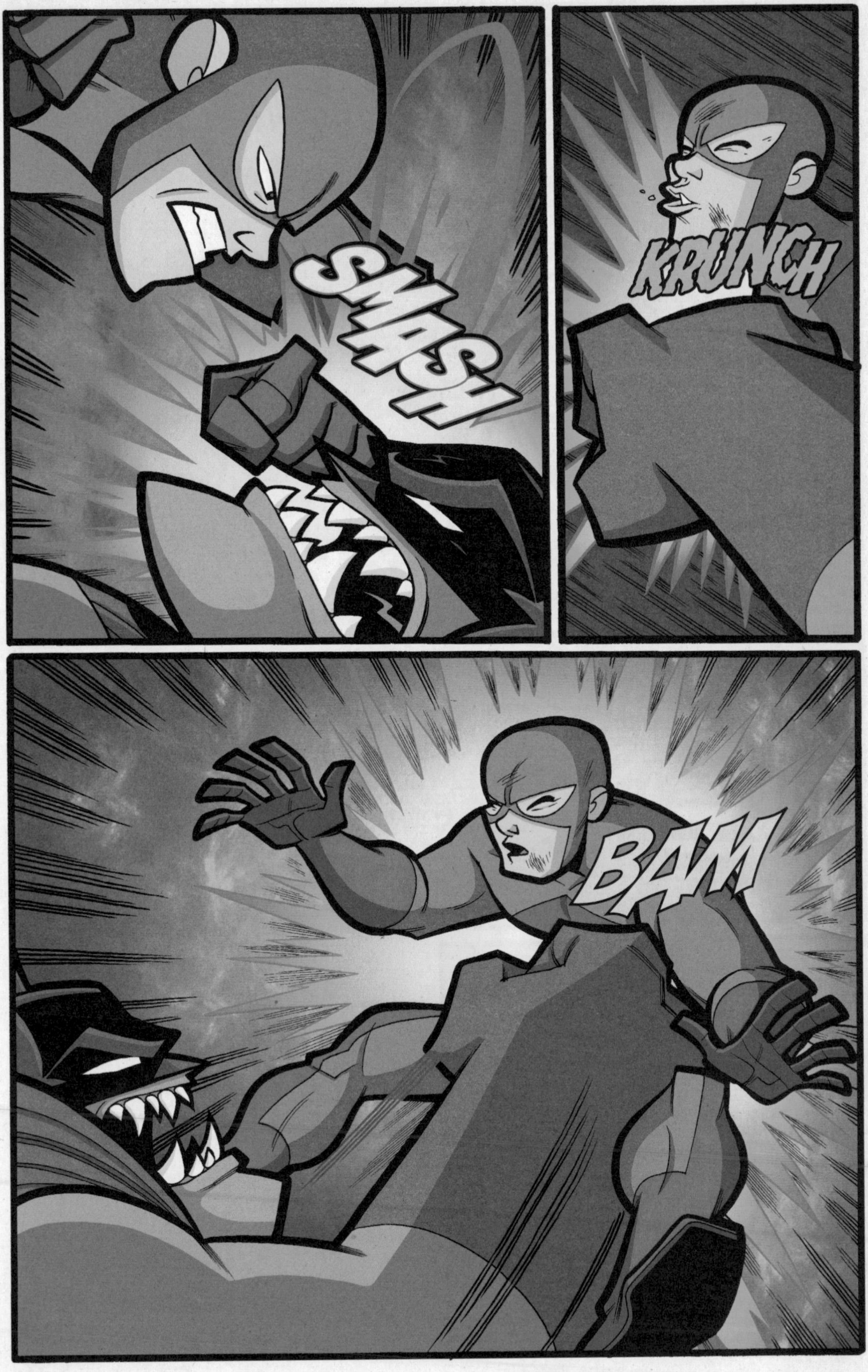
SMASH
KRUNCH
BAM

KAWHAMM

UNGH!

KRUMPLE

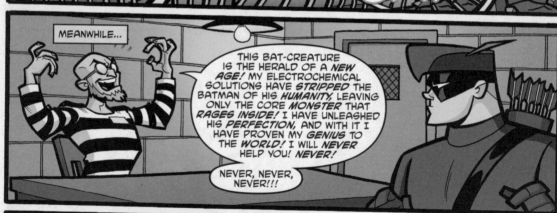

MEANWHILE...

THIS BAT-CREATURE IS THE HERALD OF A *NEW AGE!* MY ELECTROCHEMICAL SOLUTIONS HAVE *STRIPPED* THE BATMAN OF HIS *HUMANITY,* LEAVING ONLY THE CORE *MONSTER* THAT *RAGES INSIDE!* I HAVE UNLEASHED HIS *PERFECTION,* AND WITH IT I HAVE PROVEN MY *GENIUS* TO THE *WORLD!* I WILL *NEVER* HELP YOU! *NEVER!*

NEVER, NEVER, NEVER!!!

LOOK, I GOT MAYBE 15 MINUTES UNTIL A FRIEND OF MINE *EXPLODES,* AND HE'S THE ONLY THING BETWEEN THAT GIANT, ANGRY *BAT-MONSTER* AND *THIS* TINY, *EASILY SMASHABLE* PRISON.

WHAT DO YOU *THINK* IS GOING TO *HAPPEN* TO US--TO *YOU*--WHEN HE GETS HERE AND STARTS *SMASHING?*

OKAY. ONE *ANTIDOTE* COMING UP.

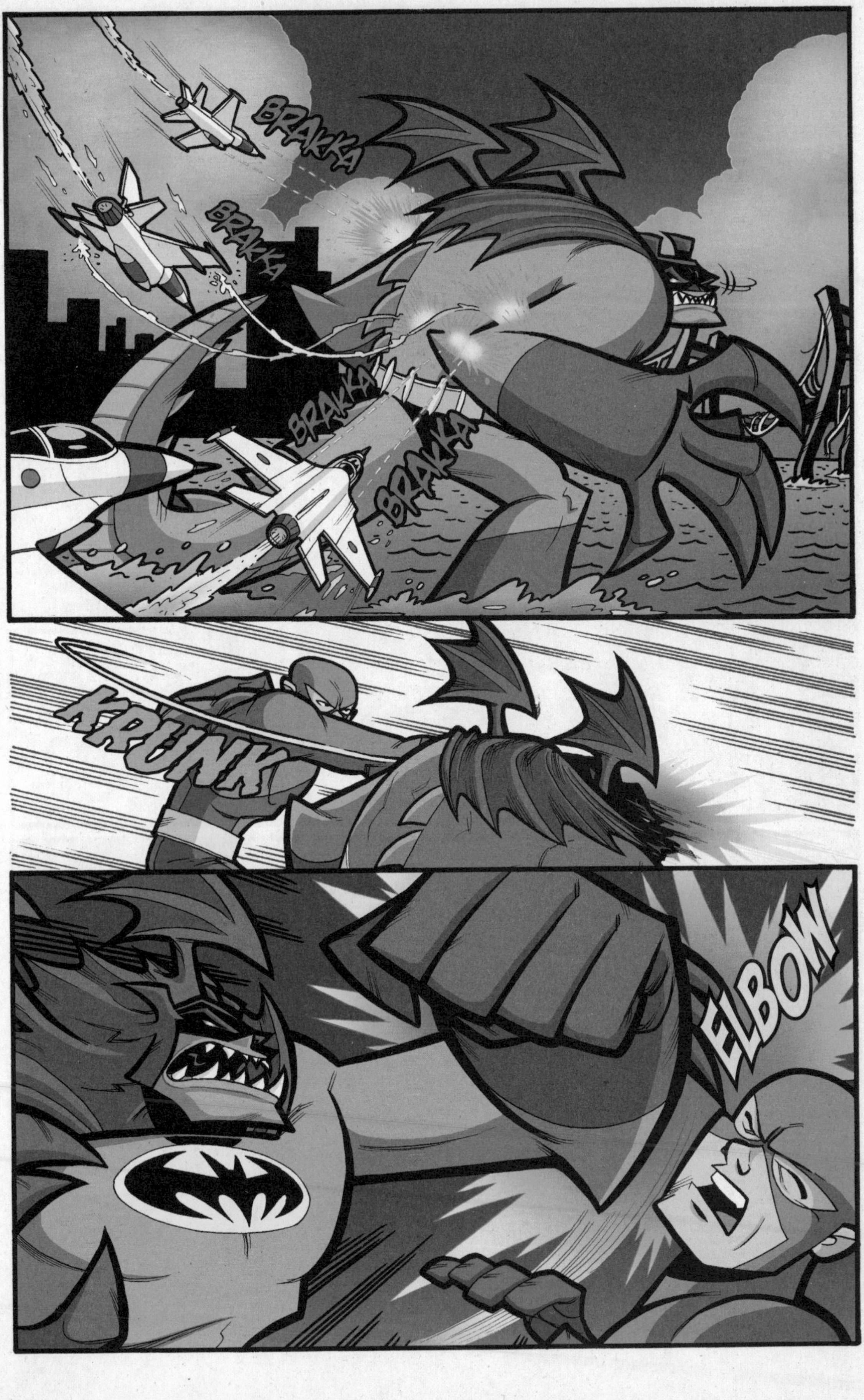
BRAKKA
BRAKKA
BRAKKA
BRAKKA
KRUNK
ELBOW

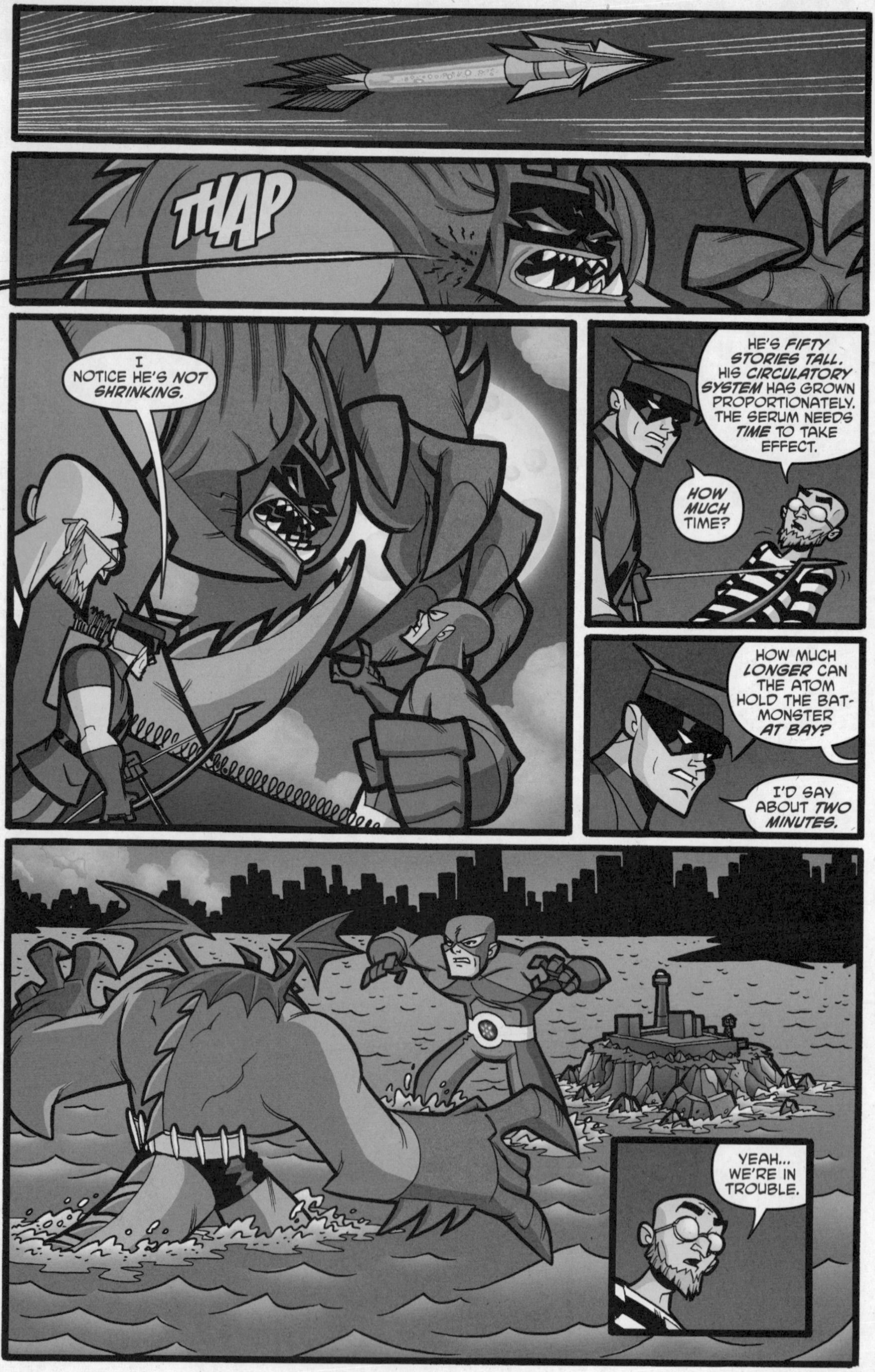
THAP
I NOTICE HE'S NOT SHRINKING.
HE'S FIFTY STORIES TALL. HIS CIRCULATORY SYSTEM HAS GROWN PROPORTIONATELY. THE SERUM NEEDS TIME TO TAKE EFFECT.
HOW MUCH TIME?
HOW MUCH LONGER CAN THE ATOM HOLD THE BAT-MONSTER AT BAY?
I'D SAY ABOUT TWO MINUTES.
YEAH... WE'RE IN TROUBLE.

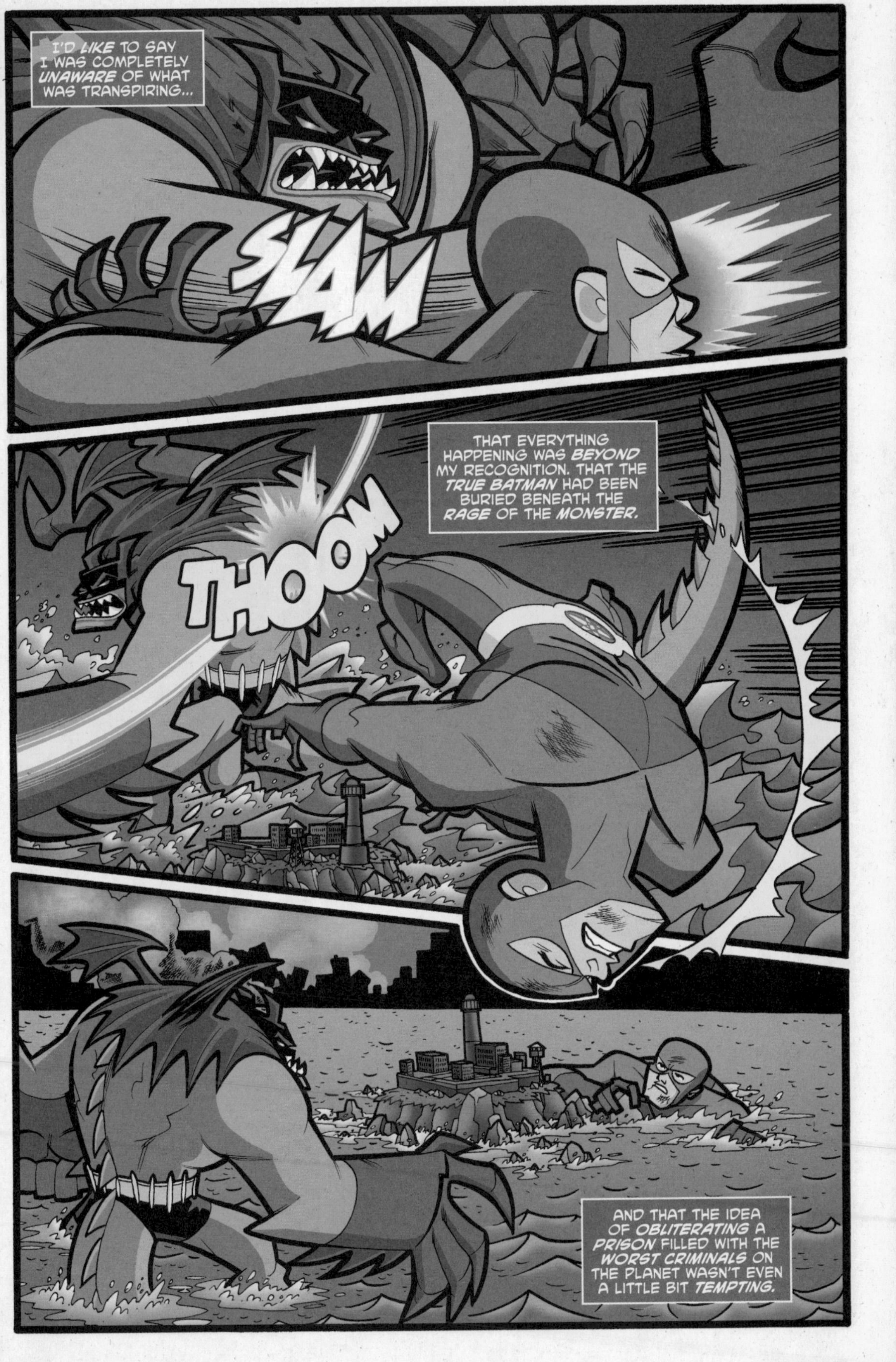
I'D LIKE TO SAY I WAS COMPLETELY UNAWARE OF WHAT WAS TRANSPIRING...
SLAM
THAT EVERYTHING HAPPENING WAS BEYOND MY RECOGNITION. THAT THE TRUE BATMAN HAD BEEN BURIED BENEATH THE RAGE OF THE MONSTER.
THOOM
AND THAT THE IDEA OF OBLITERATING A PRISON FILLED WITH THE WORST CRIMINALS ON THE PLANET WASN'T EVEN A LITTLE BIT TEMPTING.

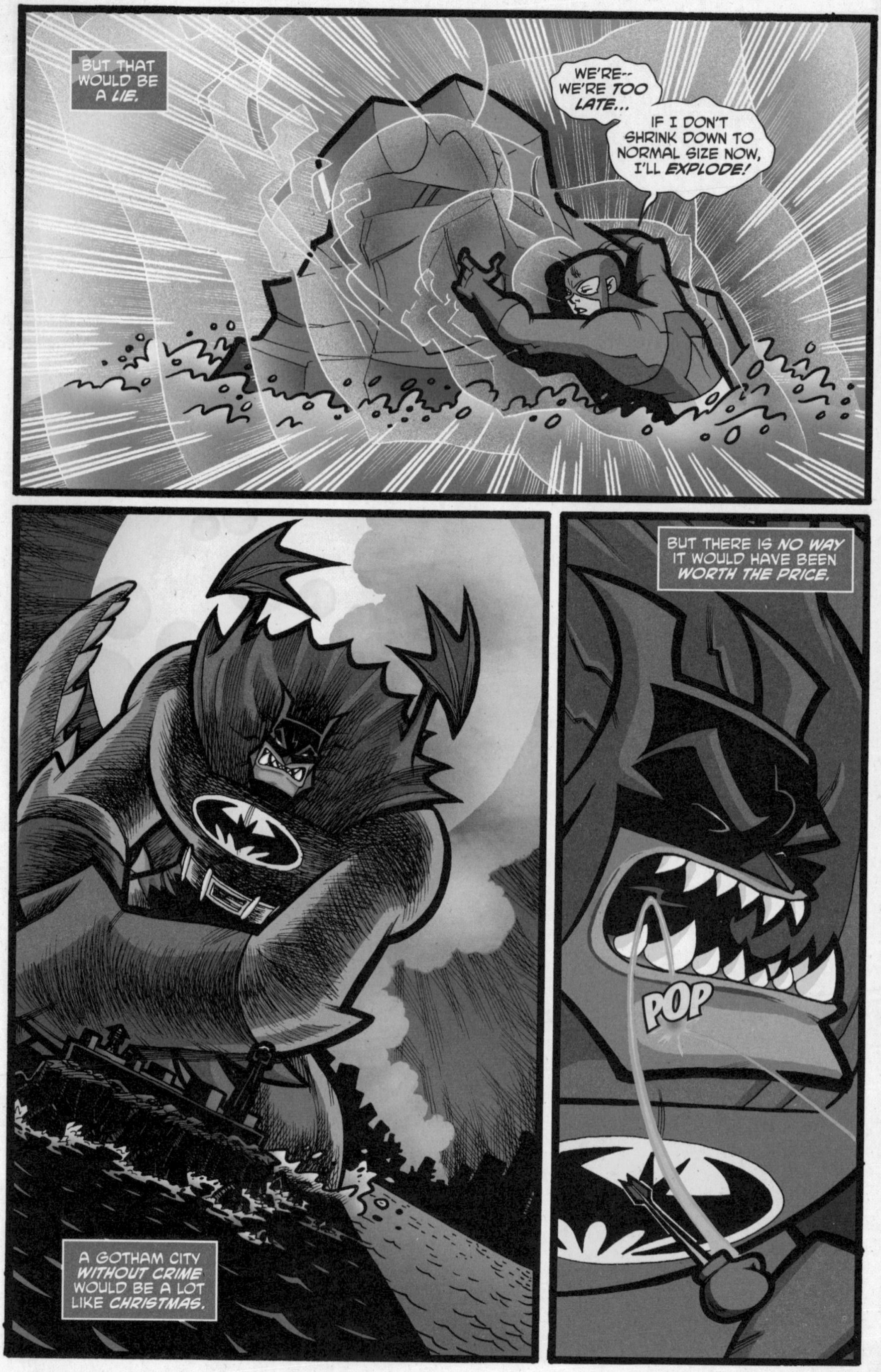
BUT THAT WOULD BE A LIE.
WE'RE-- WE'RE TOO LATE...
IF I DON'T SHRINK DOWN TO NORMAL SIZE NOW, I'LL EXPLODE!
A GOTHAM CITY WITHOUT CRIME WOULD BE A LOT LIKE CHRISTMAS.
BUT THERE IS NO WAY IT WOULD HAVE BEEN WORTH THE PRICE.
POP

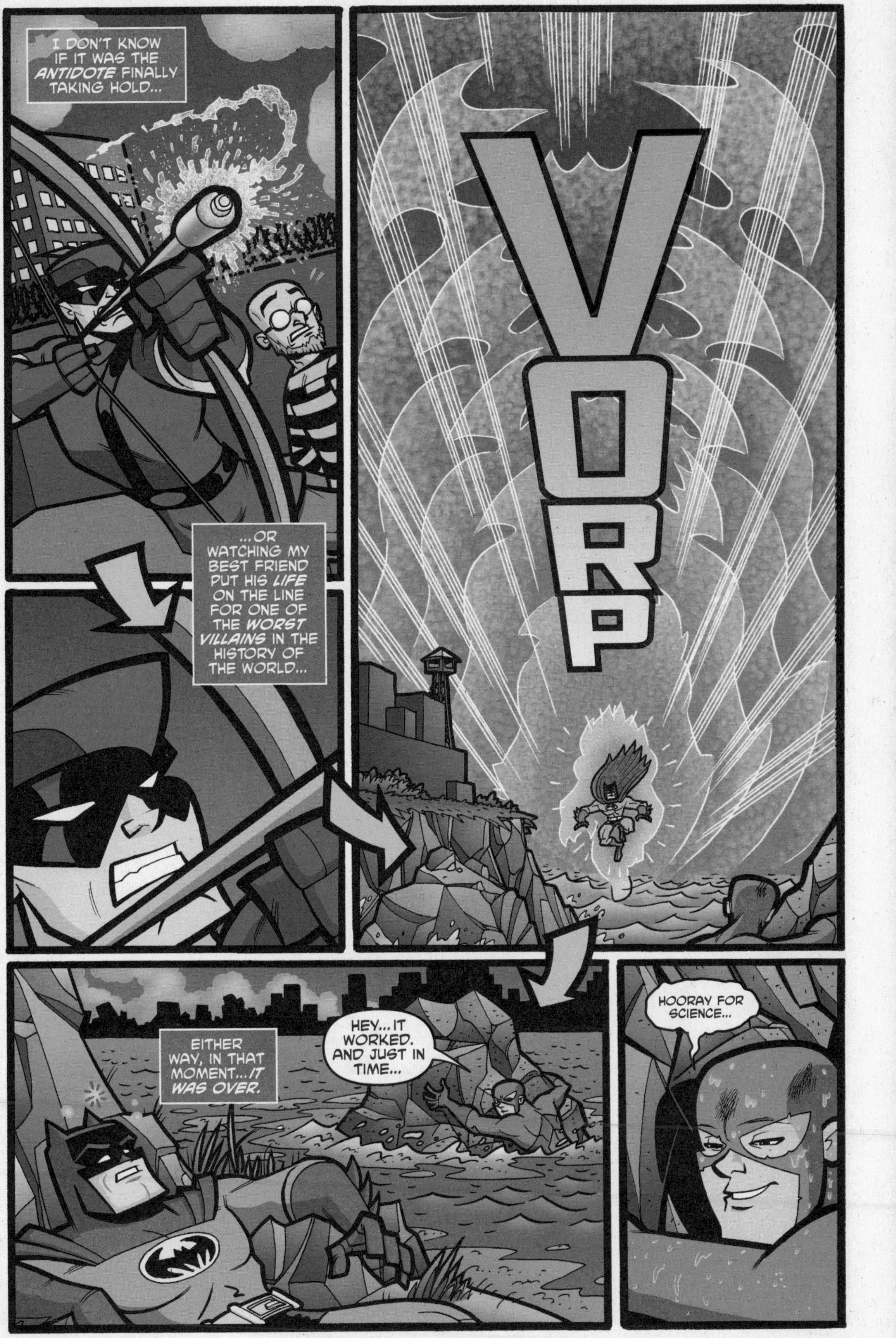
I DON'T KNOW IF IT WAS THE ANTIDOTE FINALLY TAKING HOLD...
...OR WATCHING MY BEST FRIEND PUT HIS LIFE ON THE LINE FOR ONE OF THE WORST VILLAINS IN THE HISTORY OF THE WORLD...
VORP
EITHER WAY, IN THAT MOMENT...IT WAS OVER.
HEY...IT WORKED. AND JUST IN TIME...
HOORAY FOR SCIENCE...

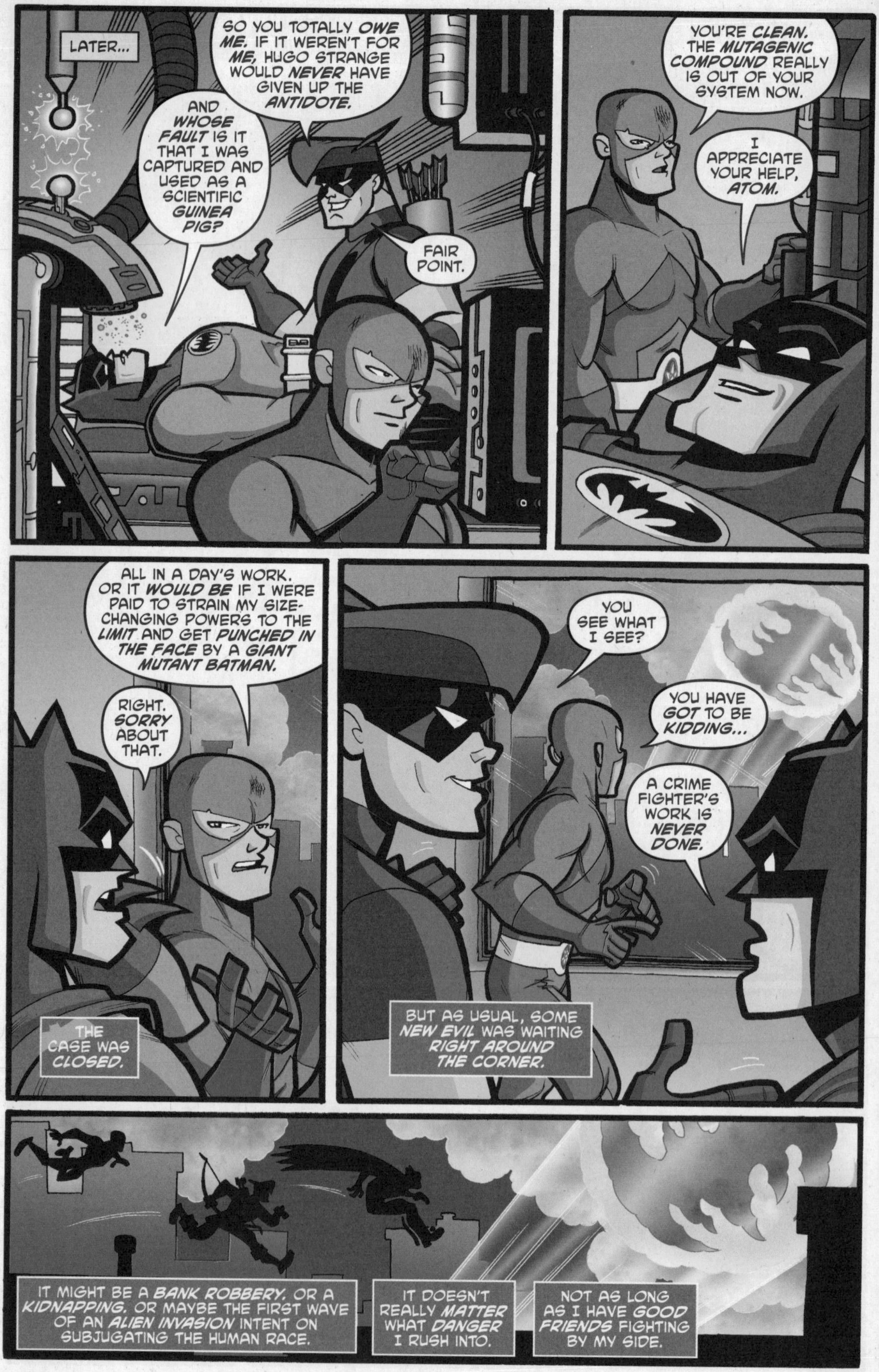
LATER...
SO YOU TOTALLY OWE ME. IF IT WEREN'T FOR ME, HUGO STRANGE WOULD NEVER HAVE GIVEN UP THE ANTIDOTE.
AND WHOSE FAULT IS IT THAT I WAS CAPTURED AND USED AS A SCIENTIFIC GUINEA PIG?
FAIR POINT.
YOU'RE CLEAN. THE MUTAGENIC COMPOUND REALLY IS OUT OF YOUR SYSTEM NOW.
I APPRECIATE YOUR HELP, ATOM.
ALL IN A DAY'S WORK. OR IT WOULD BE IF I WERE PAID TO STRAIN MY SIZE-CHANGING POWERS TO THE LIMIT AND GET PUNCHED IN THE FACE BY A GIANT MUTANT BATMAN.
RIGHT. SORRY ABOUT THAT.
THE CASE WAS CLOSED.
YOU SEE WHAT I SEE?
YOU HAVE GOT TO BE KIDDING...
A CRIME FIGHTER'S WORK IS NEVER DONE.
BUT AS USUAL, SOME NEW EVIL WAS WAITING RIGHT AROUND THE CORNER.
IT MIGHT BE A BANK ROBBERY, OR A KIDNAPPING, OR MAYBE THE FIRST WAVE OF AN ALIEN INVASION INTENT ON SUBJUGATING THE HUMAN RACE.
IT DOESN'T REALLY MATTER WHAT DANGER I RUSH INTO.
NOT AS LONG AS I HAVE GOOD FRIENDS FIGHTING BY MY SIDE.

BATMAN: THE BRAVE AND THE BOLD #11

Cover by Scott Jeralds with Hi-Fi

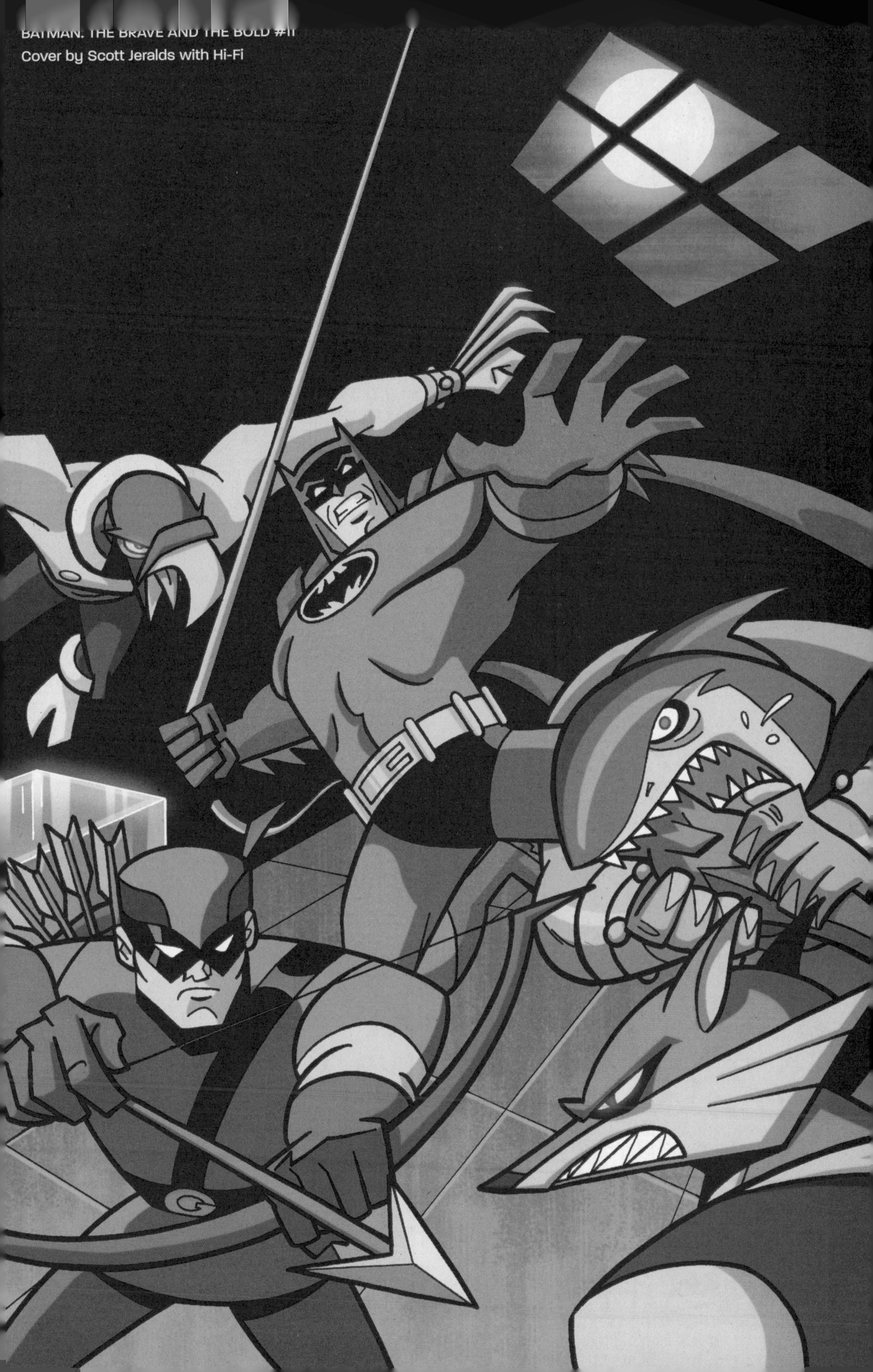

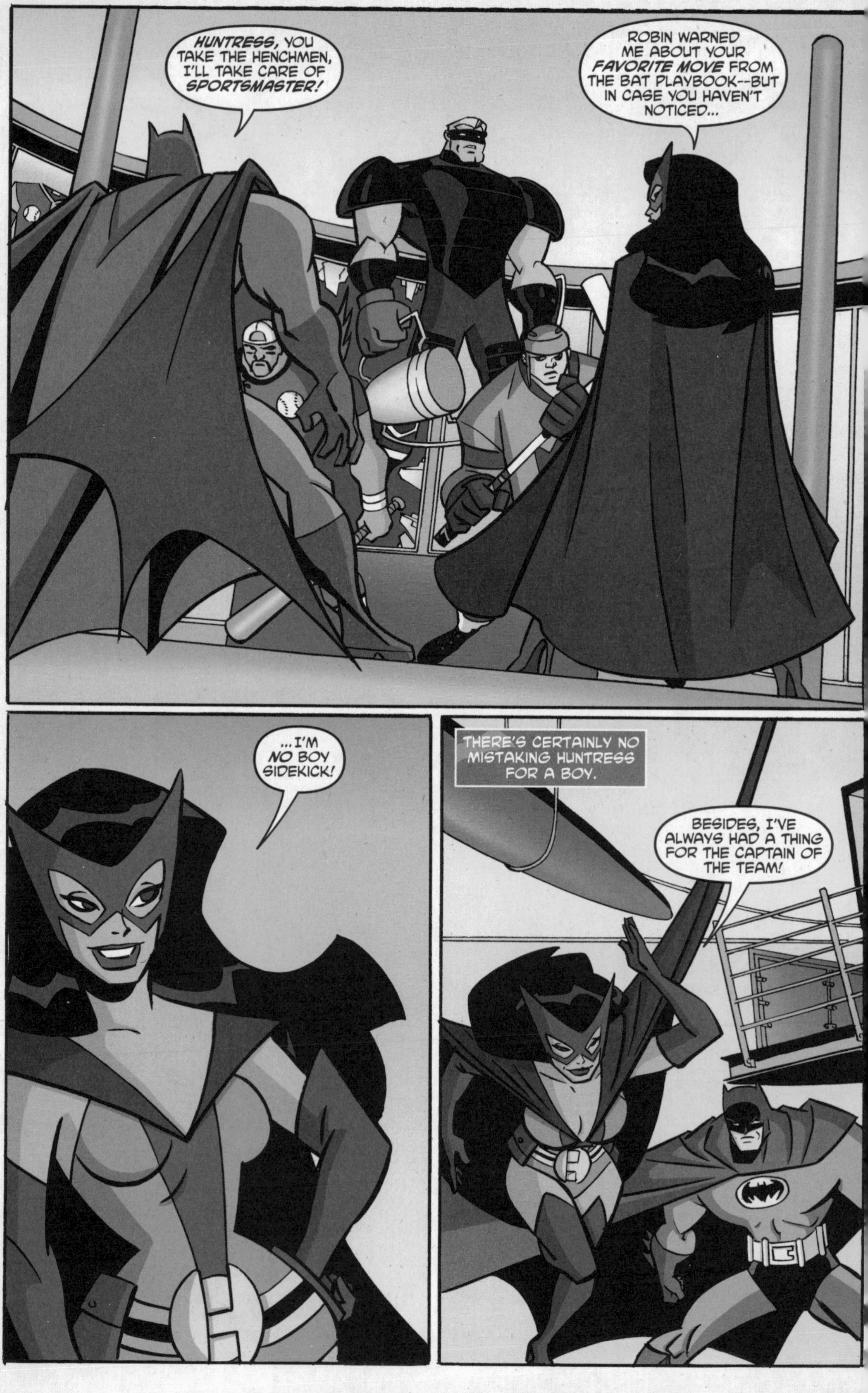
HUNTRESS, YOU TAKE THE HENCHMEN, I'LL TAKE CARE OF SPORTSMASTER!
ROBIN WARNED ME ABOUT YOUR FAVORITE MOVE FROM THE BAT PLAYBOOK--BUT IN CASE YOU HAVEN'T NOTICED...
...I'M NO BOY SIDEKICK!
THERE'S CERTAINLY NO MISTAKING HUNTRESS FOR A BOY.
BESIDES, I'VE ALWAYS HAD A THING FOR THE CAPTAIN OF THE TEAM!

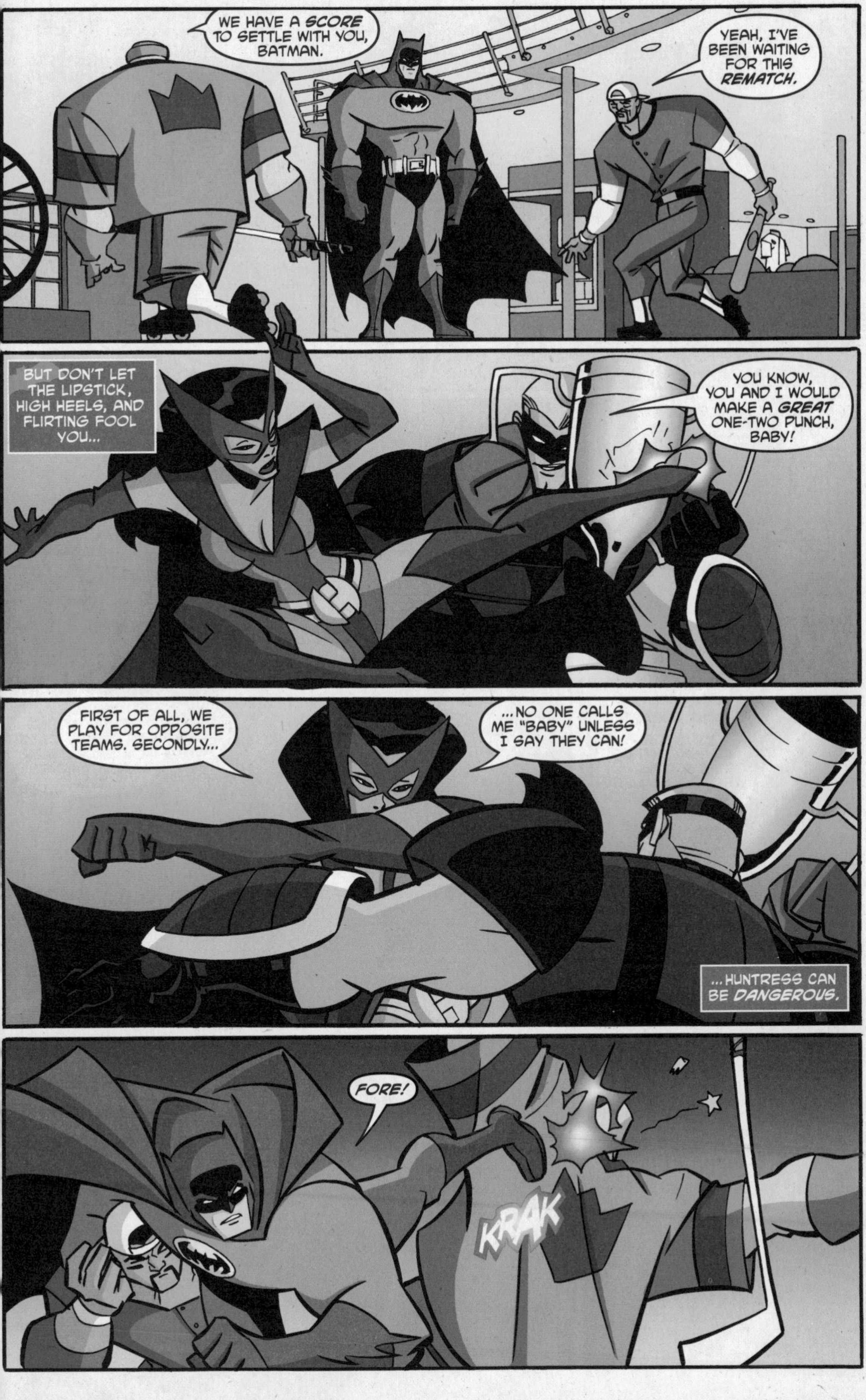
WE HAVE A SCORE TO SETTLE WITH YOU, BATMAN.
YEAH, I'VE BEEN WAITING FOR THIS REMATCH.
BUT DON'T LET THE LIPSTICK, HIGH HEELS, AND FLIRTING FOOL YOU...
YOU KNOW, YOU AND I WOULD MAKE A GREAT ONE-TWO PUNCH, BABY!
FIRST OF ALL, WE PLAY FOR OPPOSITE TEAMS. SECONDLY...
...NO ONE CALLS ME "BABY" UNLESS I SAY THEY CAN!
...HUNTRESS CAN BE DANGEROUS.
FORE!
KRAK

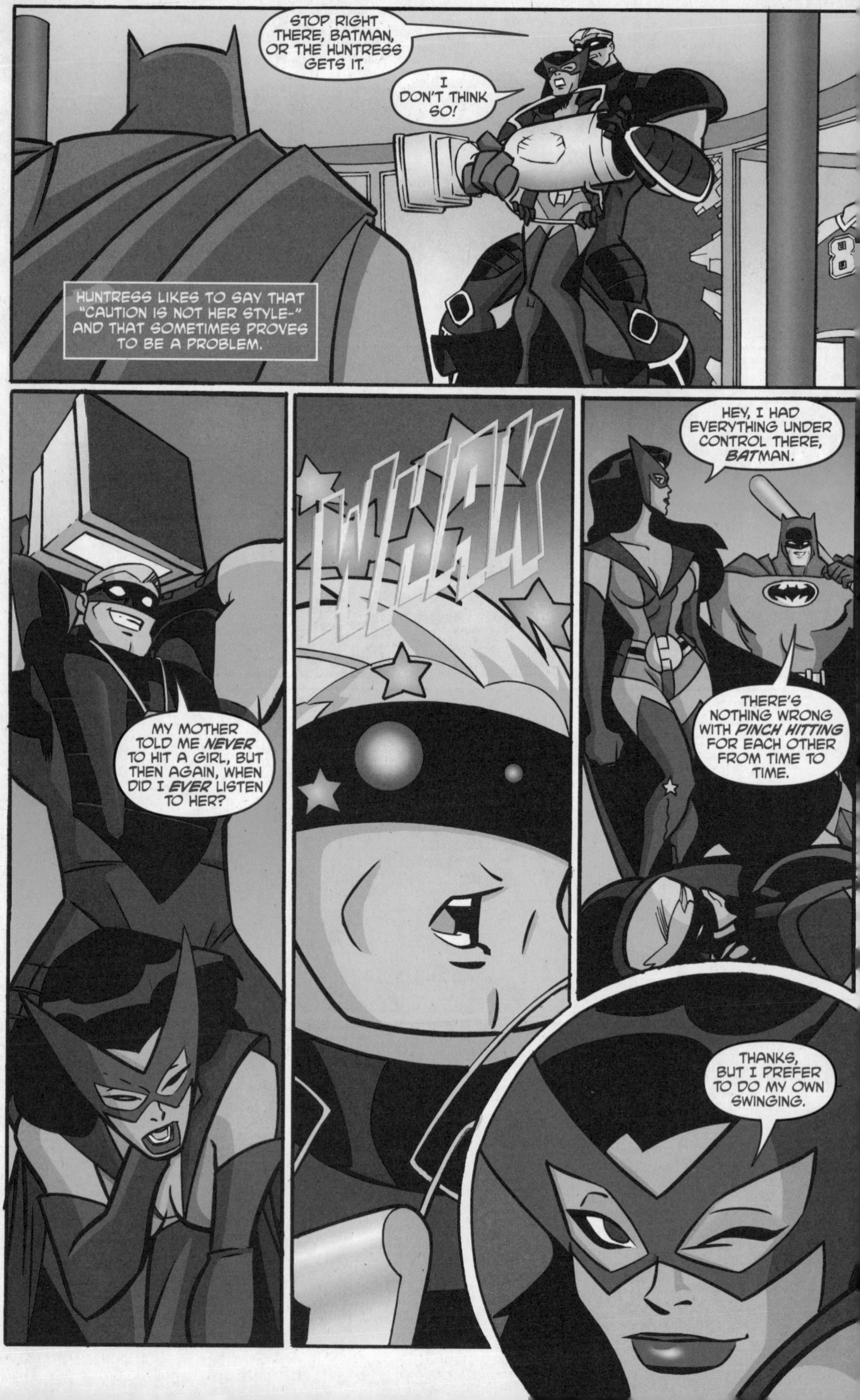
STOP RIGHT THERE, BATMAN, OR THE HUNTRESS GETS IT.
I DON'T THINK SO!
HUNTRESS LIKES TO SAY THAT "CAUTION IS NOT HER STYLE-" AND THAT SOMETIMES PROVES TO BE A PROBLEM.
MY MOTHER TOLD ME *NEVER* TO HIT A GIRL, BUT THEN AGAIN, WHEN DID I *EVER* LISTEN TO HER?
WHACK
HEY, I HAD EVERYTHING UNDER CONTROL THERE, *BAT*MAN.
THERE'S NOTHING WRONG WITH *PINCH HITTING* FOR EACH OTHER FROM TIME TO TIME.
THANKS, BUT I PREFER TO DO MY OWN SWINGING.

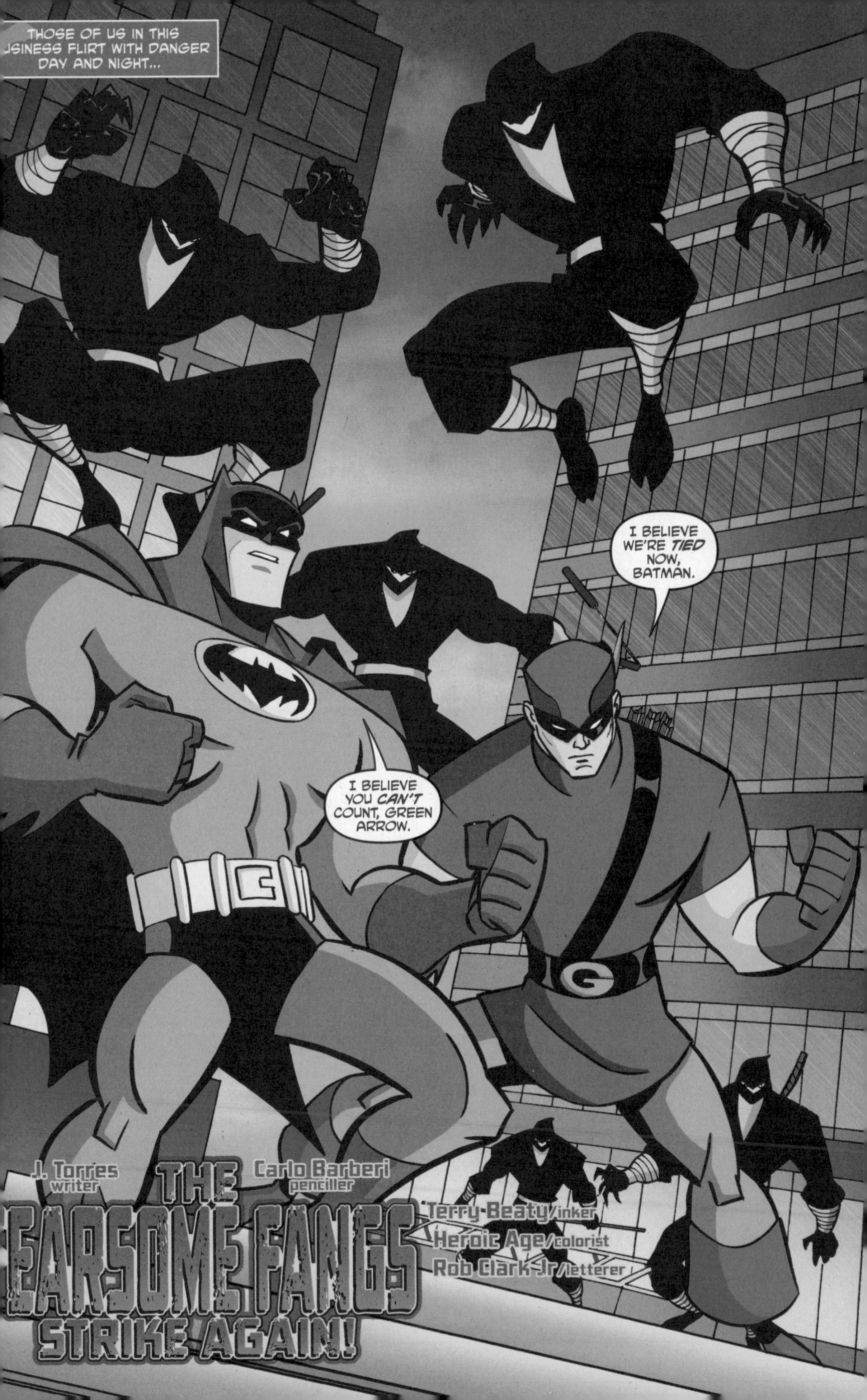
THOSE OF US IN THIS
USINESS FLIRT WITH DANGER
DAY AND NIGHT...
I BELIEVE WE'RE *TIED* NOW, BATMAN.
I BELIEVE YOU *CAN'T* COUNT, GREEN ARROW.
J. Torres writer
Carlo Barberi penciller
THE
EARSOME FANGS
STRIKE AGAIN!
Terry Beaty/inker
Heroic Age/colorist
Rob Clark Jr/letterer

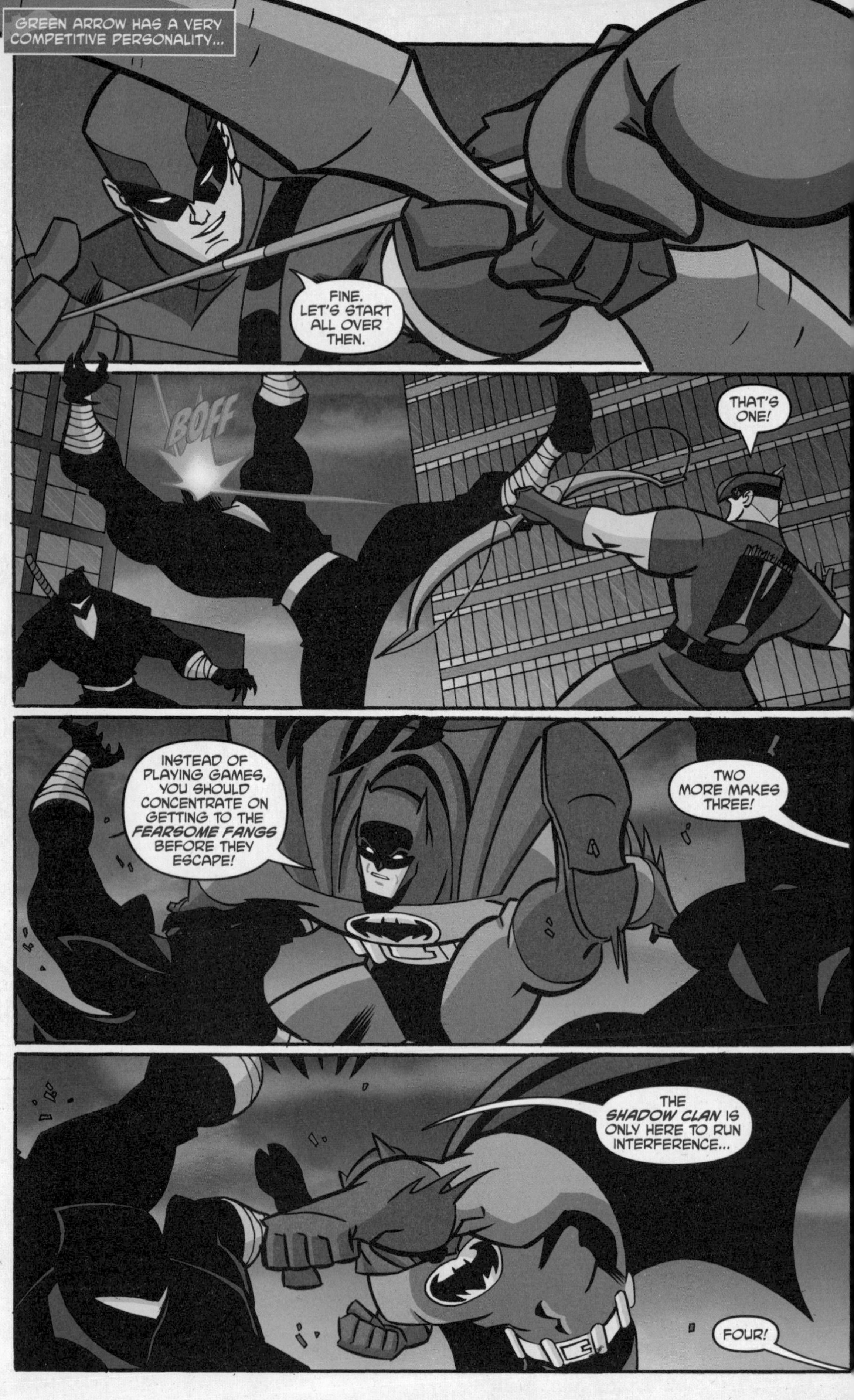
GREEN ARROW HAS A VERY COMPETITIVE PERSONALITY...
FINE. LET'S START ALL OVER THEN.
BOFF
THAT'S ONE!
INSTEAD OF PLAYING GAMES, YOU SHOULD CONCENTRATE ON GETTING TO THE *FEARSOME FANGS* BEFORE THEY ESCAPE!
TWO MORE MAKES THREE!
THE *SHADOW CLAN* IS ONLY HERE TO RUN INTERFERENCE...
FOUR!

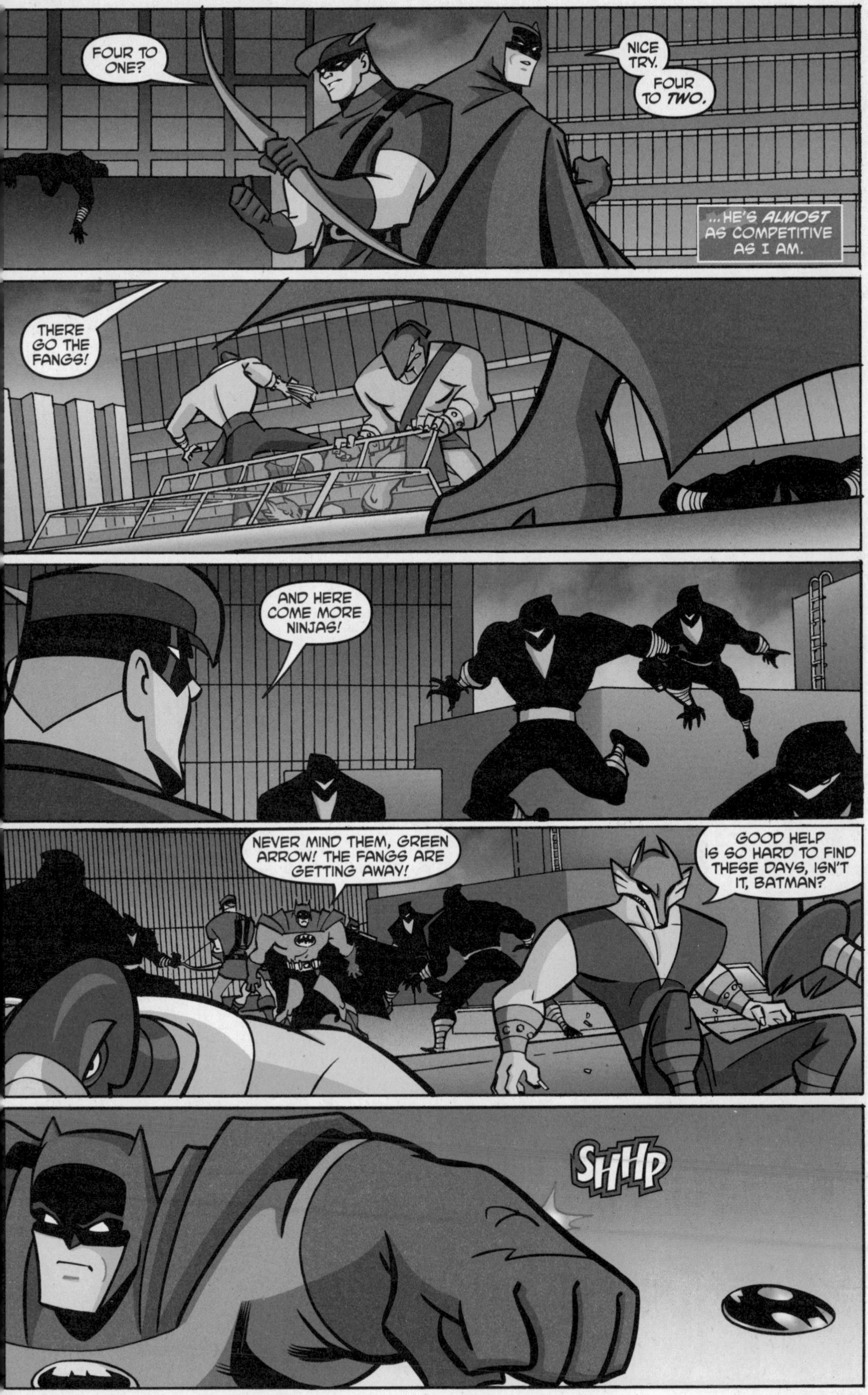

FOUR TO ONE?
NICE TRY.
FOUR TO TWO.
...HE'S ALMOST AS COMPETITIVE AS I AM.
THERE GO THE FANGS!
AND HERE COME MORE NINJAS!
NEVER MIND THEM, GREEN ARROW! THE FANGS ARE GETTING AWAY!
GOOD HELP IS SO HARD TO FIND THESE DAYS, ISN'T IT, BATMAN?
SHHP

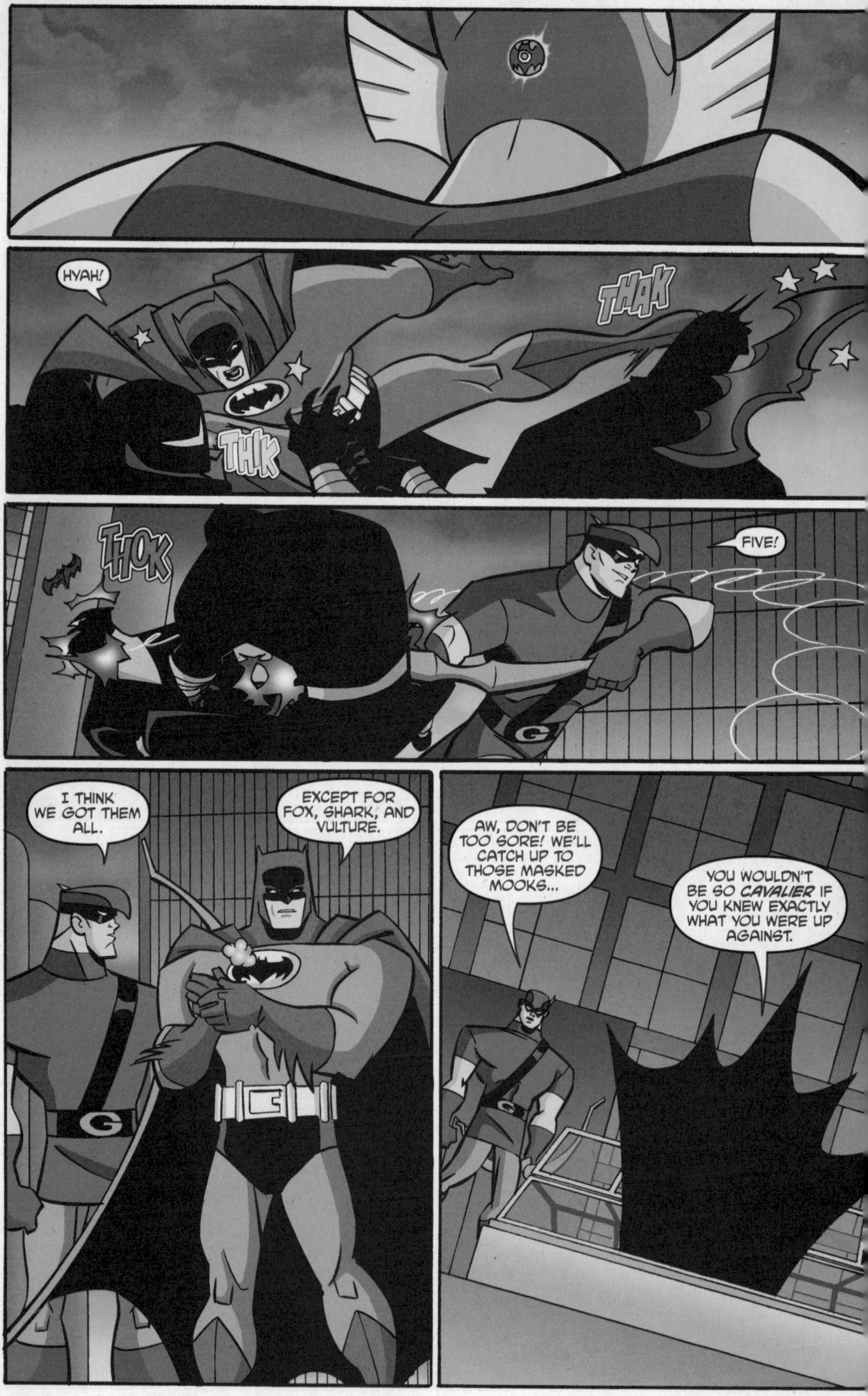
HYAH!
THAK
THIK
THOK
FIVE!
I THINK WE GOT THEM ALL.
EXCEPT FOR FOX, SHARK, AND VULTURE.
AW, DON'T BE TOO SORE! WE'LL CATCH UP TO THOSE MASKED MOOKS...
YOU WOULDN'T BE SO *CAVALIER* IF YOU KNEW EXACTLY WHAT YOU WERE UP AGAINST.

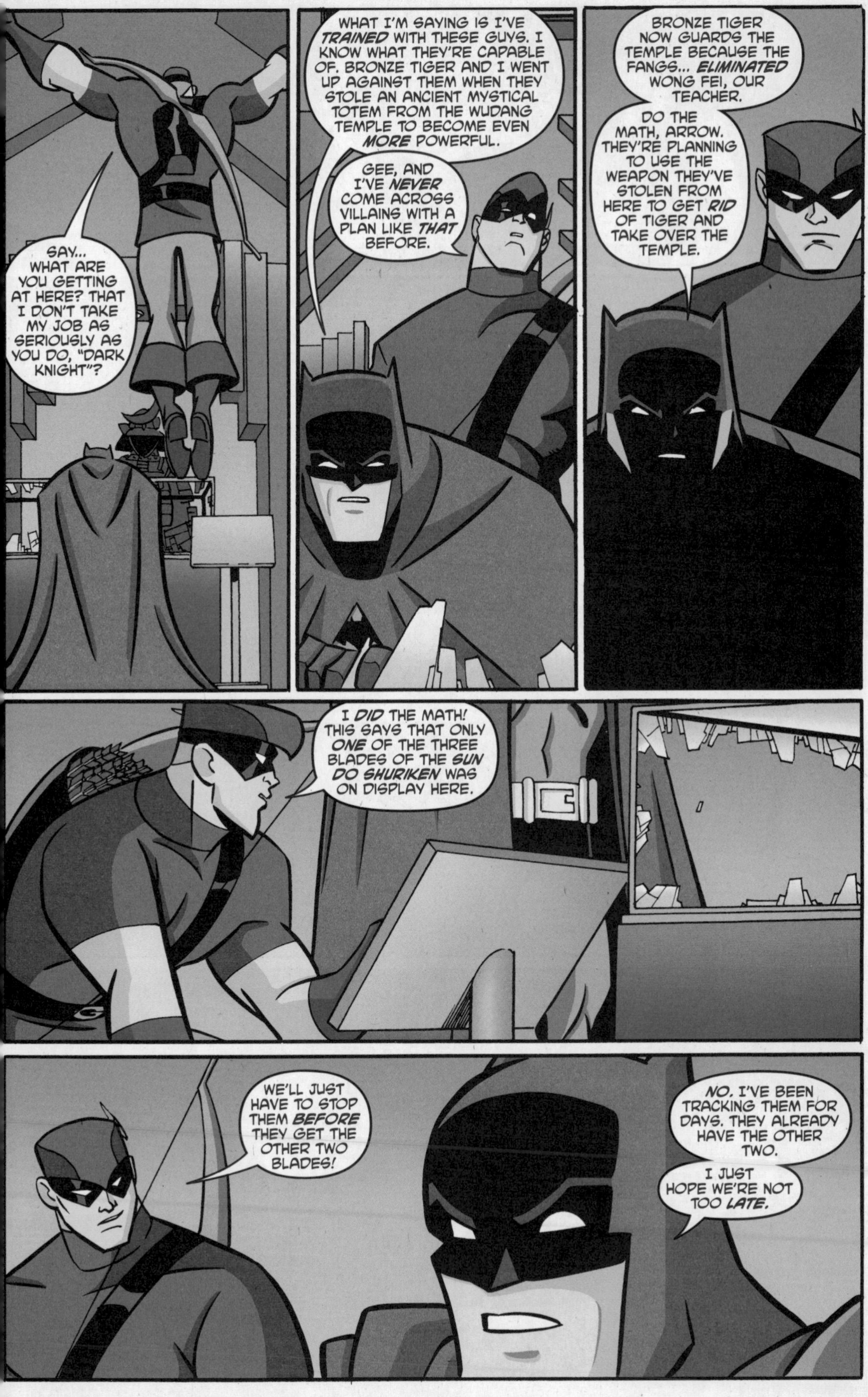
SAY... WHAT ARE YOU GETTING AT HERE? THAT I DON'T TAKE MY JOB AS SERIOUSLY AS YOU DO, "DARK KNIGHT"?
WHAT I'M SAYING IS I'VE TRAINED WITH THESE GUYS. I KNOW WHAT THEY'RE CAPABLE OF. BRONZE TIGER AND I WENT UP AGAINST THEM WHEN THEY STOLE AN ANCIENT MYSTICAL TOTEM FROM THE WUDANG TEMPLE TO BECOME EVEN MORE POWERFUL.
GEE, AND I'VE NEVER COME ACROSS VILLAINS WITH A PLAN LIKE THAT BEFORE.
BRONZE TIGER NOW GUARDS THE TEMPLE BECAUSE THE FANGS... ELIMINATED WONG FEI, OUR TEACHER.
DO THE MATH, ARROW. THEY'RE PLANNING TO USE THE WEAPON THEY'VE STOLEN FROM HERE TO GET RID OF TIGER AND TAKE OVER THE TEMPLE.
I DID THE MATH! THIS SAYS THAT ONLY ONE OF THE THREE BLADES OF THE SUN DO SHURIKEN WAS ON DISPLAY HERE.
WE'LL JUST HAVE TO STOP THEM BEFORE THEY GET THE OTHER TWO BLADES!
NO. I'VE BEEN TRACKING THEM FOR DAYS. THEY ALREADY HAVE THE OTHER TWO.
I JUST HOPE WE'RE NOT TOO LATE.

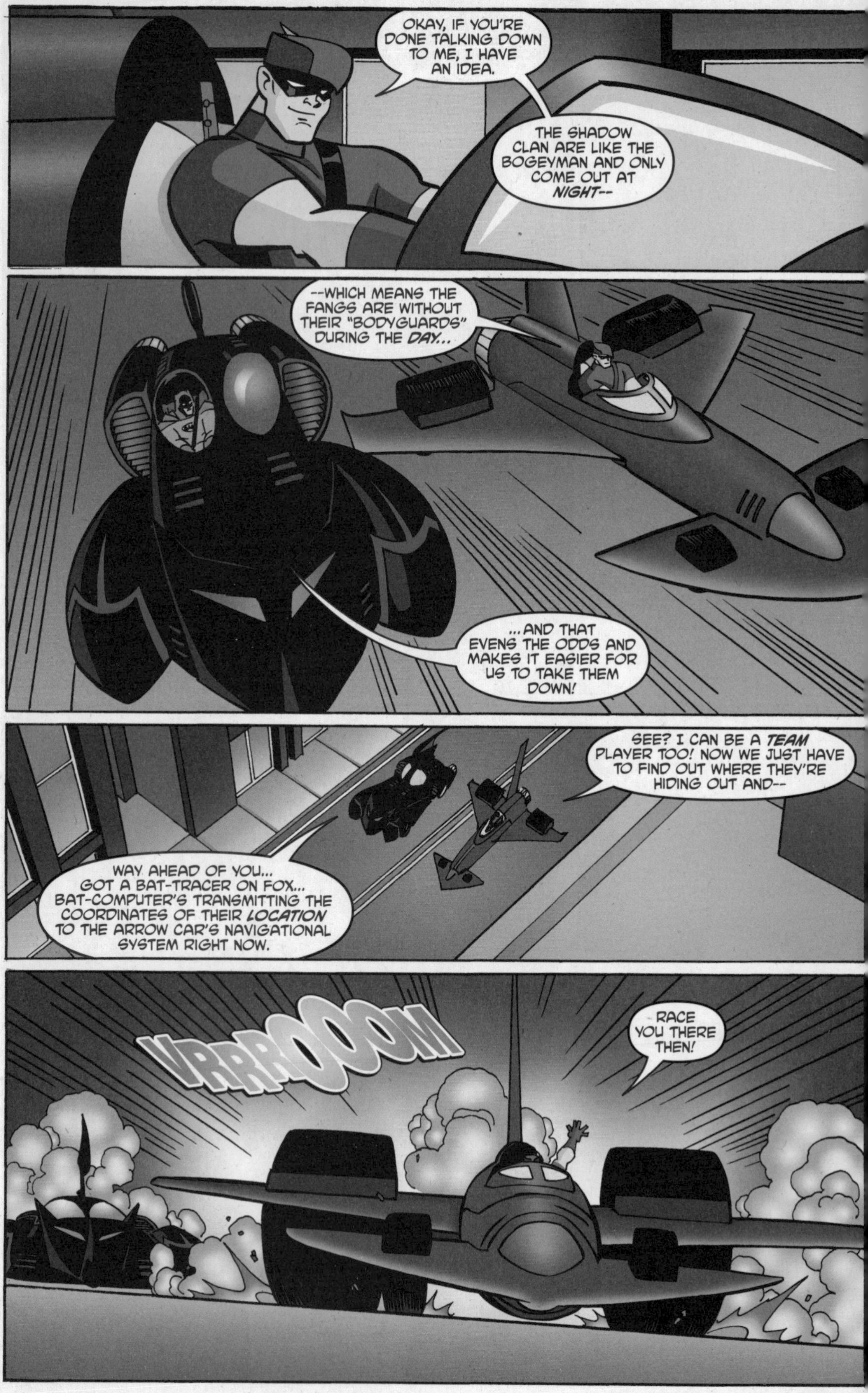
OKAY, IF YOU'RE DONE TALKING DOWN TO ME, I HAVE AN IDEA.
THE SHADOW CLAN ARE LIKE THE BOGEYMAN AND ONLY COME OUT AT NIGHT--
--WHICH MEANS THE FANGS ARE WITHOUT THEIR "BODYGUARDS" DURING THE DAY...
...AND THAT EVENS THE ODDS AND MAKES IT EASIER FOR US TO TAKE THEM DOWN!
SEE? I CAN BE A TEAM PLAYER TOO! NOW WE JUST HAVE TO FIND OUT WHERE THEY'RE HIDING OUT AND--
WAY AHEAD OF YOU... GOT A BAT-TRACER ON FOX... BAT-COMPUTER'S TRANSMITTING THE COORDINATES OF THEIR LOCATION TO THE ARROW CAR'S NAVIGATIONAL SYSTEM RIGHT NOW.
VRRROOOOM
RACE YOU THERE THEN!

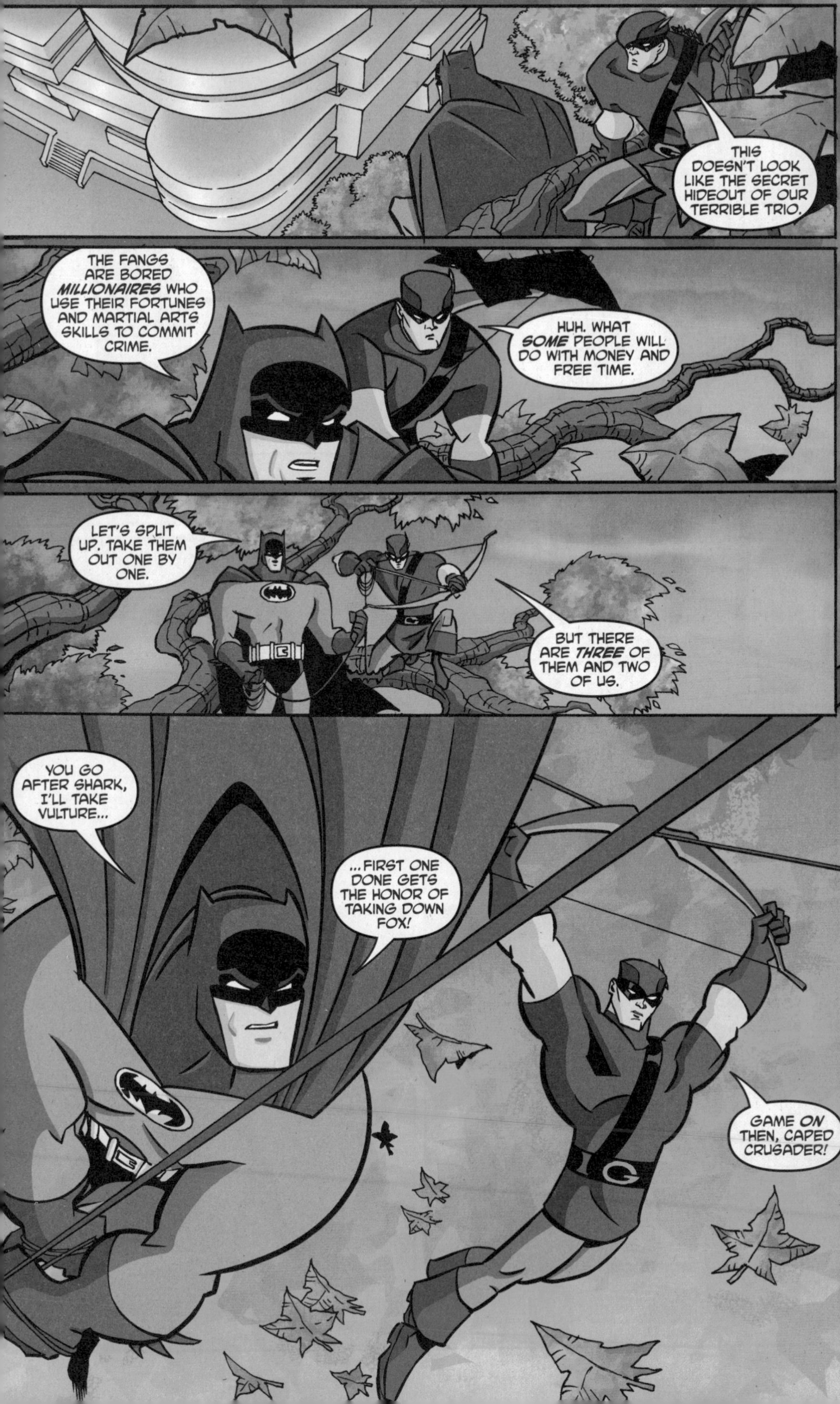
THIS DOESN'T LOOK LIKE THE SECRET HIDEOUT OF OUR TERRIBLE TRIO.
THE FANGS ARE BORED MILLIONAIRES WHO USE THEIR FORTUNES AND MARTIAL ARTS SKILLS TO COMMIT CRIME.
HUH. WHAT SOME PEOPLE WILL DO WITH MONEY AND FREE TIME.
LET'S SPLIT UP. TAKE THEM OUT ONE BY ONE.
BUT THERE ARE THREE OF THEM AND TWO OF US.
YOU GO AFTER SHARK, I'LL TAKE VULTURE...
...FIRST ONE DONE GETS THE HONOR OF TAKING DOWN FOX!
GAME ON THEN, CAPED CRUSADER!

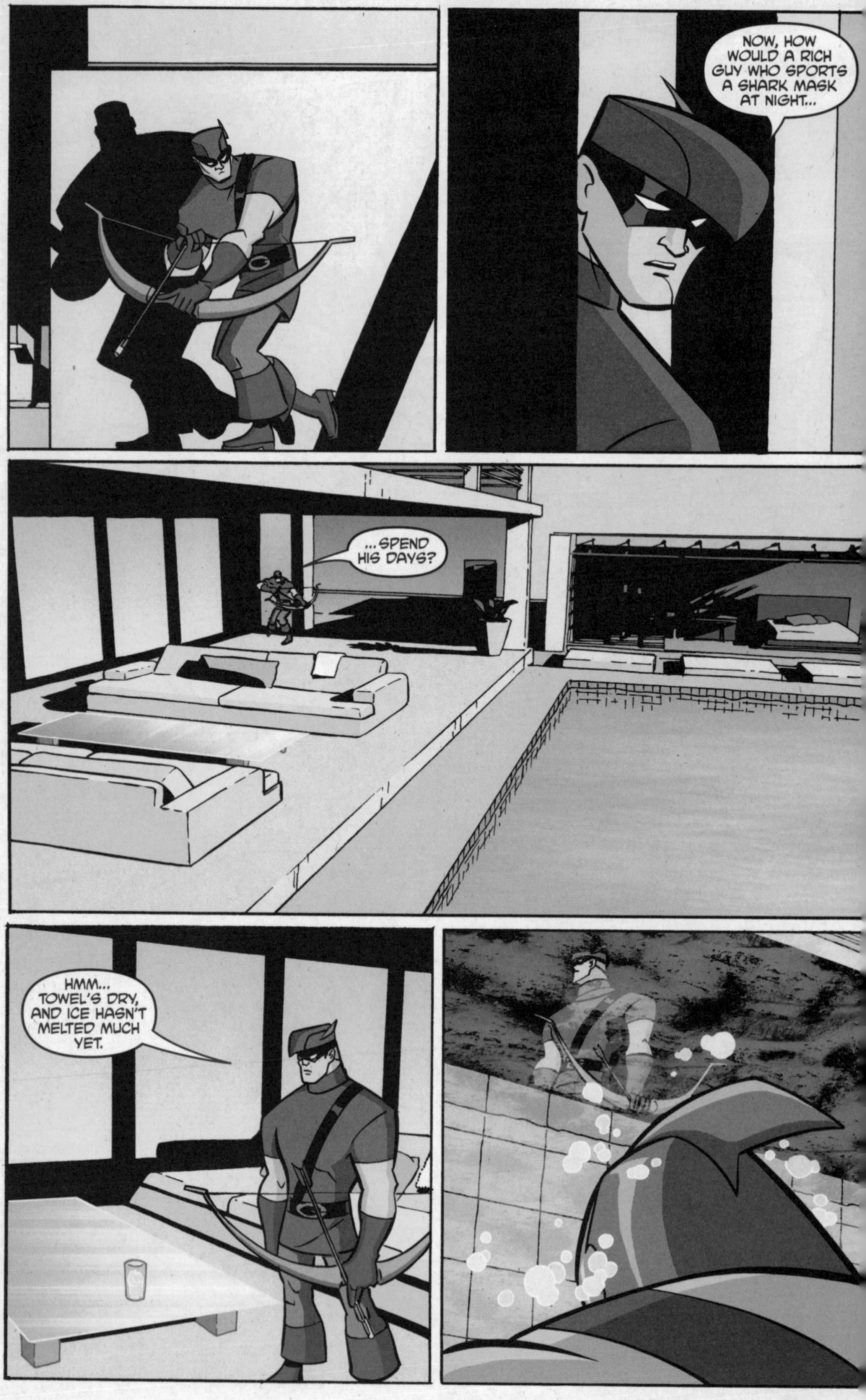
NOW, HOW WOULD A RICH GUY WHO SPORTS A SHARK MASK AT NIGHT...
...SPEND HIS DAYS?
HMM... TOWEL'S DRY, AND ICE HASN'T MELTED MUCH YET.

MASTER WONG FEI USED TO SAY...

"WHEN LOOKING FOR A BIRD...

"...SEARCH THE TREES..."

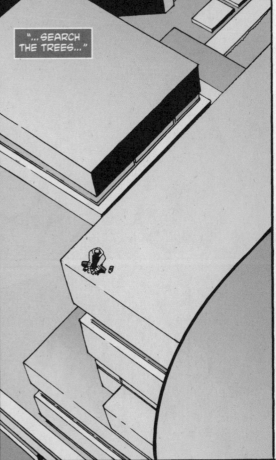

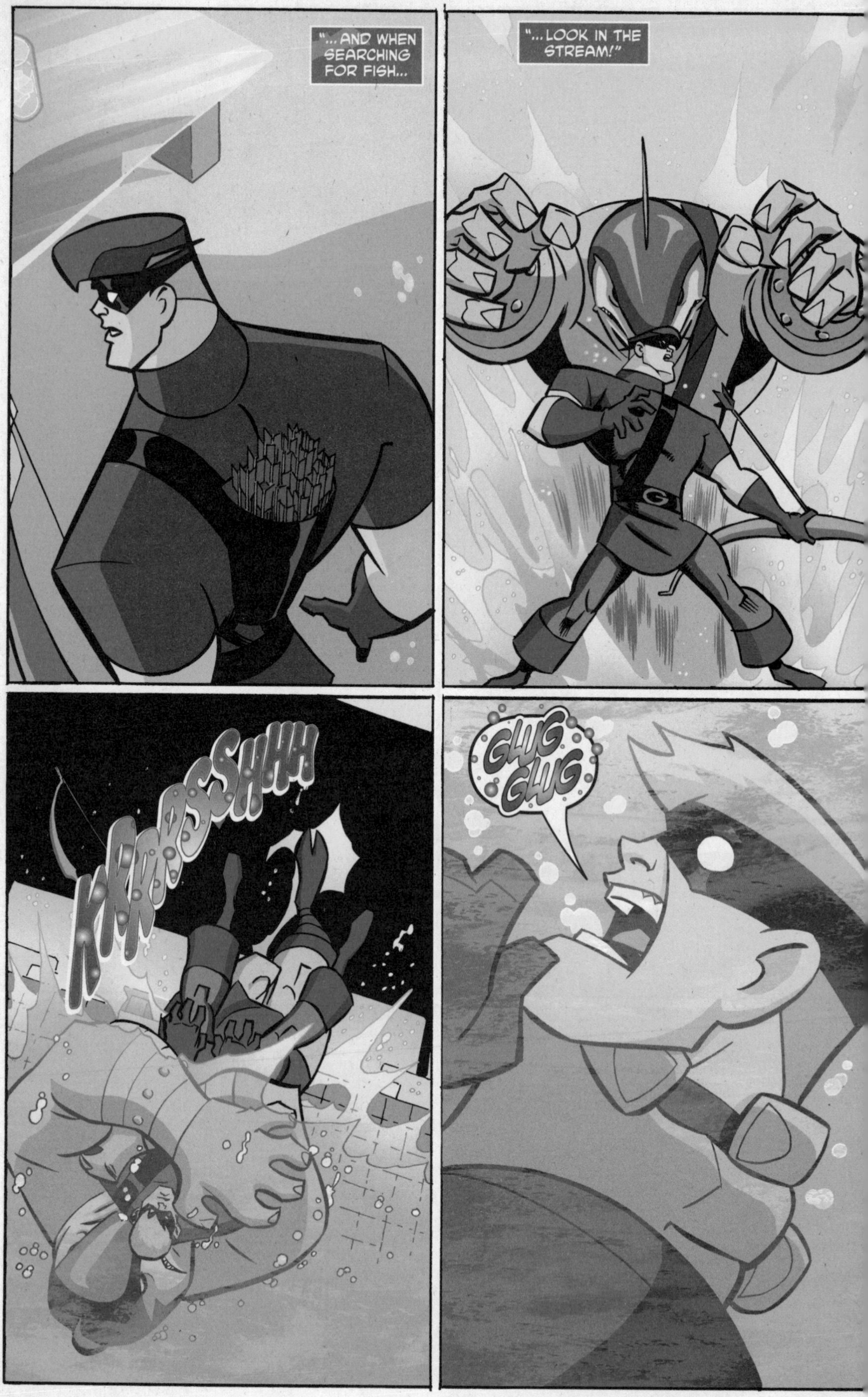
"...AND WHEN SEARCHING FOR FISH...
"...LOOK IN THE STREAM!"
KRRRSSHHH
GLUG GLUG

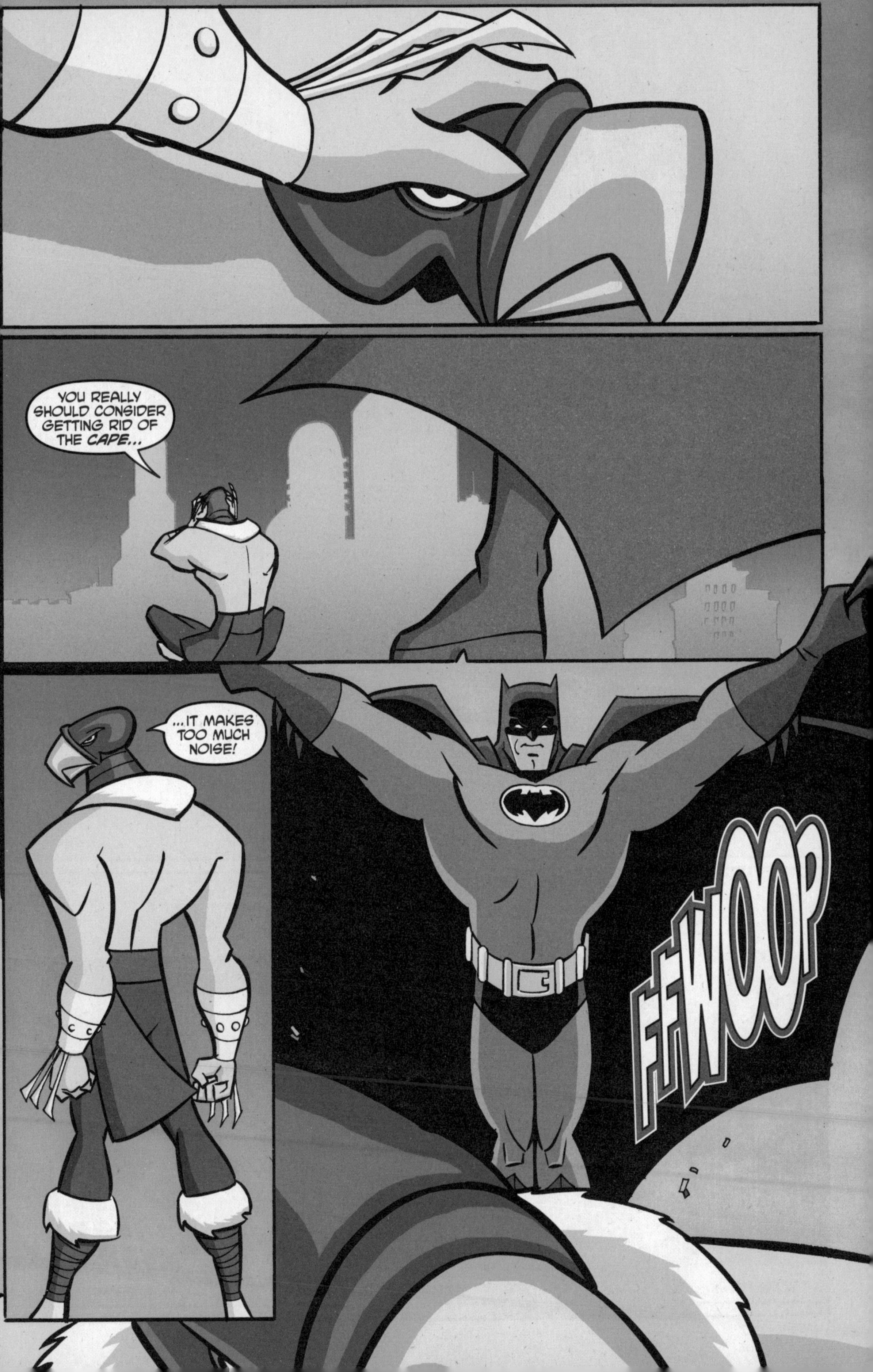
YOU REALLY SHOULD CONSIDER GETTING RID OF THE *CAPE*...
...IT MAKES TOO MUCH NOISE!
FFWOOP

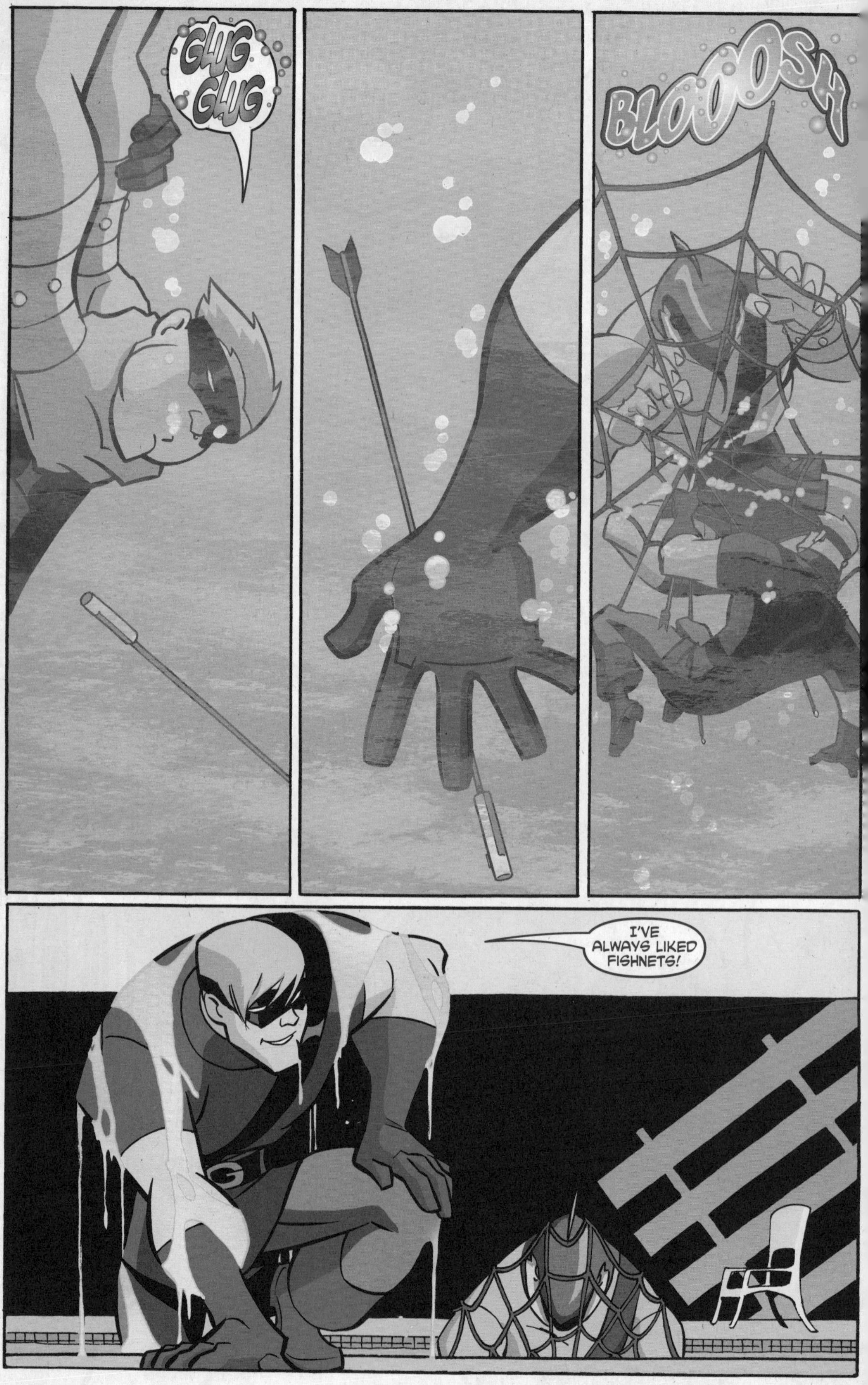
GLUG GLUG
BLOOOOSH
I'VE ALWAYS LIKED FISHNETS!

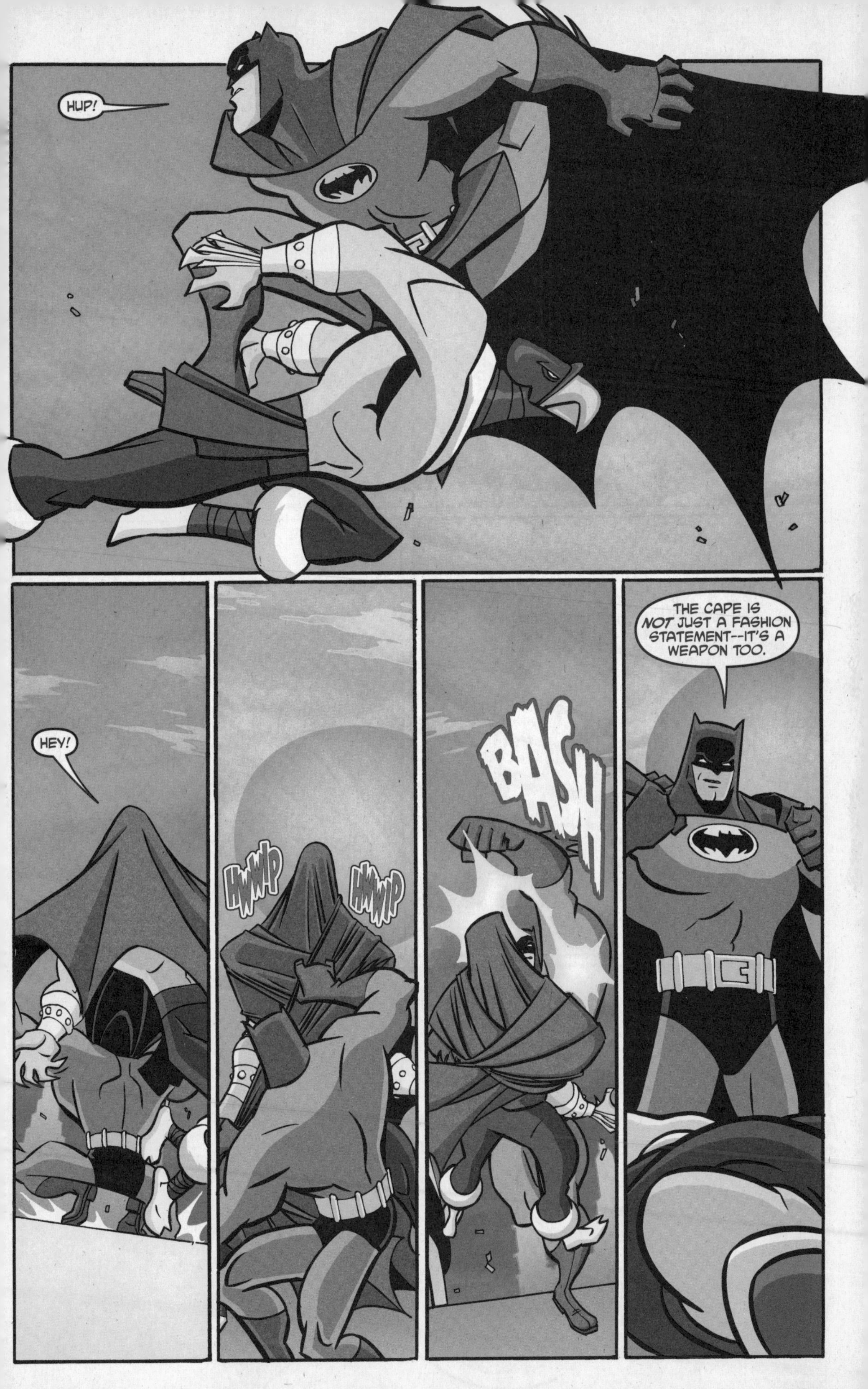
HUP!
HEY!
HWWIP
HWWIP
BASH
THE CAPE IS NOT JUST A FASHION STATEMENT--IT'S A WEAPON TOO.

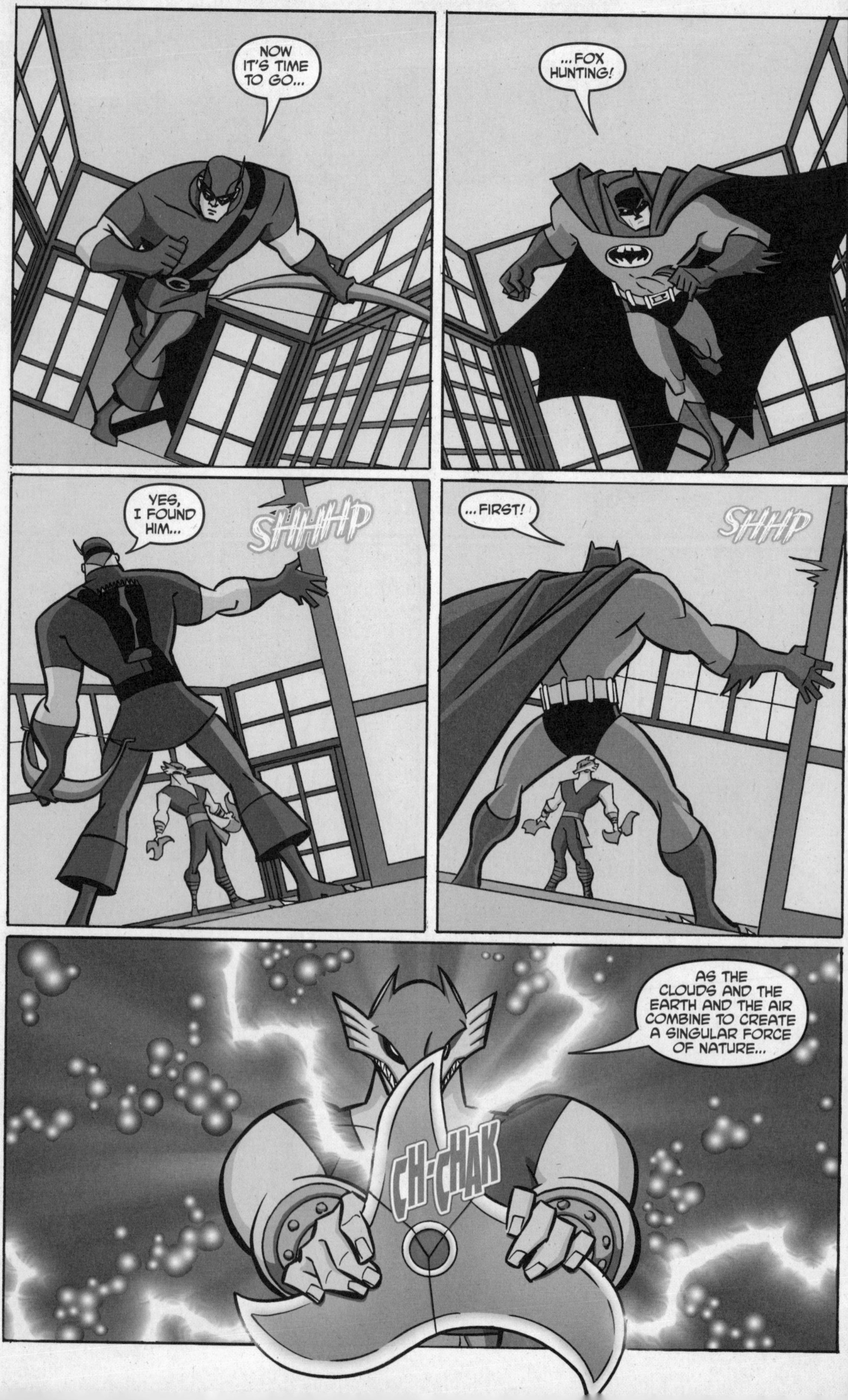
NOW IT'S TIME TO GO...
...FOX HUNTING!
YES, I FOUND HIM...
SHHHP
...FIRST!
SHHP
AS THE CLOUDS AND THE EARTH AND THE AIR COMBINE TO CREATE A SINGULAR FORCE OF NATURE...
CH-CHAK

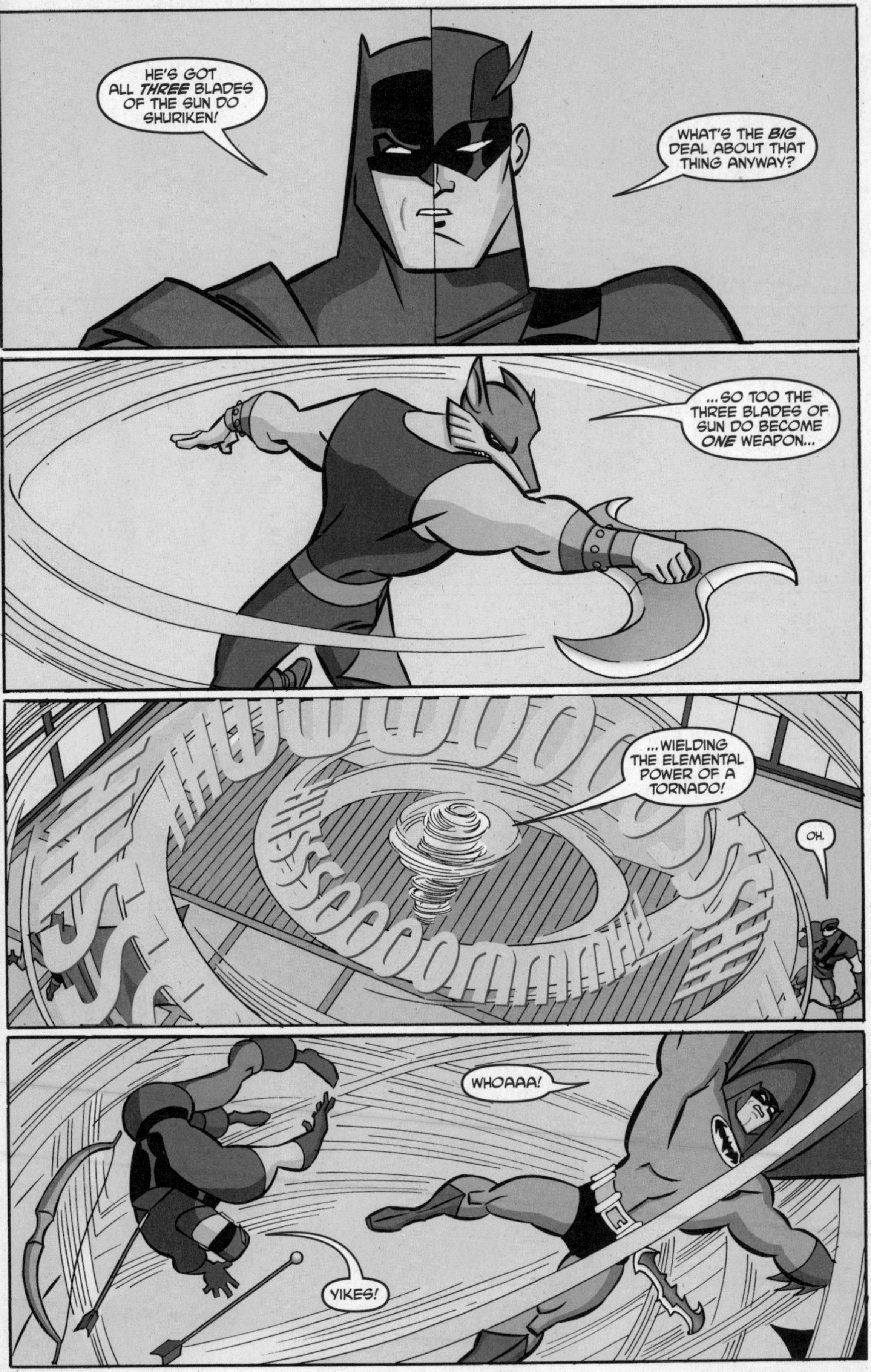
HE'S GOT ALL *THREE* BLADES OF THE SUN DO SHURIKEN!
WHAT'S THE *BIG* DEAL ABOUT THAT THING ANYWAY?
...SO TOO THE THREE BLADES OF SUN DO BECOME *ONE* WEAPON...
...WIELDING THE ELEMENTAL POWER OF A TORNADO!
OH.
WHOAAA!
YIKES!

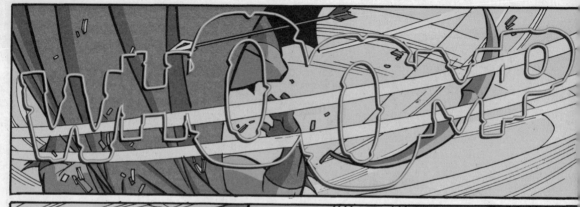

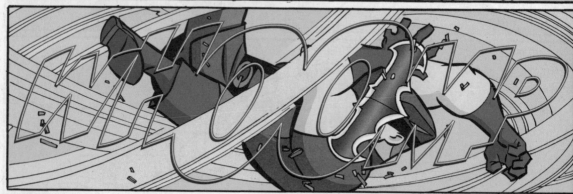

NOW DO YOU *SEE* THE BIG DEAL ABOUT THE SUN DO SHURIKEN?

WITH THIS KIND OF *POWER*, THE WUDANG TEMPLE IS MINE FOR THE TAKING!

BUT YOU FORGET WHAT WONG FEI TAUGHT US: WEAPONS ARE ONLY TOOLS...

...AND YOU SHOULDN'T ALLOW YOURSELF TO BECOME DEPENDENT OR *DISTRACTED* BY THEM!

HEY, FOXY! OVER HERE!

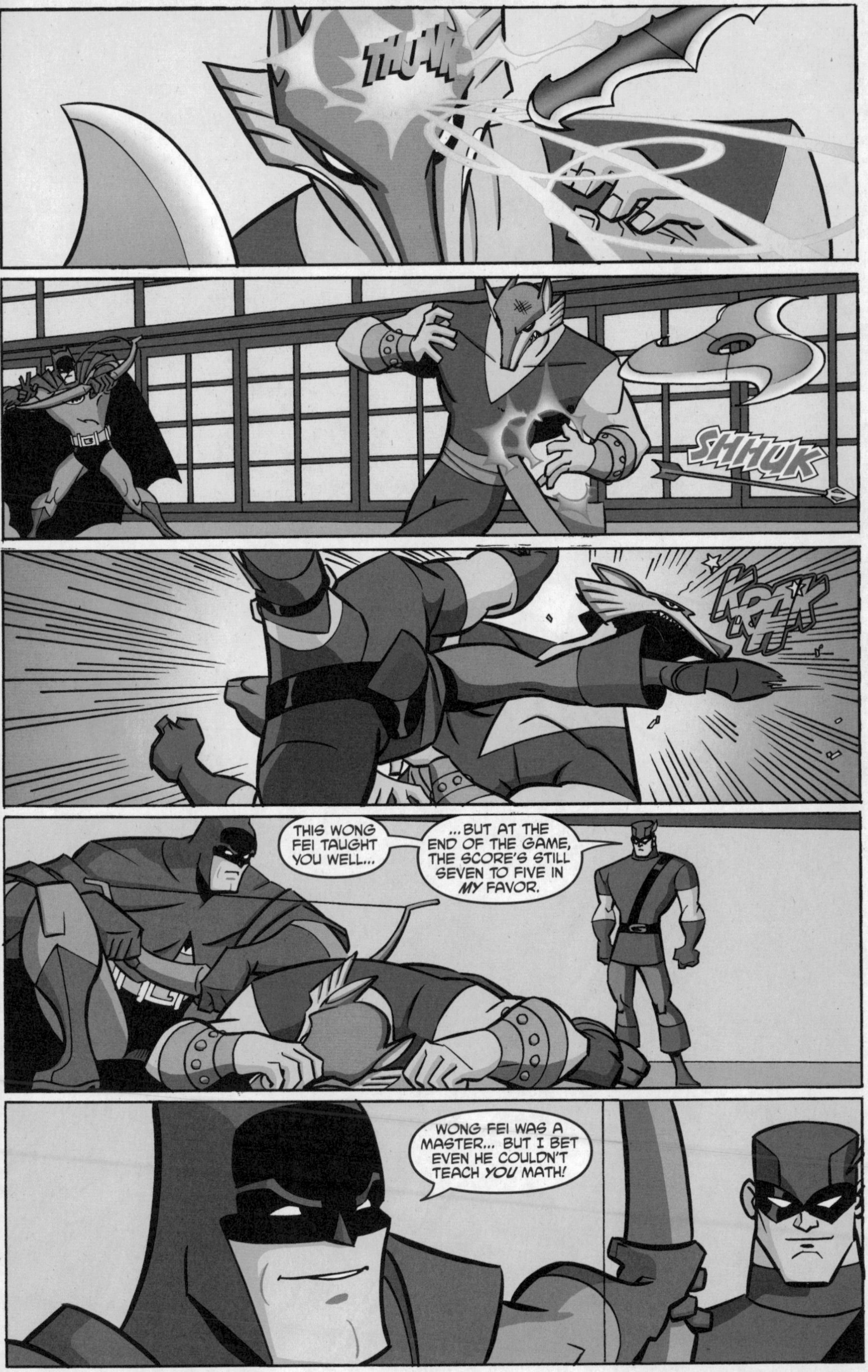
THUNK
SHHUK
KRAK
THIS WONG FEI TAUGHT YOU WELL...
...BUT AT THE END OF THE GAME, THE SCORE'S STILL SEVEN TO FIVE IN MY FAVOR.
WONG FEI WAS A MASTER... BUT I BET EVEN HE COULDN'T TEACH YOU MATH!

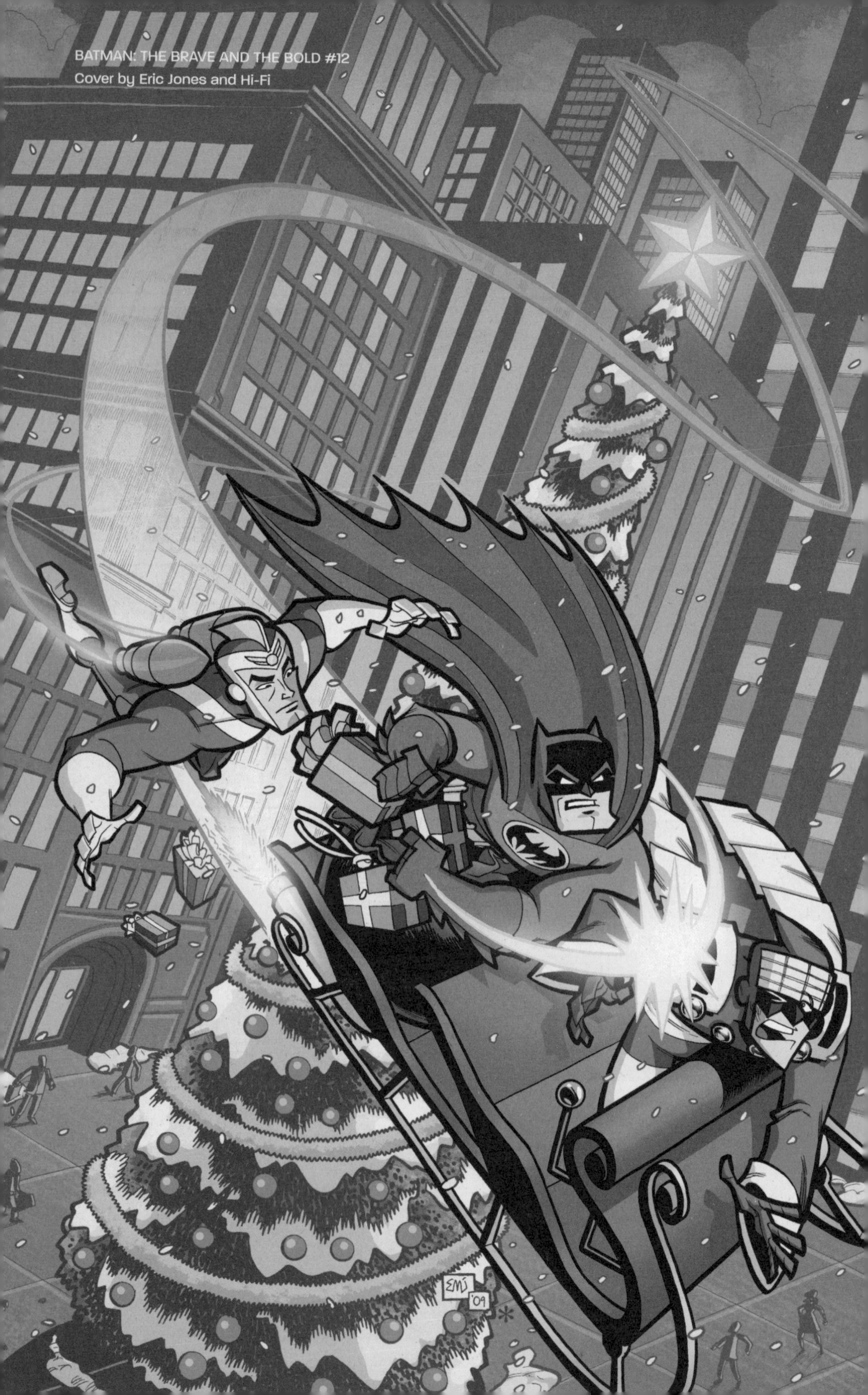

BATMAN: THE BRAVE AND THE BOLD #12
Cover by Eric Jones and Hi-Fi

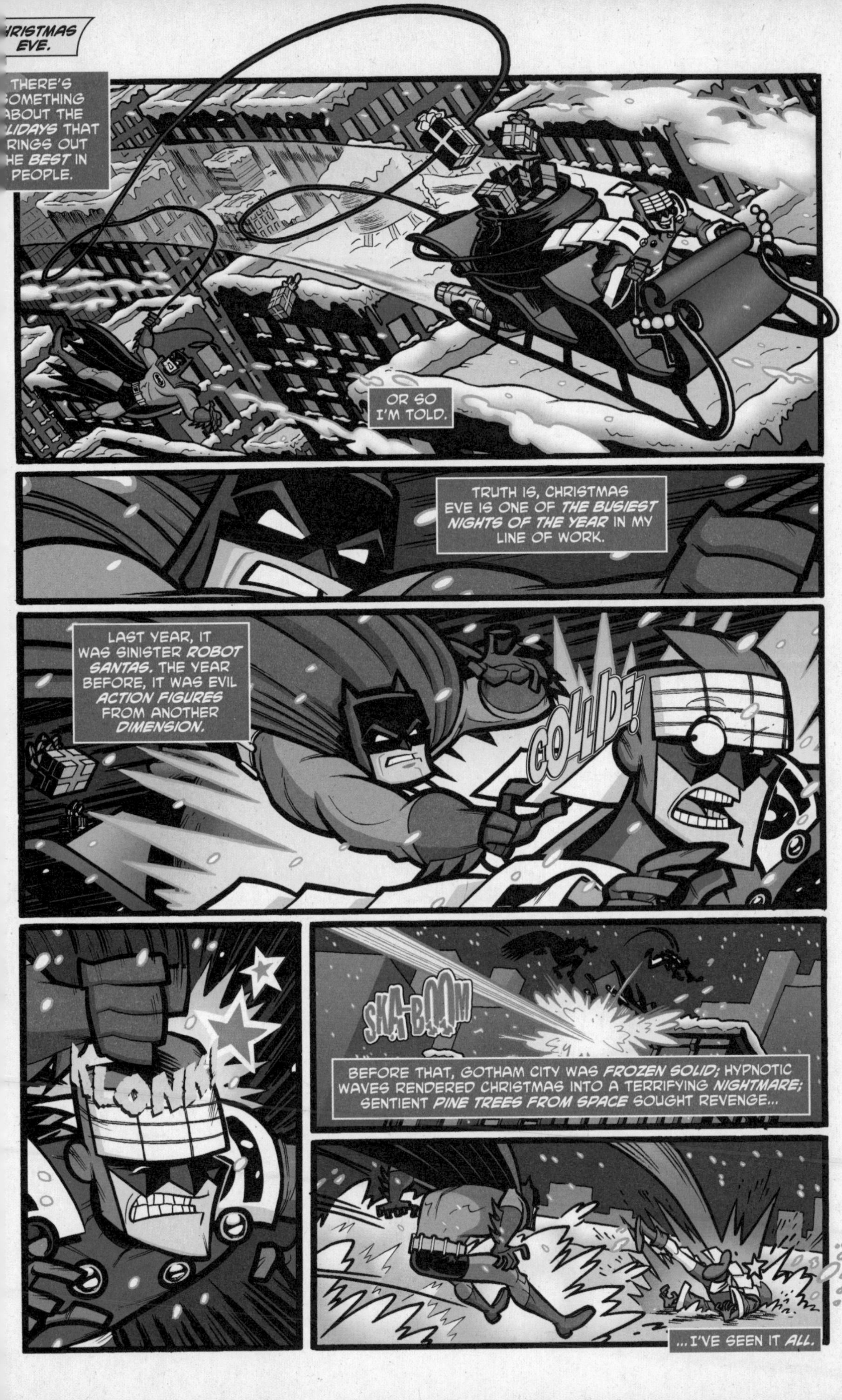

CHRISTMAS EVE.
THERE'S SOMETHING ABOUT THE HOLIDAYS THAT BRINGS OUT THE BEST IN PEOPLE.
OR SO I'M TOLD.
TRUTH IS, CHRISTMAS EVE IS ONE OF THE BUSIEST NIGHTS OF THE YEAR IN MY LINE OF WORK.
LAST YEAR, IT WAS SINISTER ROBOT SANTAS. THE YEAR BEFORE, IT WAS EVIL ACTION FIGURES FROM ANOTHER DIMENSION.
COLLIDE!
KLONK!
SKA-BOOM
BEFORE THAT, GOTHAM CITY WAS FROZEN SOLID; HYPNOTIC WAVES RENDERED CHRISTMAS INTO A TERRIFYING NIGHTMARE; SENTIENT PINE TREES FROM SPACE SOUGHT REVENGE...
...I'VE SEEN IT ALL.

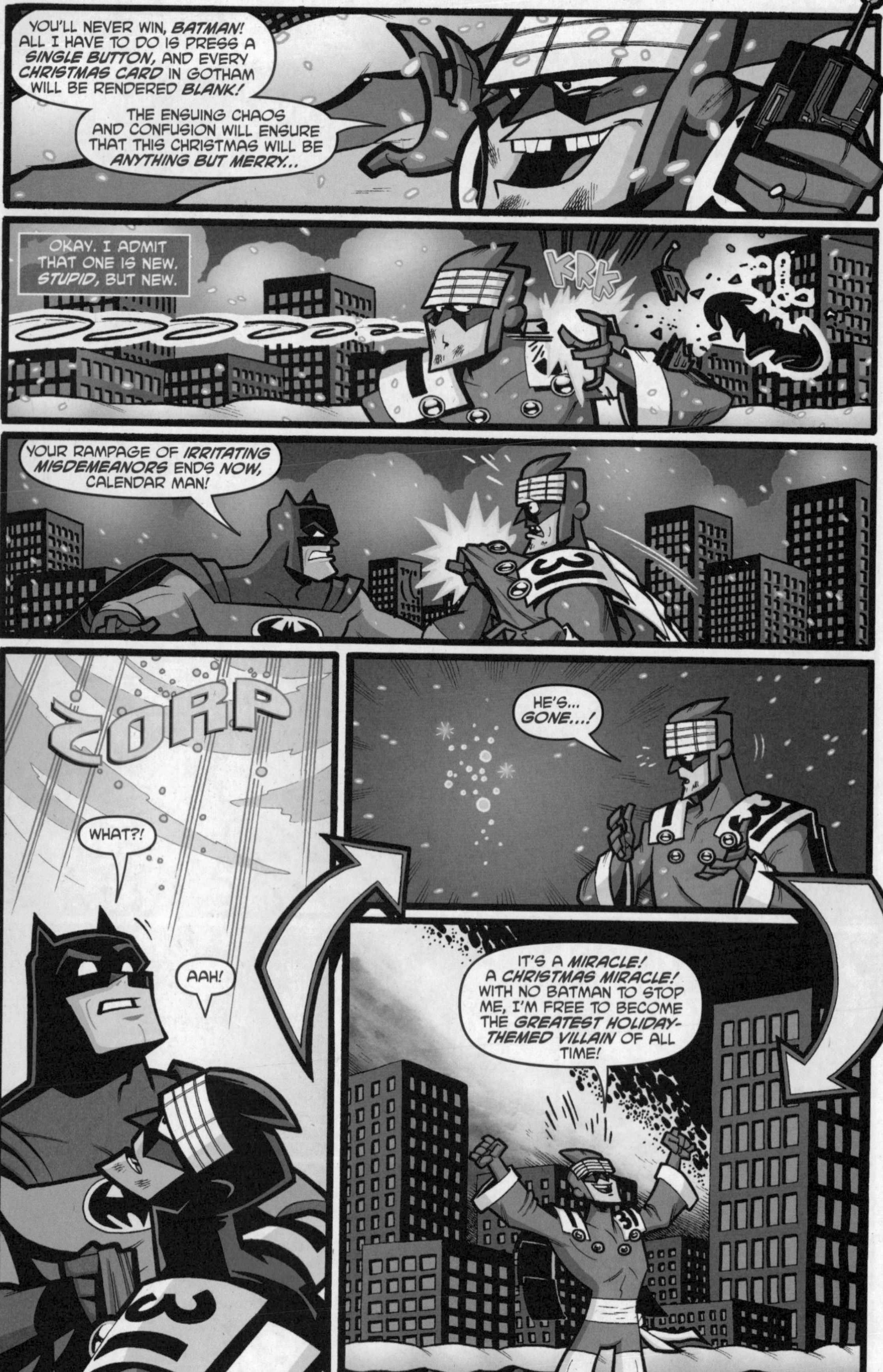
YOU'LL NEVER WIN, BATMAN! ALL I HAVE TO DO IS PRESS A SINGLE BUTTON, AND EVERY CHRISTMAS CARD IN GOTHAM WILL BE RENDERED BLANK!
THE ENSUING CHAOS AND CONFUSION WILL ENSURE THAT THIS CHRISTMAS WILL BE ANYTHING BUT MERRY...
OKAY. I ADMIT THAT ONE IS NEW. STUPID, BUT NEW.
KRK
YOUR RAMPAGE OF IRRITATING MISDEMEANORS ENDS NOW, CALENDAR MAN!
ZORP
WHAT?!
AAH!
HE'S... GONE...!
IT'S A MIRACLE! A CHRISTMAS MIRACLE! WITH NO BATMAN TO STOP ME, I'M FREE TO BECOME THE GREATEST HOLIDAY-THEMED VILLAIN OF ALL TIME!

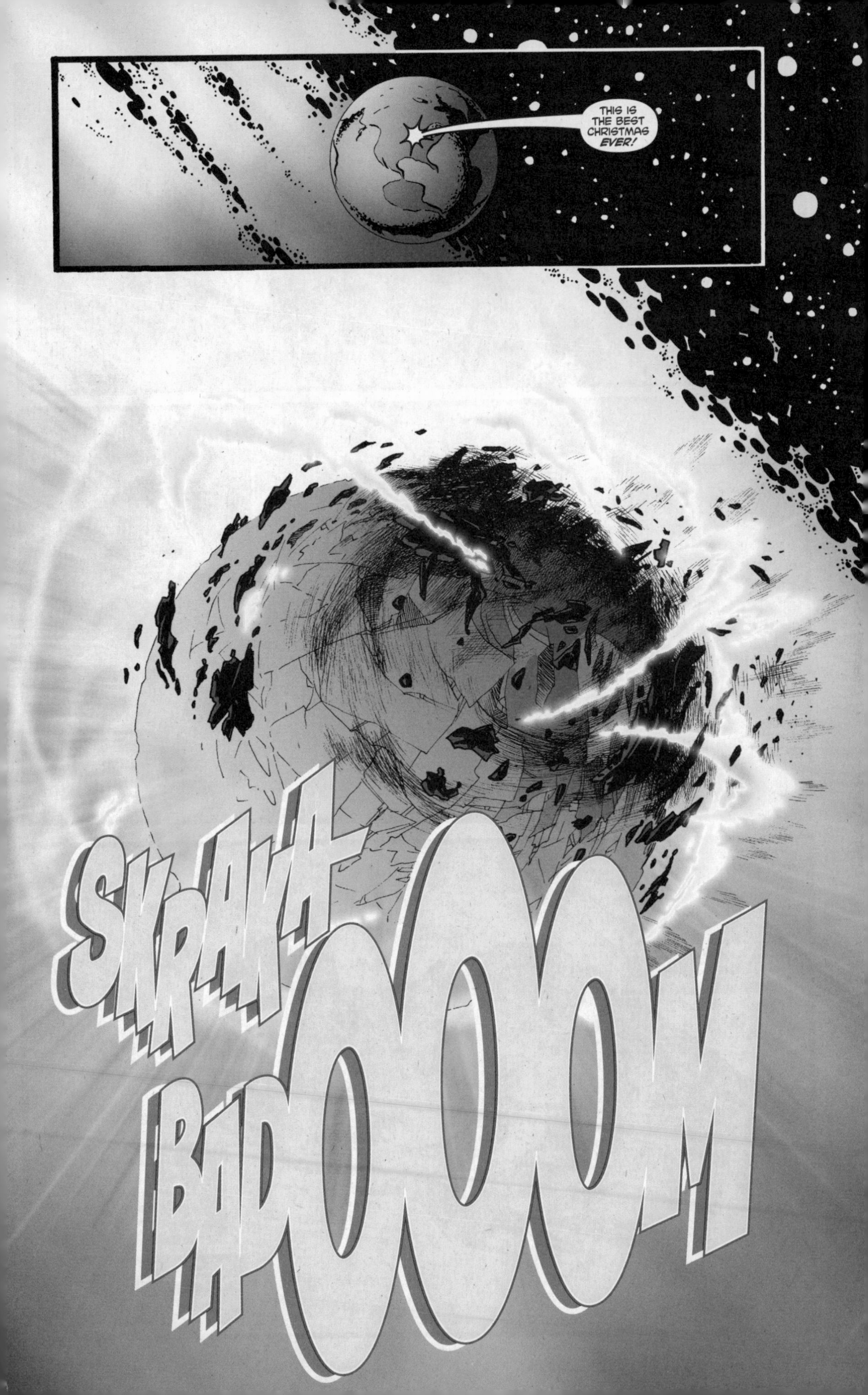
THIS IS THE BEST CHRISTMAS *EVER!*
SKRAKA-BADOOOOM

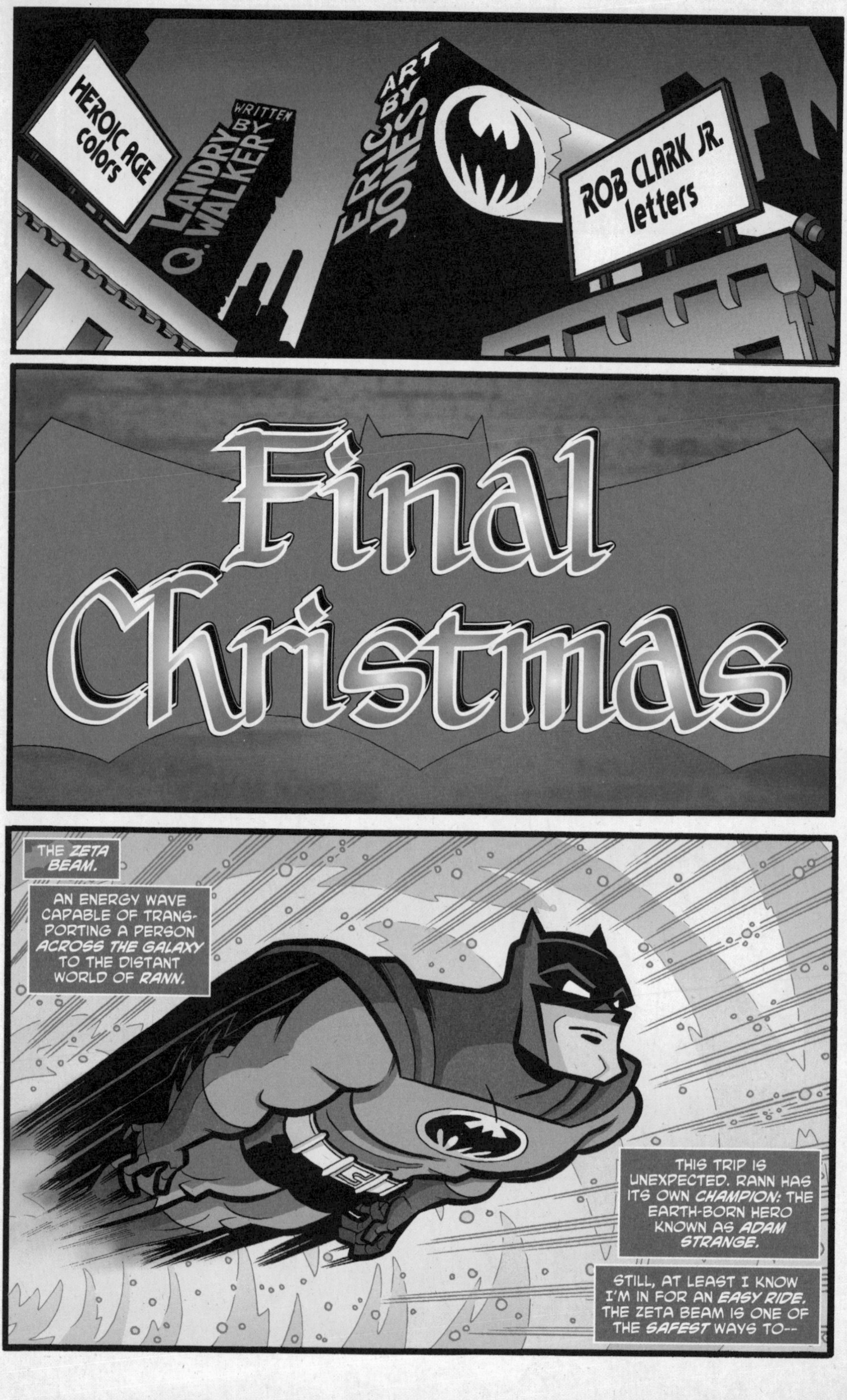
HEROIC AGE colors
WRITTEN BY LANDRY Q. WALKER
ART BY ERIC JONES
ROB CLARK JR. letters
Final Christmas
THE ZETA BEAM.
AN ENERGY WAVE CAPABLE OF TRANSPORTING A PERSON ACROSS THE GALAXY TO THE DISTANT WORLD OF RANN.
THIS TRIP IS UNEXPECTED. RANN HAS ITS OWN CHAMPION: THE EARTH-BORN HERO KNOWN AS ADAM STRANGE.
STILL, AT LEAST I KNOW I'M IN FOR AN EASY RIDE. THE ZETA BEAM IS ONE OF THE SAFEST WAYS TO--

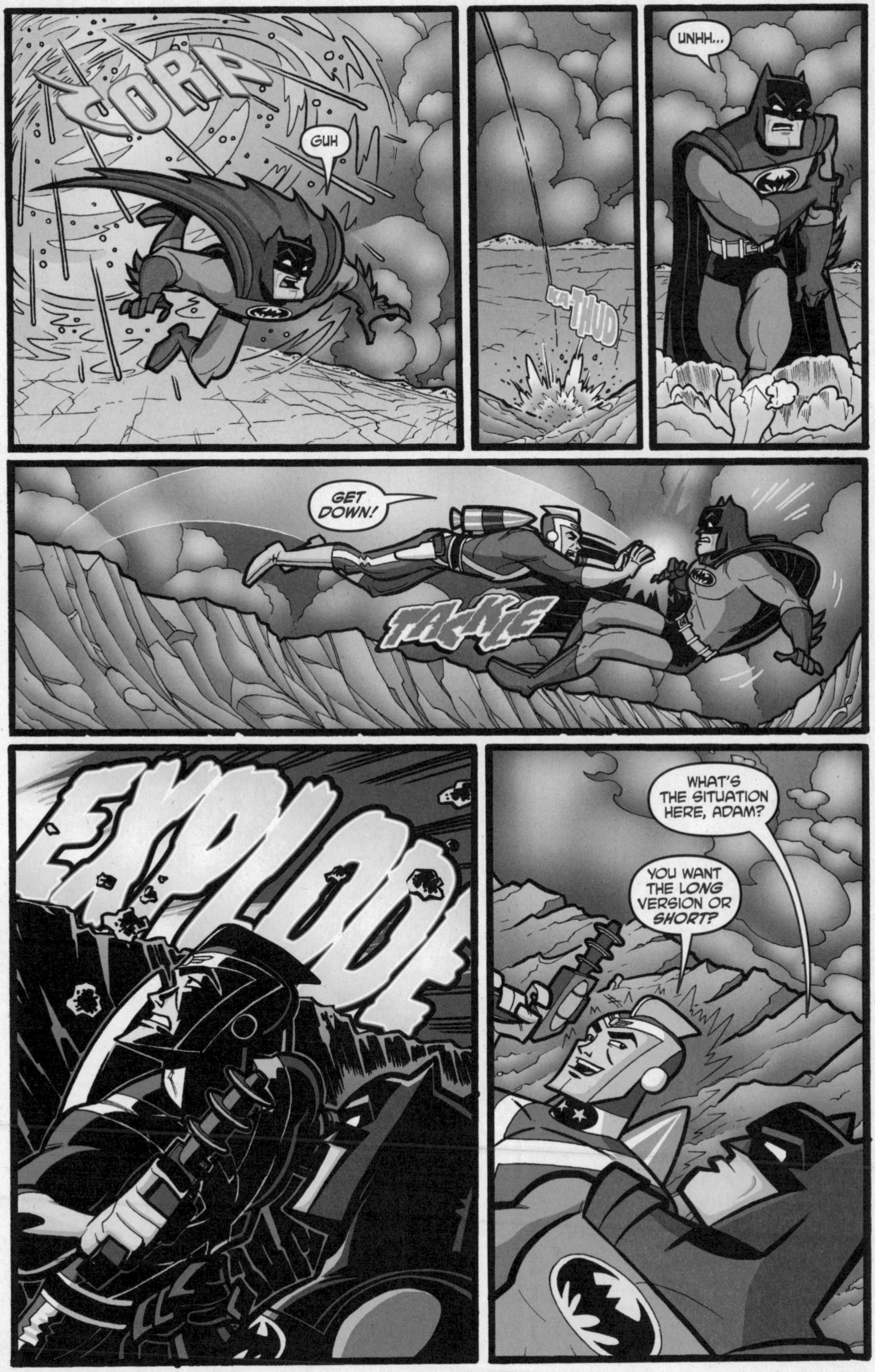
CORP
GUH
KA-THUD
UNHH...
GET DOWN!
TACKLE
EXPLOOF
WHAT'S THE SITUATION HERE, ADAM?
YOU WANT THE LONG VERSION OR SHORT?

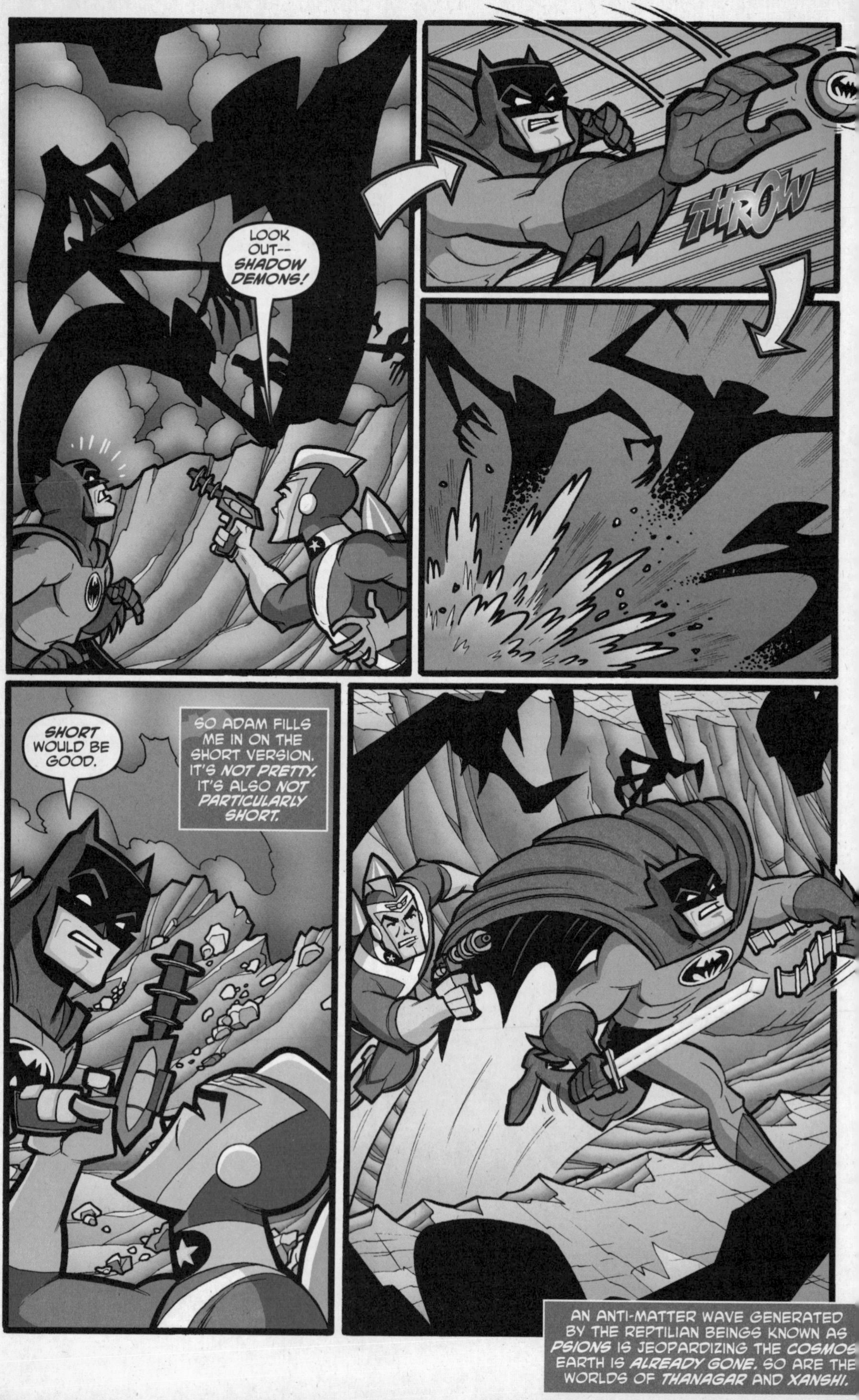
LOOK OUT-- SHADOW DEMONS!
THROW
SHORT WOULD BE GOOD.
SO ADAM FILLS ME IN ON THE SHORT VERSION. IT'S NOT PRETTY. IT'S ALSO NOT PARTICULARLY SHORT.
AN ANTI-MATTER WAVE GENERATED BY THE REPTILIAN BEINGS KNOWN AS PSIONS IS JEOPARDIZING THE COSMOS. EARTH IS ALREADY GONE. SO ARE THE WORLDS OF THANAGAR AND XANSHI.

...S A NATURAL GENERATOR OF *ZETA RADIATION*, RANN WAS SPARED COMPLETE DESTRUCTION.

INSTEAD, THE PLANET HAS BECOME AN *ARCTIC WASTELAND* FILLED WITH STRANGE *SHADOW CREATURES* COMPRISED OF PURE ANTI-MATTER.

ADAM AND HIS WIFE *ALANA* WERE ABLE TO TRANSFER ME HERE, BEFORE THE *EARTH* WAS *DESTROYED*.

BUT WE DON'T HAVE LONG. BY SUNRISE THE ANTI-MATTER WAVE WILL TRIGGER A GALAXY-WIDE *CHAIN REACTION*.

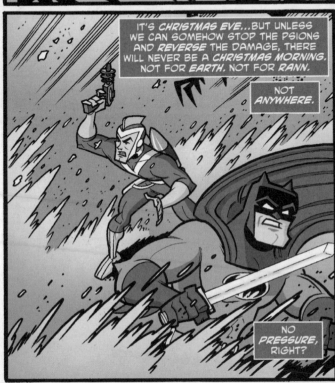

IT'S *CHRISTMAS EVE*...BUT UNLESS WE CAN SOMEHOW STOP THE PSIONS AND *REVERSE* THE DAMAGE, THERE WILL NEVER BE A *CHRISTMAS MORNING*, NOT FOR *EARTH*. NOT FOR *RANN*.

NOT ANYWHERE.

NO *PRESSURE*, RIGHT?

THE *ANTI-MATTER CREATURES* WILL REGROUP! HURRY!

IT'S THE MRS.!

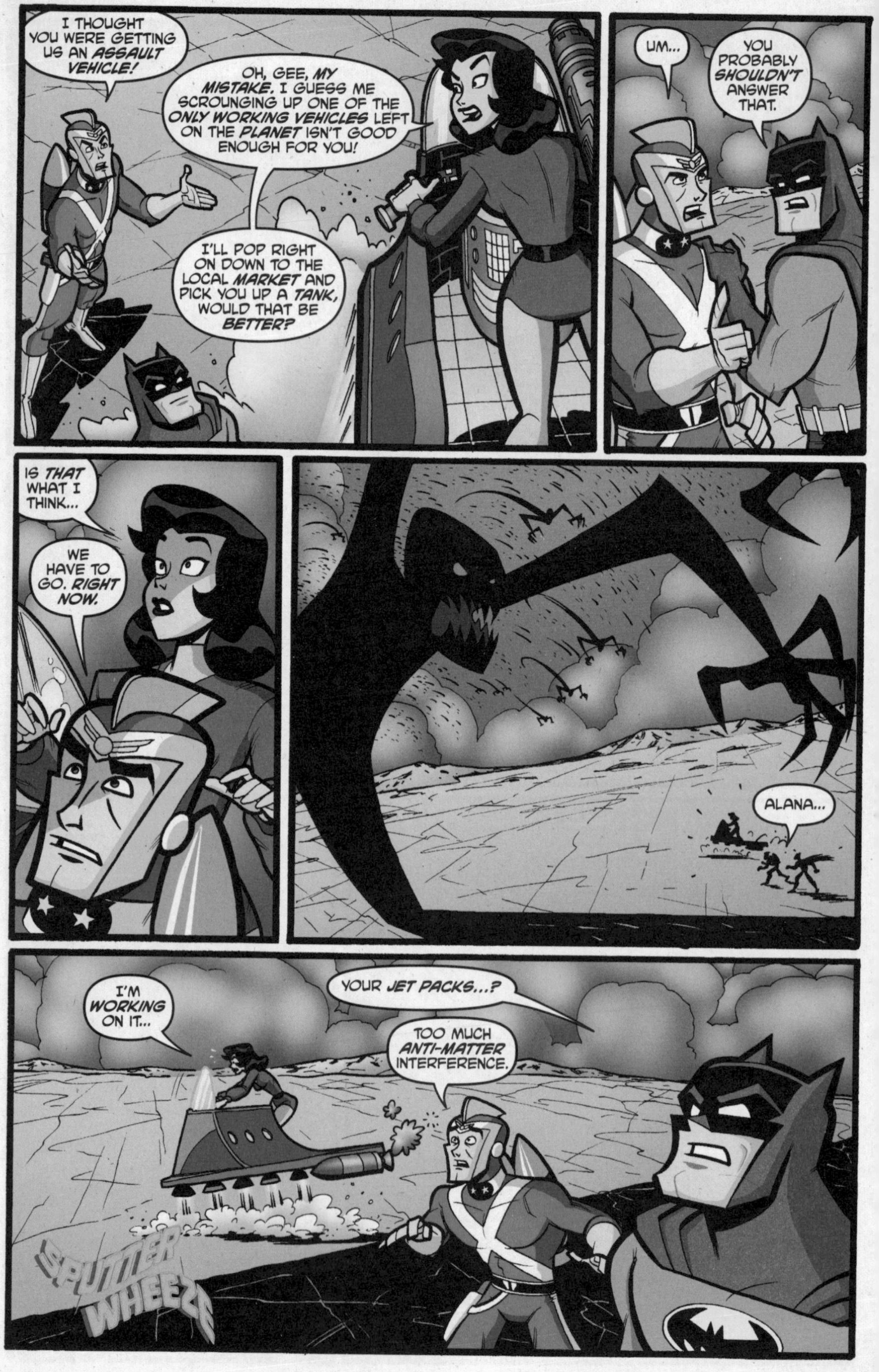

I THOUGHT YOU WERE GETTING US AN ASSAULT VEHICLE!
OH, GEE, MY MISTAKE. I GUESS ME SCROUNGING UP ONE OF THE ONLY WORKING VEHICLES LEFT ON THE PLANET ISN'T GOOD ENOUGH FOR YOU!
I'LL POP RIGHT ON DOWN TO THE LOCAL MARKET AND PICK YOU UP A TANK, WOULD THAT BE BETTER?
UM...
YOU PROBABLY SHOULDN'T ANSWER THAT.
IS THAT WHAT I THINK...
WE HAVE TO GO. RIGHT NOW.
ALANA...
I'M WORKING ON IT...
YOUR JET PACKS...?
TOO MUCH ANTI-MATTER INTERFERENCE.
SPUTTER
WHEEZE

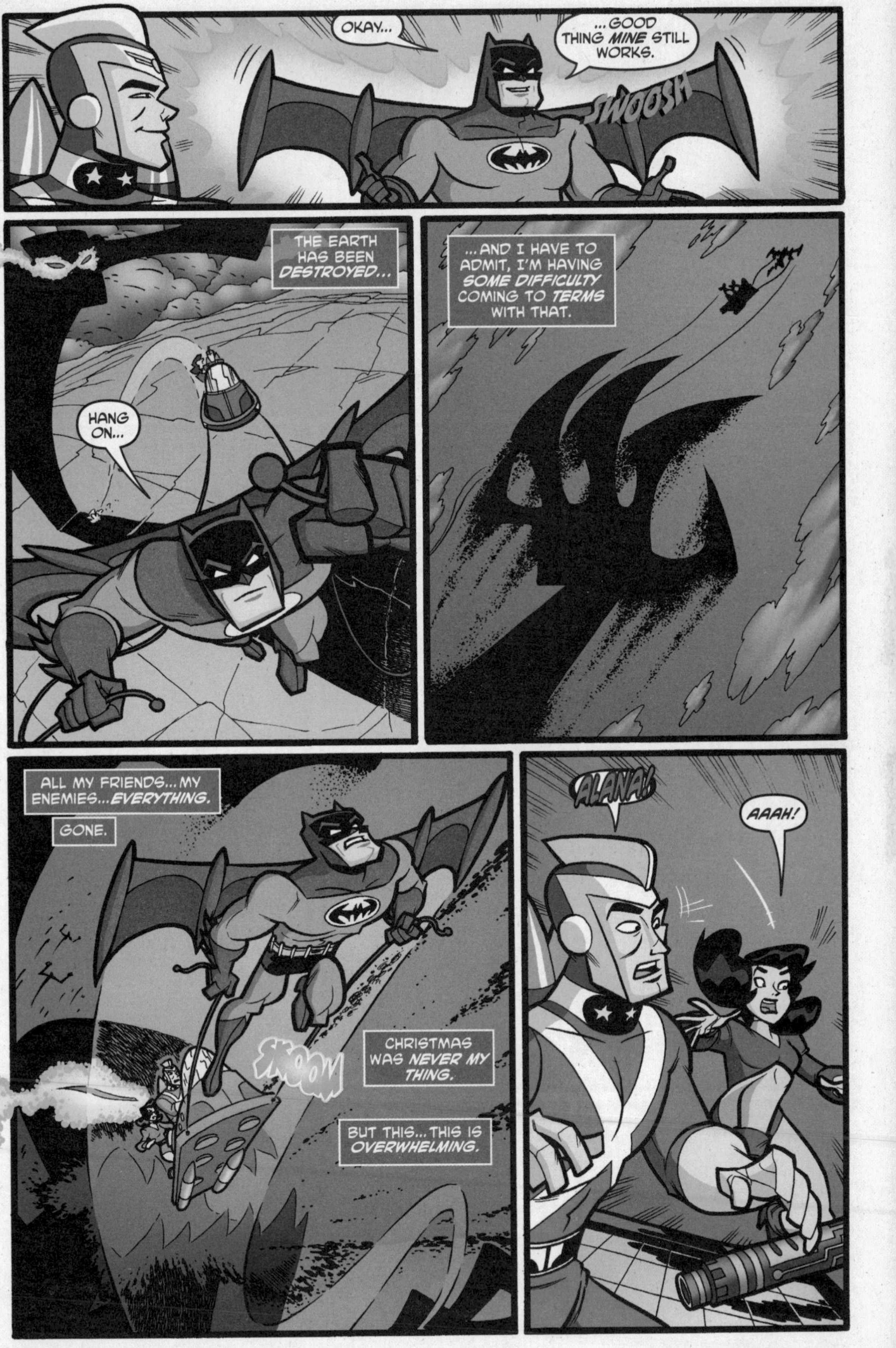

OKAY...
...GOOD THING MINE STILL WORKS.
SWOOSH
THE EARTH HAS BEEN DESTROYED...
HANG ON...
...AND I HAVE TO ADMIT, I'M HAVING SOME DIFFICULTY COMING TO TERMS WITH THAT.
ALL MY FRIENDS... MY ENEMIES... EVERYTHING.
GONE.
SKOOM
CHRISTMAS WAS NEVER MY THING.
BUT THIS... THIS IS OVERWHELMING.
ALANA!
AAAH!

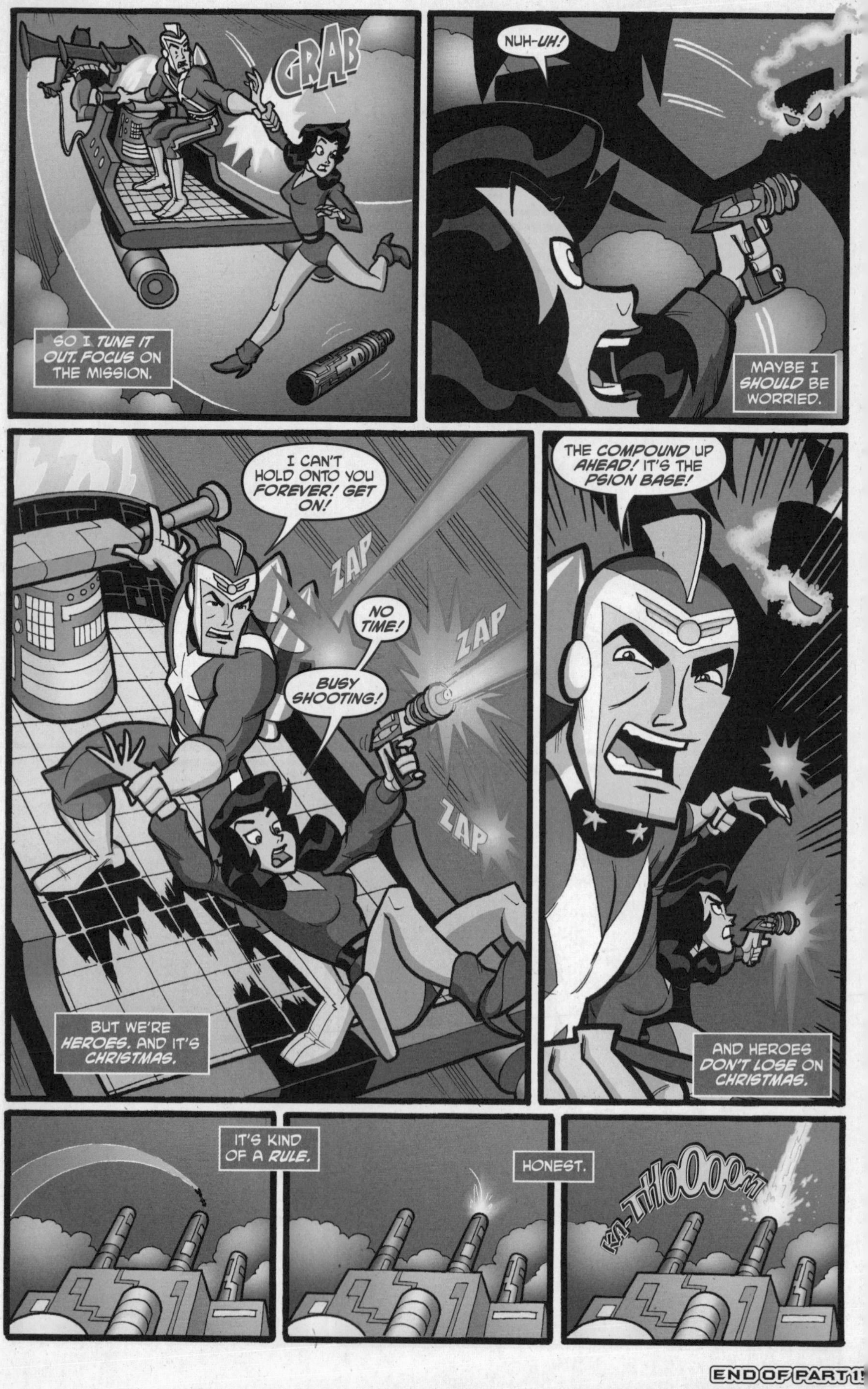
GRAB
SO I TUNE IT OUT. FOCUS ON THE MISSION.
NUH-UH!
MAYBE I SHOULD BE WORRIED.
I CAN'T HOLD ONTO YOU FOREVER! GET ON!
ZAP
NO TIME!
BUSY SHOOTING!
ZAP
ZAP
BUT WE'RE HEROES. AND IT'S CHRISTMAS.
THE COMPOUND UP AHEAD! IT'S THE PSION BASE!
AND HEROES DON'T LOSE ON CHRISTMAS.
IT'S KIND OF A RULE.
HONEST.
KA-THOOOOM
END OF PART 1!

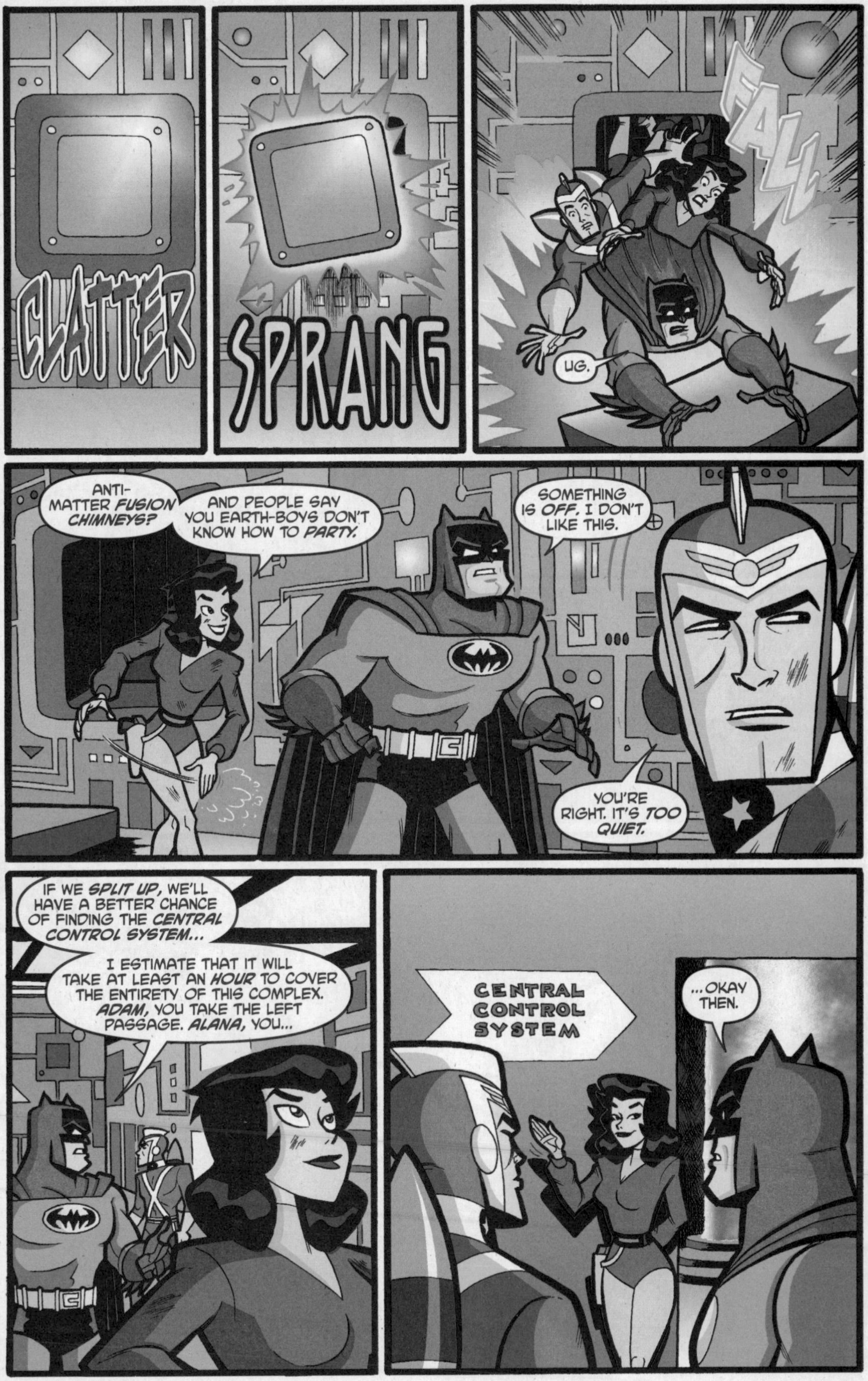
CLATTER
SPRANG
FALL
UG.
ANTI-MATTER FUSION CHIMNEYS?
AND PEOPLE SAY YOU EARTH-BOYS DON'T KNOW HOW TO PARTY.
SOMETHING IS OFF. I DON'T LIKE THIS.
YOU'RE RIGHT. IT'S TOO QUIET.
IF WE SPLIT UP, WE'LL HAVE A BETTER CHANCE OF FINDING THE CENTRAL CONTROL SYSTEM...
I ESTIMATE THAT IT WILL TAKE AT LEAST AN HOUR TO COVER THE ENTIRETY OF THIS COMPLEX. ADAM, YOU TAKE THE LEFT PASSAGE. ALANA, YOU...
CENTRAL CONTROL SYSTEM
...OKAY THEN.

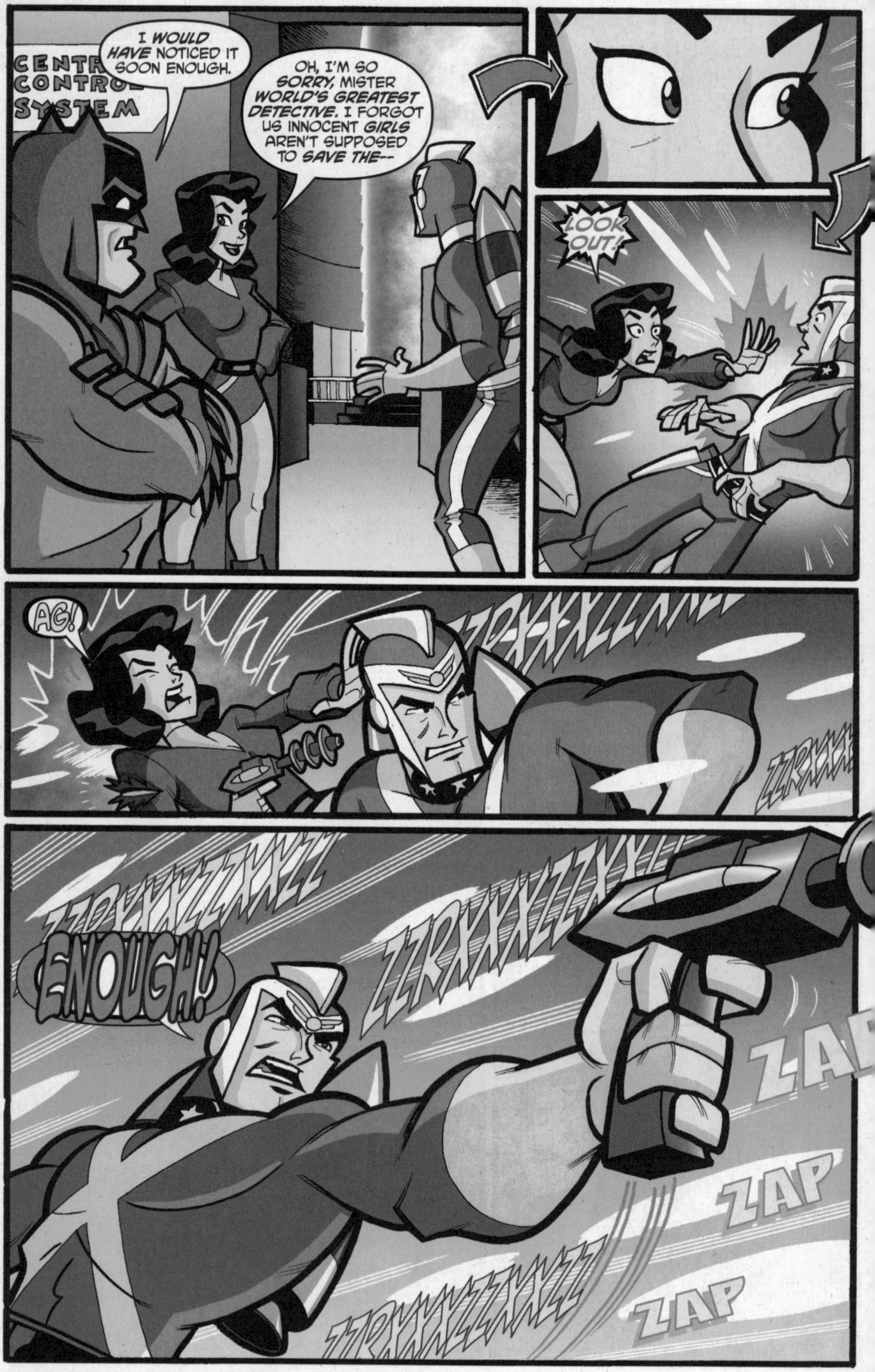
CENTRAL CONTROL SYSTEM
I WOULD HAVE NOTICED IT SOON ENOUGH.
OH, I'M SO SORRY, MISTER WORLD'S GREATEST DETECTIVE. I FORGOT US INNOCENT GIRLS AREN'T SUPPOSED TO SAVE THE--
LOOK OUT!
AG!
ZZRXXXZZZXXZZ
ZZRXXX
ENOUGH!
ZZRXXXXZZXXZZ
ZZRXXXXZZZXXZZ
ZAP
ZAP
ZAP
ZZRXXXXZZZXXZZ

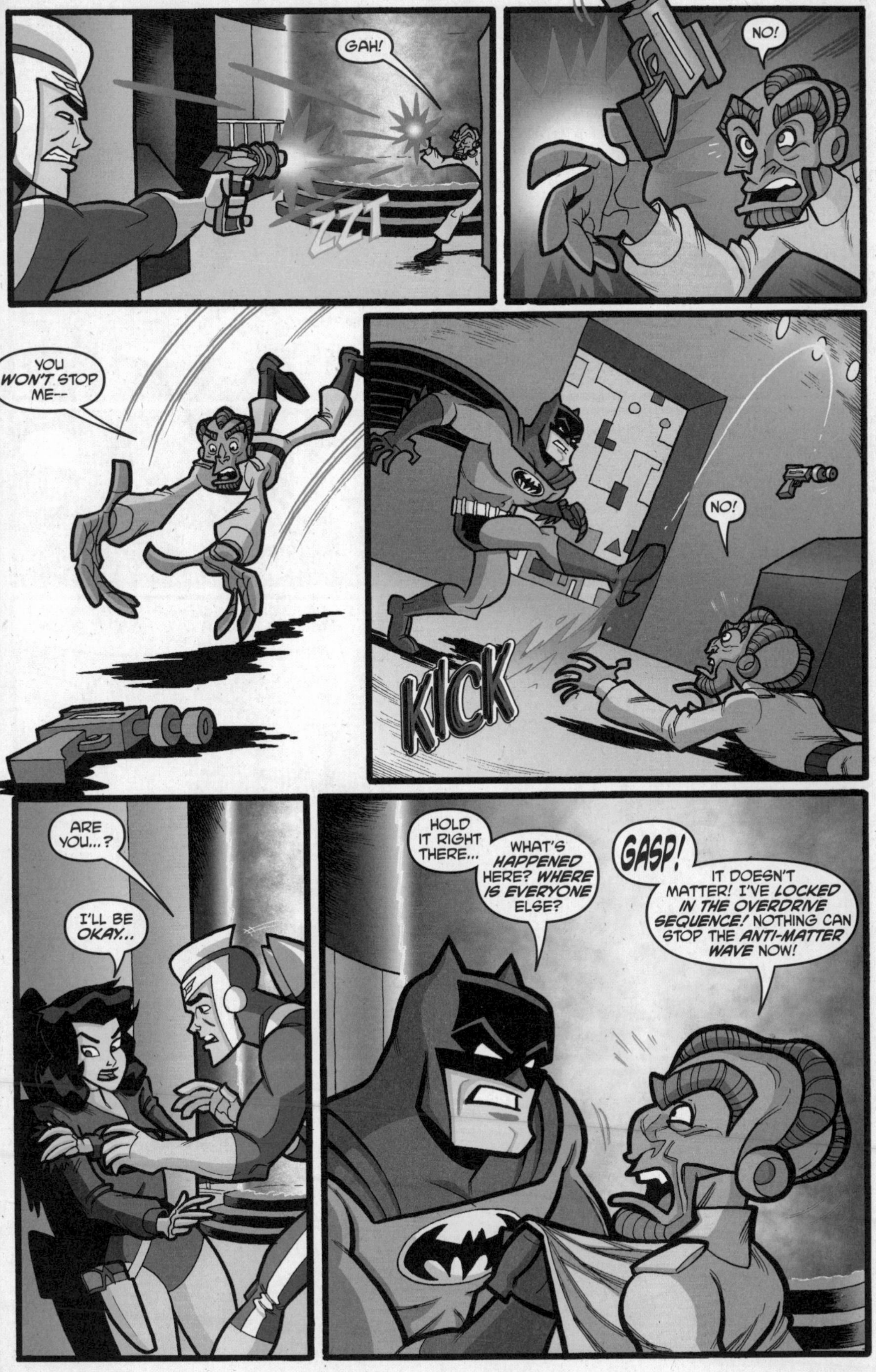
GAH!
ZZZT
NO!
YOU WON'T STOP ME--
NO!
KICK
ARE YOU...?
I'LL BE OKAY...
HOLD IT RIGHT THERE...
WHAT'S HAPPENED HERE? WHERE IS EVERYONE ELSE?
GASP!
IT DOESN'T MATTER! I'VE LOCKED IN THE OVERDRIVE SEQUENCE! NOTHING CAN STOP THE ANTI-MATTER WAVE NOW!

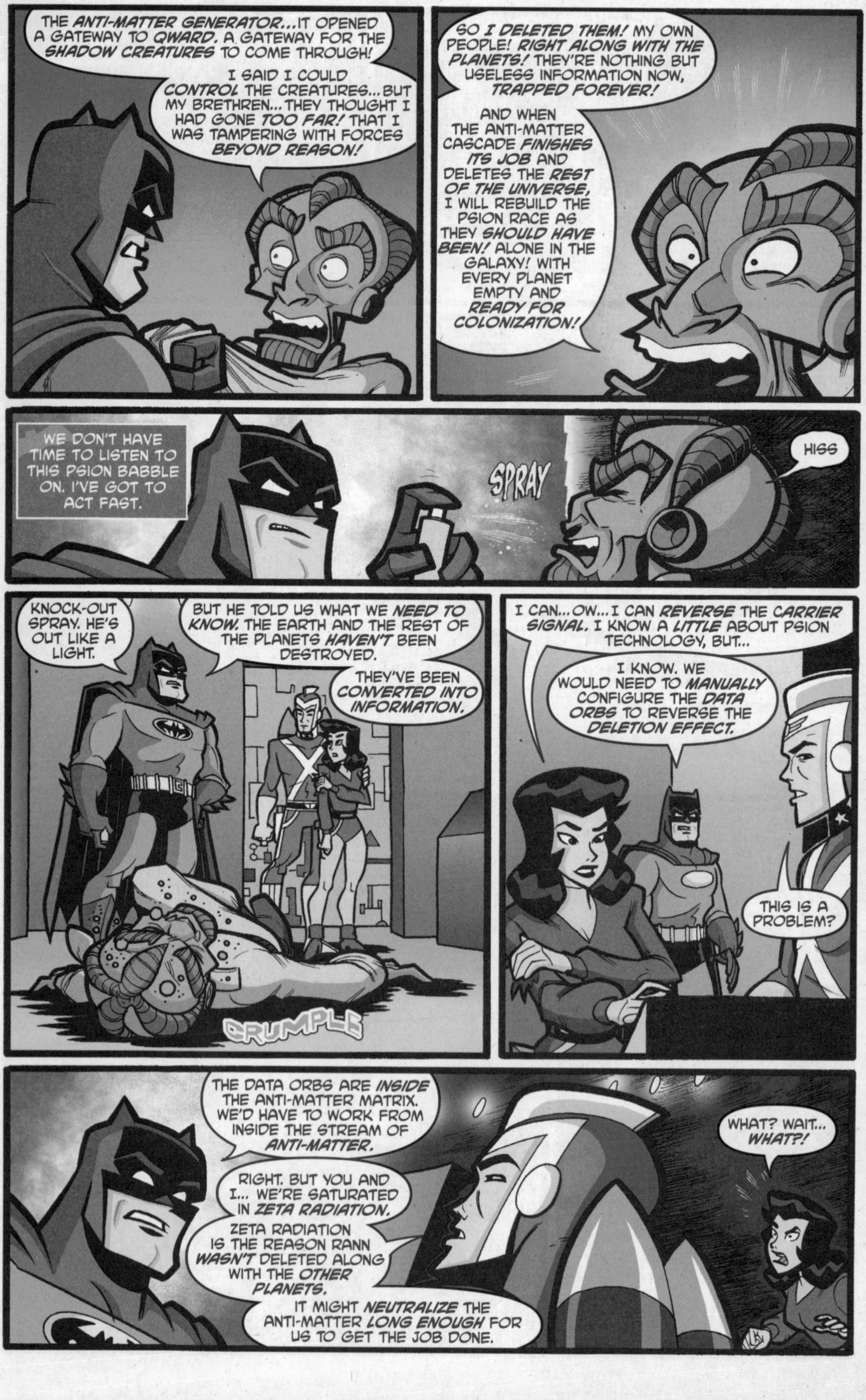
THE ANTI-MATTER GENERATOR... IT OPENED A GATEWAY TO QWARD. A GATEWAY FOR THE SHADOW CREATURES TO COME THROUGH!
I SAID I COULD CONTROL THE CREATURES... BUT MY BRETHREN... THEY THOUGHT I HAD GONE TOO FAR! THAT I WAS TAMPERING WITH FORCES BEYOND REASON!
SO I DELETED THEM! MY OWN PEOPLE! RIGHT ALONG WITH THE PLANETS! THEY'RE NOTHING BUT USELESS INFORMATION NOW, TRAPPED FOREVER!
AND WHEN THE ANTI-MATTER CASCADE FINISHES ITS JOB AND DELETES THE REST OF THE UNIVERSE, I WILL REBUILD THE PSION RACE AS THEY SHOULD HAVE BEEN! ALONE IN THE GALAXY! WITH EVERY PLANET EMPTY AND READY FOR COLONIZATION!
WE DON'T HAVE TIME TO LISTEN TO THIS PSION BABBLE ON. I'VE GOT TO ACT FAST.
SPRAY
HISS
KNOCK-OUT SPRAY. HE'S OUT LIKE A LIGHT.
BUT HE TOLD US WHAT WE NEED TO KNOW. THE EARTH AND THE REST OF THE PLANETS HAVEN'T BEEN DESTROYED.
THEY'VE BEEN CONVERTED INTO INFORMATION.
CRUMPLE
I CAN... OW... I CAN REVERSE THE CARRIER SIGNAL. I KNOW A LITTLE ABOUT PSION TECHNOLOGY, BUT...
I KNOW. WE WOULD NEED TO MANUALLY CONFIGURE THE DATA ORBS TO REVERSE THE DELETION EFFECT.
THIS IS A PROBLEM?
THE DATA ORBS ARE INSIDE THE ANTI-MATTER MATRIX. WE'D HAVE TO WORK FROM INSIDE THE STREAM OF ANTI-MATTER.
WHAT? WAIT... WHAT?!
RIGHT. BUT YOU AND I... WE'RE SATURATED IN ZETA RADIATION.
ZETA RADIATION IS THE REASON RANN WASN'T DELETED ALONG WITH THE OTHER PLANETS.
IT MIGHT NEUTRALIZE THE ANTI-MATTER LONG ENOUGH FOR US TO GET THE JOB DONE.

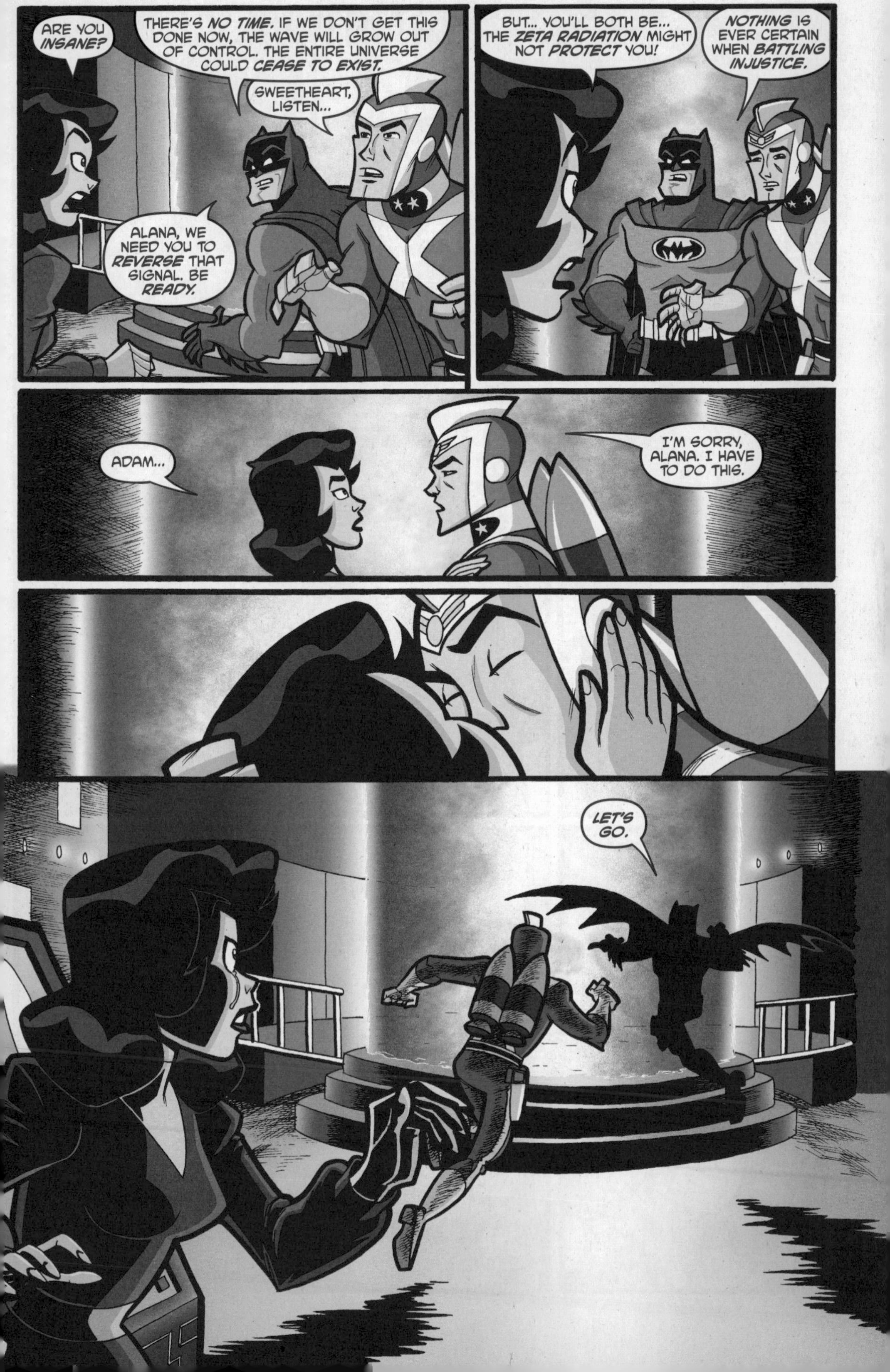
ARE YOU INSANE?
THERE'S NO TIME. IF WE DON'T GET THIS DONE NOW, THE WAVE WILL GROW OUT OF CONTROL. THE ENTIRE UNIVERSE COULD CEASE TO EXIST.
SWEETHEART, LISTEN...
ALANA, WE NEED YOU TO REVERSE THAT SIGNAL. BE READY.
BUT... YOU'LL BOTH BE... THE ZETA RADIATION MIGHT NOT PROTECT YOU!
NOTHING IS EVER CERTAIN WHEN BATTLING INJUSTICE.
ADAM...
I'M SORRY, ALANA. I HAVE TO DO THIS.
LET'S GO.

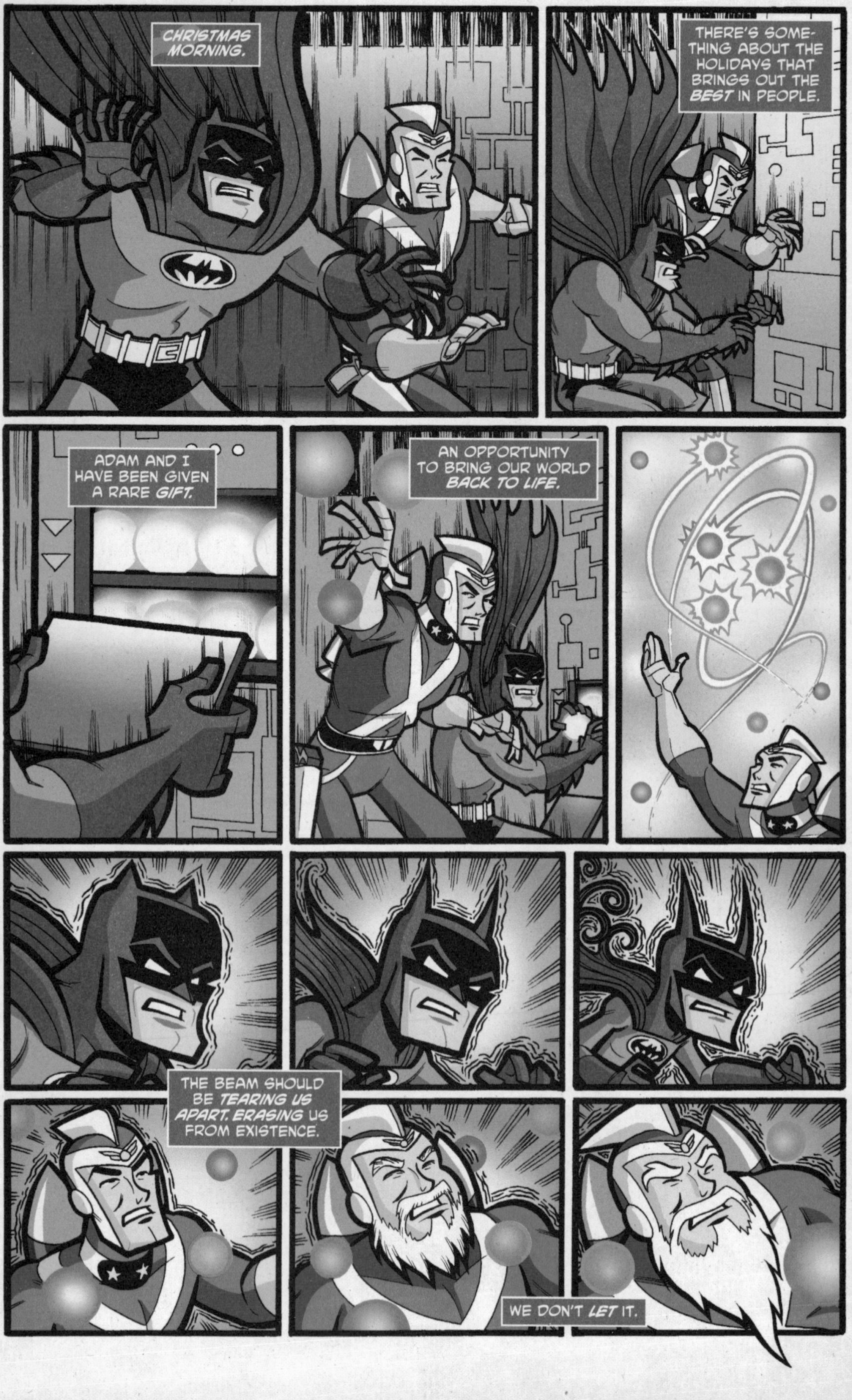
CHRISTMAS MORNING.
THERE'S SOMETHING ABOUT THE HOLIDAYS THAT BRINGS OUT THE BEST IN PEOPLE.
ADAM AND I HAVE BEEN GIVEN A RARE GIFT.
AN OPPORTUNITY TO BRING OUR WORLD BACK TO LIFE.
THE BEAM SHOULD BE TEARING US APART. ERASING US FROM EXISTENCE.
WE DON'T LET IT.

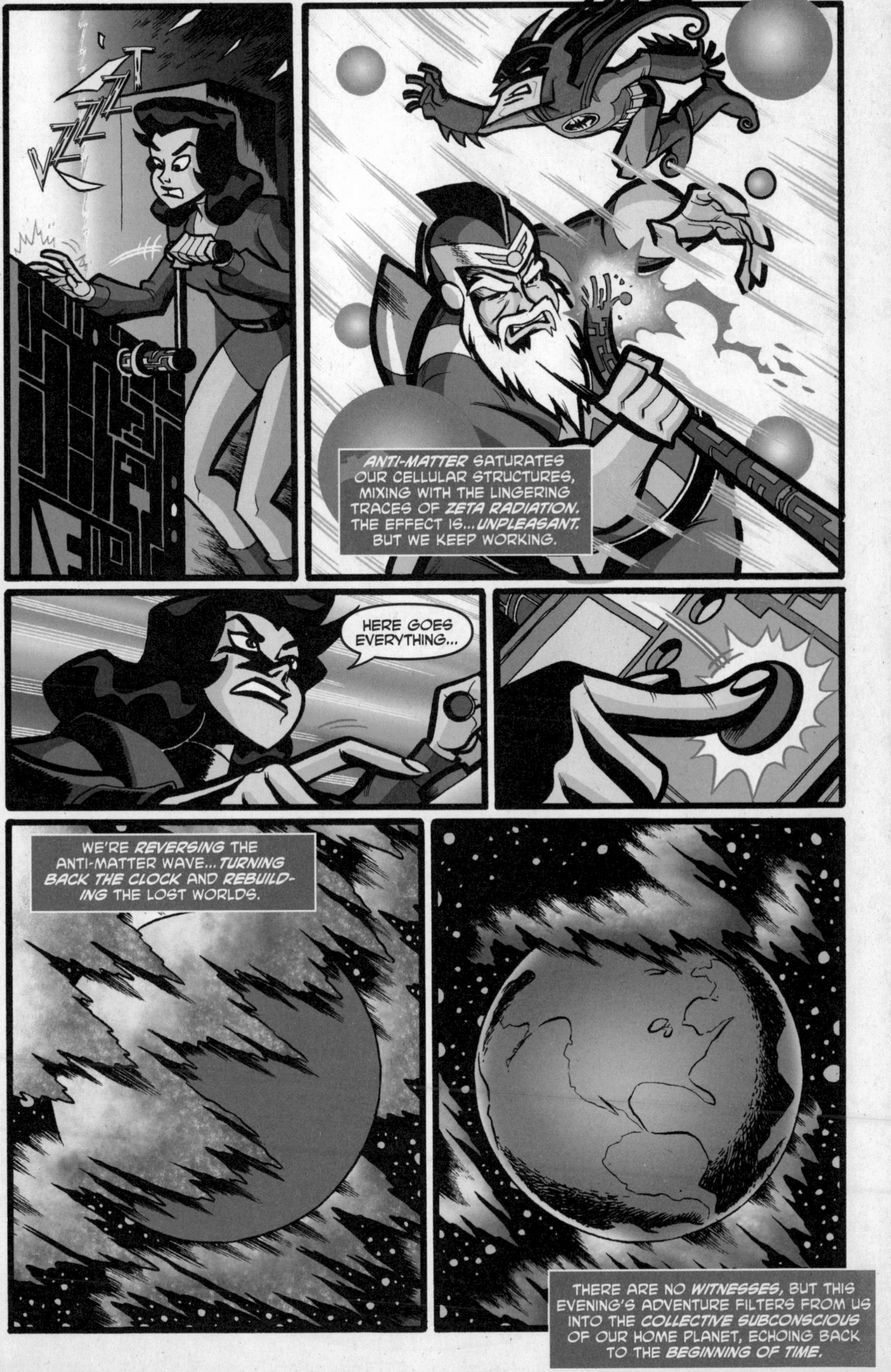
VZZZZZT
ANTI-MATTER SATURATES OUR CELLULAR STRUCTURES, MIXING WITH THE LINGERING TRACES OF ZETA RADIATION. THE EFFECT IS...UNPLEASANT. BUT WE KEEP WORKING.
HERE GOES EVERYTHING...
WE'RE REVERSING THE ANTI-MATTER WAVE...TURNING BACK THE CLOCK AND REBUILDING THE LOST WORLDS.
THERE ARE NO WITNESSES, BUT THIS EVENING'S ADVENTURE FILTERS FROM US INTO THE COLLECTIVE SUBCONSCIOUS OF OUR HOME PLANET, ECHOING BACK TO THE BEGINNING OF TIME.

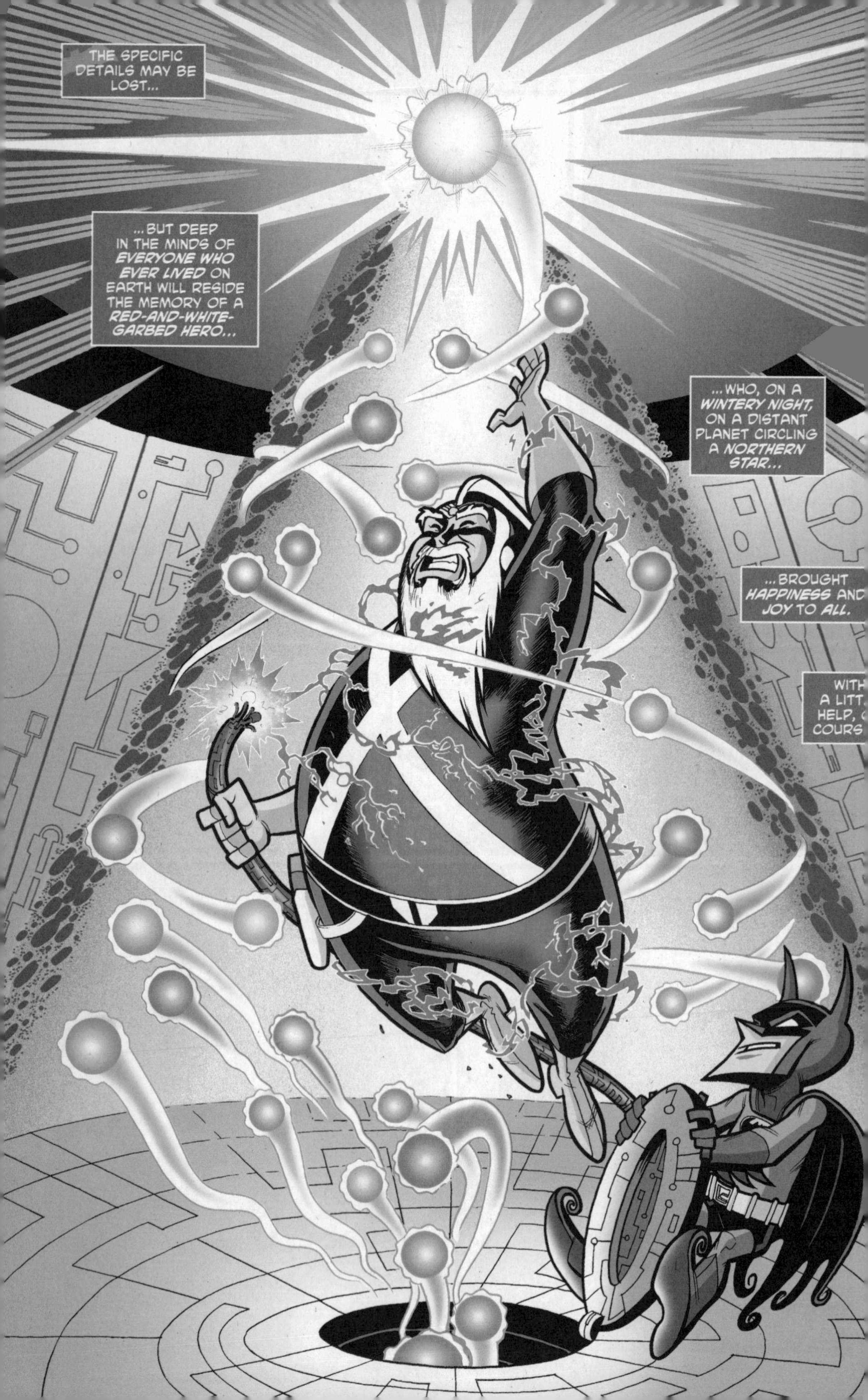
THE SPECIFIC DETAILS MAY BE LOST...
...BUT DEEP IN THE MINDS OF EVERYONE WHO EVER LIVED ON EARTH WILL RESIDE THE MEMORY OF A RED-AND-WHITE-GARBED HERO...
...WHO, ON A WINTERY NIGHT, ON A DISTANT PLANET CIRCLING A NORTHERN STAR...
...BROUGHT HAPPINESS AND JOY TO ALL.

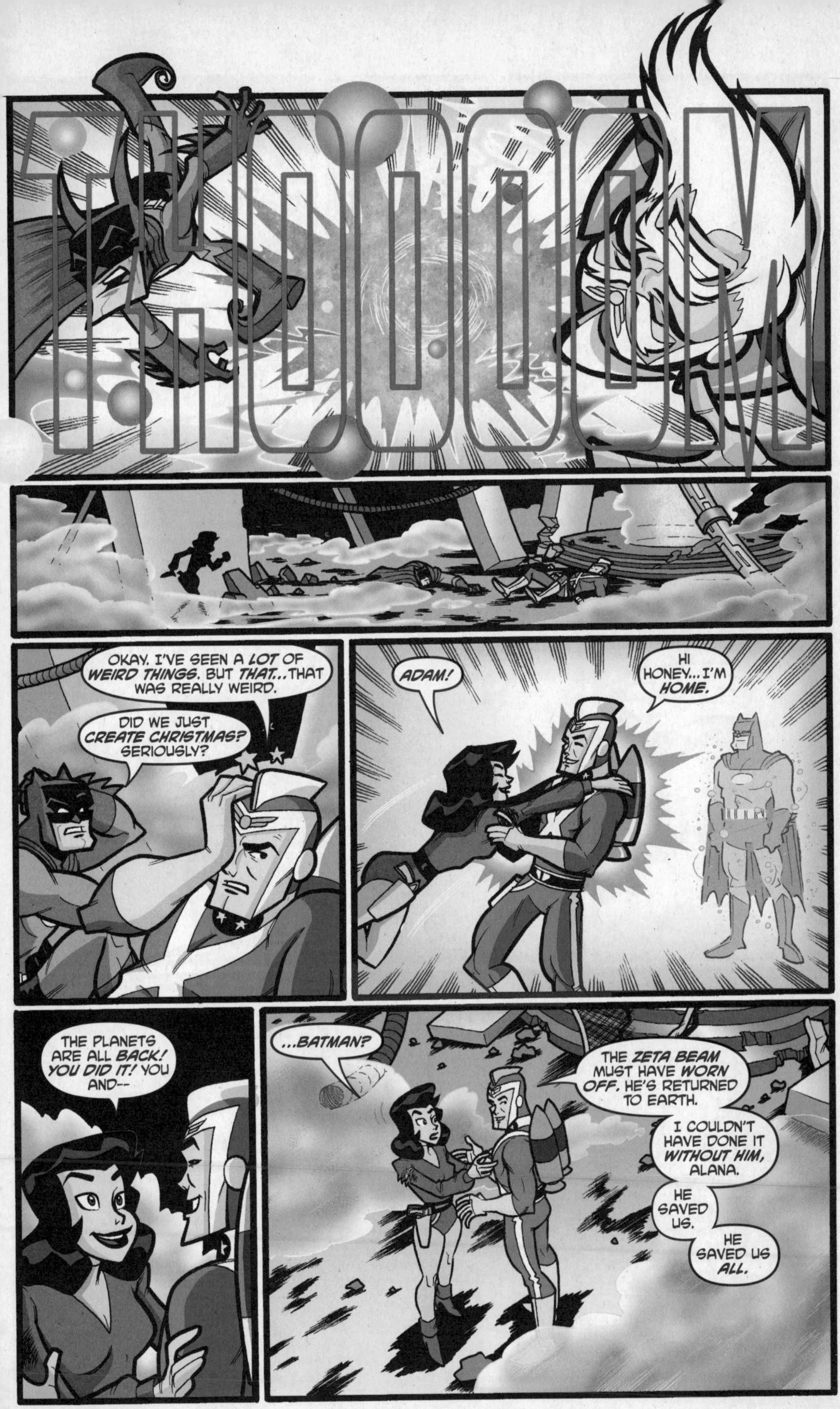
THOOOOOM
OKAY. I'VE SEEN A LOT OF WEIRD THINGS. BUT THAT... THAT WAS REALLY WEIRD.
DID WE JUST CREATE CHRISTMAS? SERIOUSLY?
ADAM!
HI HONEY... I'M HOME.
THE PLANETS ARE ALL BACK! YOU DID IT! YOU AND--
...BATMAN?
THE ZETA BEAM MUST HAVE WORN OFF. HE'S RETURNED TO EARTH.
I COULDN'T HAVE DONE IT WITHOUT HIM, ALANA.
HE SAVED US.
HE SAVED US ALL.

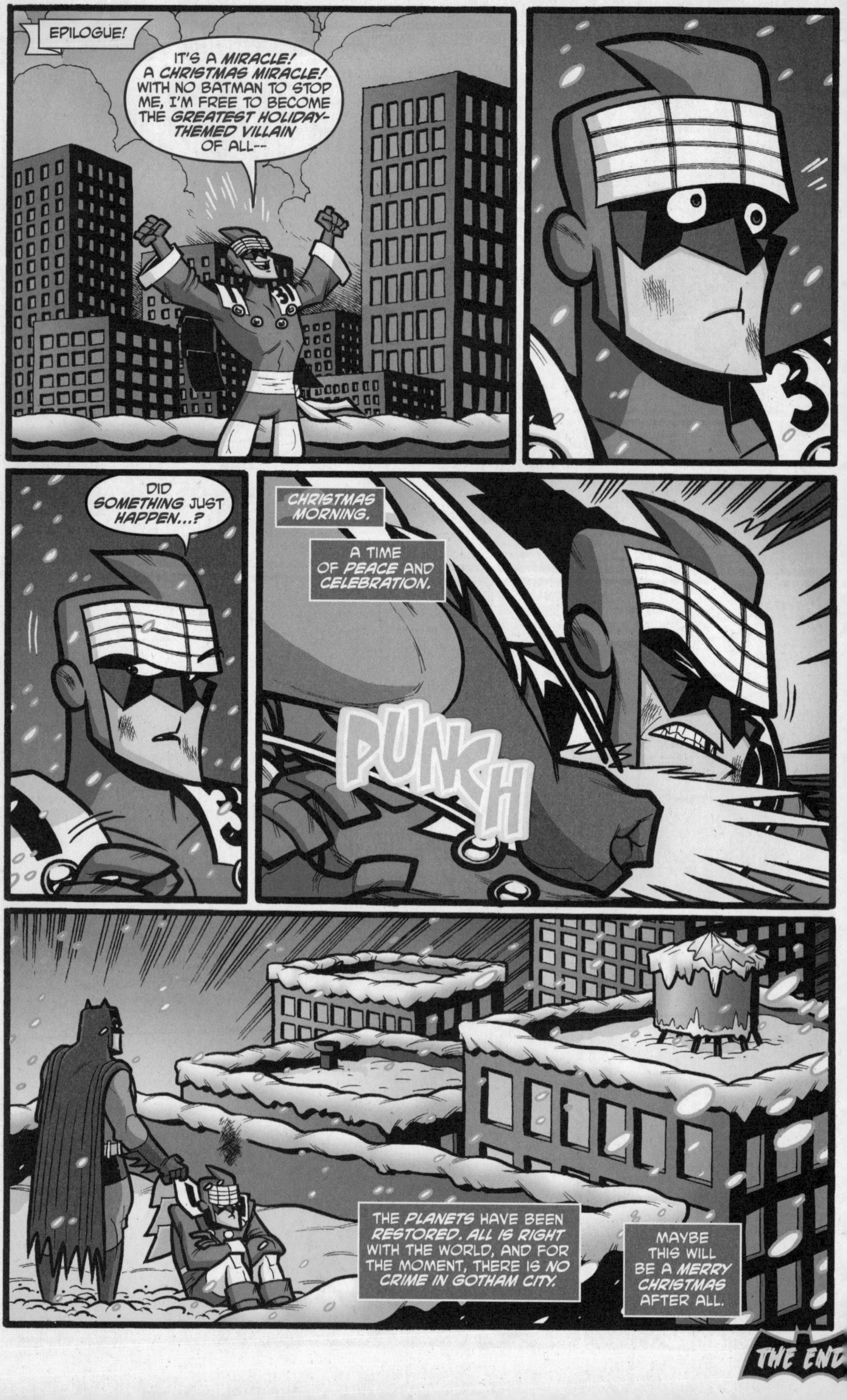
EPILOGUE!
IT'S A MIRACLE! A CHRISTMAS MIRACLE! WITH NO BATMAN TO STOP ME, I'M FREE TO BECOME THE GREATEST HOLIDAY-THEMED VILLAIN OF ALL--
DID SOMETHING JUST HAPPEN...?
CHRISTMAS MORNING.
A TIME OF PEACE AND CELEBRATION.
PUNCH
THE PLANETS HAVE BEEN RESTORED. ALL IS RIGHT WITH THE WORLD, AND FOR THE MOMENT, THERE IS NO CRIME IN GOTHAM CITY.
MAYBE THIS WILL BE A MERRY CHRISTMAS AFTER ALL.
THE END